Islam:
What Catholics
Need to Know

Resources for Catholic Administrators
and Religious Educators in Serving
Interreligious Dialogue

Rev. Elias D. Mallon, Ph.D.

A revised and expanded second edition

www.NCEA.org

ISBN No. 978-1-55833-665-0
Part No. REL-30-1593

Dedicated to Tom Powell

and the staff of the

Catholic Near East Welfare Association (CNEWA)

Contents

Index of Maps

Index of Photos

Preface

Clearly, the cultural landscape of the United States grows ever more plural. To help Catholics know, celebrate, live and express in prayer their faith in a diverse society, the *General Directory for Catechesis* (1997) identifies six universal tasks for catechesis: catechesis promotes knowledge of the faith, catechesis promotes knowledge of the meaning of the Liturgy and the Sacraments, catechesis promotes moral formation in Jesus Christ, catechesis teaches Christians how to pray with Christ, catechesis prepares Christians how to live in community and to participate in the life and mission of the Church, and catechesis promotes a missionary spirit that prepares the faithful to be present as Christians in society.

The *National Directory for Catechesis* (2005) names the sixth task of catechesis as an essential element that is part of a unified whole by which we form disciples of Jesus Christ. It states that "Catholics need to be familiar with the history of Islam especially the conflicts between Christians and Muslims." (p. 214) Taking its cue from the *Declaration on the Relation of the Church to Non-Christian Religions (Nostra Aetate)*, the NDC reminds us that the Church urges Catholics and Muslims to work for mutual understanding and to promote justice and moral welfare as well as peace and freedom. To support this holistic approach to catechesis, the Department of Religious Education presents this publication in the series titled, *For Religious Educators,* as a resource in support of the sixth task of catechesis.

I thank Fr. Elias D. Mallon for writing *Islam: What*

Catholics Need to Know. Drawing upon his training in biblical studies and his many years of experience in interreligious dialogue, he has given Catholics an accessible introduction into the world and beliefs of Islam. This book is sure to be an essential resource for those who form others in faith as well as for any adult who remains a lifelong disciple ever striving to grow in faith and to be a witness to that faith in the market place.

I also thank and acknowledge Christina Gergits in the Department of Religious Education for assisting me in managing the project, Fr. Phillip B. Cover, Shawna Rose Madison and Mary Hinshelwood for editorial assistance, and Mary Twillman for her expertise with the cover, design and production of the text.

Diana Dudoit Raiche
Executive Director
Department of Religious Education

Foreword

So much has happened in the world since Atonement Friar Elias D. Mallon, Ph.D., K.H.S., first wrote this enlightening book a little over 10 years ago. Back then, there was an "almost calm" that permeated through much of the areas now torn apart by violence — particularly the Middle East. This is not to say there were no issues or challenges or conflicts beneath the eerie calm; for a majority of the land was ruled, in some cases, by "terror and brutality."

Father Elias opened his book echoing "Nostra Aetate," a declaration of the fathers of the Second Vatican Council concerning the Catholic Church's relationship with non-Christians promulgated by Pope Paul VI in 1965. He believed the council was calling for Catholics and Muslims to face their history together: "To face the mutual humiliations, the mutual aggressions and overcome them for the glory of God and the benefit of humility."

Nothing could be more poignant for our world today.

Only by stepping into the shoes of "the other," and by listening and observing from their vantage point, will we hear and come to understand the perspectives of our brothers and sisters. This is necessary if we are to possess the respect that is necessary to coexist in this ever-changing world.

Father Elias, by documenting our shared history in such a detailed and skillful way, will enable us all — hopefully — to learn from our mistakes in our past.

In 2009, I was privileged to be part of a small group trekking across the Sinai desert, something that would not be possible to me today I am sure. There, near the peninsula's southern tip, lies one of the oldest functioning Christian monasteries. Built by the Byzantine emperor, Justinian I, between the years 548 and 565 A.D., St. Catherine is a jewel box, its church, chapels and library enshrine gems precious to all humanity.

Following my predawn ascent to the summit of Mount Sinai, and my sunrise descent, I was honored by the monastery's Orthodox monks to visit their library. There, I saw a copy of the Ashtiname of Muhammad, in which the Muslim prophet bestowed his protection upon the monastery. Signed with a fading handprint of the prophet himself, the document contains several clauses covering all aspects of human rights, including such topics as the protection of Christians living under Islamic rule.

One prays that such a covenant could become a model for rebuilding bridges of dialogue between Christians and Muslims — indeed among all peoples of good will.

During his two-day visit to Egypt earlier in 2017, Pope Francis, pulled no punches as he called on Christian and Muslim religious leaders in Egypt and throughout the Middle East to join in building "a new civilization of peace" by declaring together "a firm and clear 'no' to every form of violence, vengeance and hatred carried out in the name of religion and in the name of God" and to "affirm the incompatibility of violence and faith, belief and hatred."

His words drew applause, not just in Al Azhar, the most prestigious center of learning in Sunni Islam, but around the world.

"What is needed is peacemakers," he continued, "not fomenters of conflict; firefighters not arsonists; preachers of reconciliation and not instigators of destruction."

The past two decades have seen cataclysmic changes in our world, and in how Christians, Jews and Muslims see one another. In the new chapters added to his original manuscript, Father Elias has succinctly and adeptly brought us up-to-date.

I would encourage all those charged with responsibility in Catholic education to read this work in the hopes that it might lead to greater understanding and mutual respect of our fellow believers in the One God.

Vicki Downey, D.G.C.H.S.,
Lieutenant, Eastern Lieutenancy USA
Equestrian Order of the Holy Sepulchre of Jerusalem

Islam:
What Catholics
Need to Know

Resources for Catholic Administrators
and Religious Educators in Serving
Interreligious Dialogue

A Brief Timeline of the History of Islam

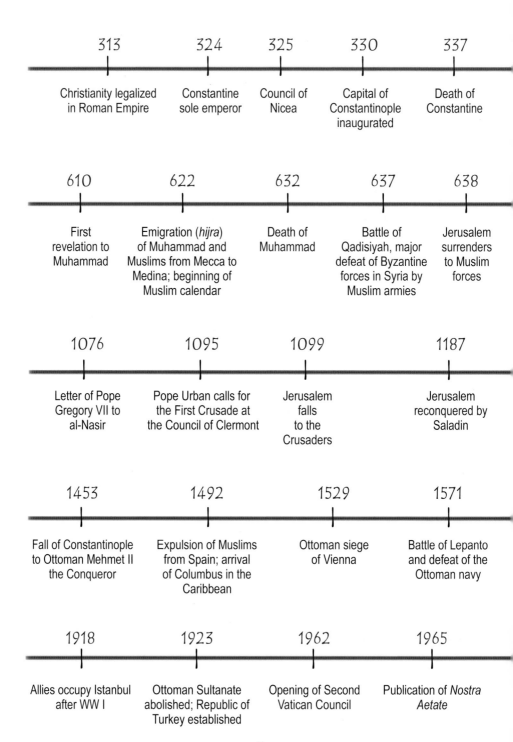

313 — Christianity legalized in Roman Empire

324 — Constantine sole emperor

325 — Council of Nicea

330 — Capital of Constantinople inaugurated

337 — Death of Constantine

610 — First revelation to Muhammad

622 — Emigration (*hijra*) of Muhammad and Muslims from Mecca to Medina; beginning of Muslim calendar

632 — Death of Muhammad

637 — Battle of Qadisiyah, major defeat of Byzantine forces in Syria by Muslim armies

638 — Jerusalem surrenders to Muslim forces

1076 — Letter of Pope Gregory VII to al-Nasir

1095 — Pope Urban calls for the First Crusade at the Council of Clermont

1099 — Jerusalem falls to the Crusaders

1187 — Jerusalem reconquered by Saladin

1453 — Fall of Constantinople to Ottoman Mehmet II the Conqueror

1492 — Expulsion of Muslims from Spain; arrival of Columbus in the Caribbean

1529 — Ottoman siege of Vienna

1571 — Battle of Lepanto and defeat of the Ottoman navy

1918 — Allies occupy Istanbul after WW I

1923 — Ottoman Sultanate abolished; Republic of Turkey established

1962 — Opening of Second Vatican Council

1965 — Publication of *Nostra Aetate*

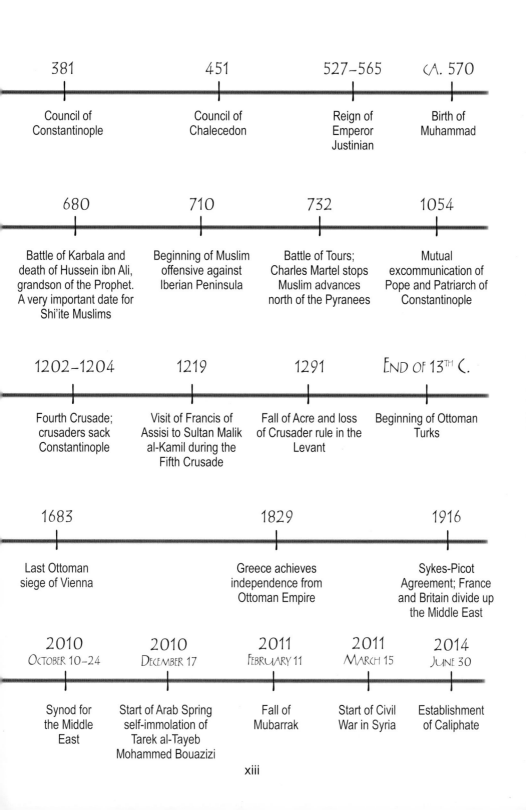

381 — Council of Constantinople

451 — Council of Chalecedon

527–565 — Reign of Emperor Justinian

ca. 570 — Birth of Muhammad

680 — Battle of Karbala and death of Hussein ibn Ali, grandson of the Prophet. A very important date for Shi'ite Muslims

710 — Beginning of Muslim offensive against Iberian Peninsula

732 — Battle of Tours; Charles Martel stops Muslim advances north of the Pyranees

1054 — Mutual excommunication of Pope and Patriarch of Constantinople

1202–1204 — Fourth Crusade; crusaders sack Constantinople

1219 — Visit of Francis of Assisi to Sultan Malik al-Kamil during the Fifth Crusade

1291 — Fall of Acre and loss of Crusader rule in the Levant

End of 13th c. — Beginning of Ottoman Turks

1683 — Last Ottoman siege of Vienna

1829 — Greece achieves independence from Ottoman Empire

1916 — Sykes-Picot Agreement; France and Britain divide up the Middle East

2010 October 10–24 — Synod for the Middle East

2010 December 17 — Start of Arab Spring self-immolation of Tarek al-Tayeb Mohammed Bouazizi

2011 February 11 — Fall of Mubarrak

2011 March 15 — Start of Civil War in Syria

2014 June 30 — Establishment of Caliphate

A Brief Timeline of the History of Islam (continued)

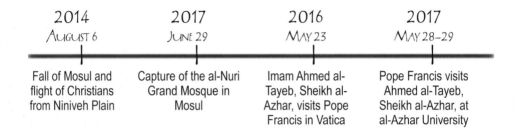

2014	2017	2016	2017
AUGUST 6	JUNE 29	MAY 23	MAY 28–29
Fall of Mosul and flight of Christians from Niniveh Plain	Capture of the al-Nuri Grand Mosque in Mosul	Imam Ahmed al-Tayeb, Sheikh al-Azhar, visits Pope Francis in Vatica	Pope Francis visits Ahmed al-Tayeb, Sheikh al-Azhar, at al-Azhar University

Why This? Why Now?

Current Context

In writing a book, *Islam for Religious Educators*, and specifically Roman Catholic religious educators, one can immediately hear the questions arising: "Why this? Why now?" This is entirely understandable. Religious educators are often overwhelmed by the task which faces them. Curricula are becoming more complicated and the amount of material to be taught is becoming greater and greater. The era of "question and answer" religious education is past and religious educators are under tremendous pressure to continue their own religious education and to deal with topics which were never part of the religious education curriculum previously. If in the past religious education dealt solely with what Roman Catholics believed and never ventured into what others believed, since the Second Vatican Council we know that ecumenism and interreligious dialogue are part of the mission of the Church.[1] This expands the horizons of Roman Catholic education considerably. If one looks at the ecumenical involvement of the Roman Catholic Churches, there are dozens of bilateral dialogues that have been in progress for more than 60 years which have generated volumes of documents and have impacted how we Roman Catholics understand ourselves. The number of Christian churches is staggering—there are more than 300 member churches of the World Council of Churches—and many will have beliefs and theologies which differ more or less from each other and from the beliefs and theology of the Roman Catholic Church. Being faced with understanding this situation and presenting it within the larger context of Roman Catholic religious education is indeed a daunting, if not frightening, task. It is no wonder that many religious educators become frustrated at the constantly increasing demands made upon them and their curricula.

Interreligious Dialogue

When we begin to speak about interreligious dialogue the complexity increases exponentially. If ecumenical dialogues are varied and complicated, they at least all deal with a shared and basic set of Christian beliefs and perhaps also with shared assumptions. Ecumenical dialogue is by definition a dialogue *between Christians.* That is not the case at all with interreligious dialogue. If ecumenical dialogue could be compared to studying the planets of our solar system, interreligious dialogue can be compared to studying all the galaxies of the universe. Some religious traditions such as Hinduism can be even more diverse than Christianity. The beliefs, symbol systems, and rituals of Hinduism, Jainism, Shintoism, and Buddhism, to say nothing of indigenous faith traditions, are often radically different one from another. Academically, a student would limit herself or himself to achieving expertise in only one of these traditions and even that is the goal of a lifetime of work. Yet the religious educator is expected to be able to impart some knowledge about interreligious dialogue with each of these religious traditions to the Roman Catholic student. Interreligious dialogue is not something superficial to Catholic life. Pope John Paul II in a 1984 address to the Plenary Assembly of the Pontifical Council for Interreligious Dialogue stated: "[Interreligious] dialogue is fundamental to the Church, which is called to collaborate in God's plan with her methods of presence, respect and love towards all persons."[2]

Why This? Why Islam?

Why then should it be necessary or even advisable to produce a book on only *one* of the "galaxies" of the religious universe of humanity? Given the immensity of the task of conveying even the broadest outline of interreligious dialogue which involves so many different religious traditions,[3] why would we single out Islam for special treatment? Is not the field overly crowded as it is? Is there something about Islam that calls for special treatment that other religious traditions —at least at this point—do not require? Lastly, why does this have to be done precisely at this juncture in history?

In the history of the Roman Catholic Church's involvement in interreligious dialogue, special place has been given to particular dialogues. Thus the dialogue between the Roman Catholic Church and the Jews enjoys a special status that is even reflected administratively. The Catholic-Jewish dialogue is the responsibility of the Pontifical Council for Promoting Christian Unity, while all dialogue with other religions is the responsibility of the Pontifical Council for Interreligious Dialogue.

Having said the above, the original questions still remain: "Why this? Why now?" In attempting to answer these questions, two things should be kept in mind. Firstly, the answers to the questions will be located in the larger context of the worldwide Roman Catholic Church. Secondly, however, the specific context of Roman Catholic religious education in the United States will be kept in mind.

Catholic-Muslim Relations Since Vatican II

"Why this? Why Islam?" As a religion that believes in one God, Islam immediately stands in a special relationship with Christianity and Judaism. On October 28, 1965, the Second Vatican Council published *Nostra Aetate, The Declaration on the Relation of the Church to Non-Christian Religions.* After a general introduction, the first religion that the Council mentions in detail is Islam. The Council expresses its "high regard" for Muslims and notes that they "worship God, who is one, living and subsistent, merciful and almighty, the Creator of heaven and earth..." (¶3). The Council also notes the Muslim belief in revelation, final judgment, reward and punishment, their reverence for Jesus as a prophet, and their practices of prayer, almsgiving, and fasting. The Council implies correctly that Muslims and Christians (as well as Jews) worship the same God and recognizes that Muslims link their faith to that of Abraham. Thus, Christianity, Judaism and Islam are often referred to as the "Abrahamic religions."[4] For Roman Catholics, therefore, Islam and Judaism stand in a relationship to Christianity which other religious traditions of the world do not enjoy. Islam shares commonalities with

Christianity which other religious traditions do not: belief in the one God of Abraham, belief in a final judgment, belief in a revealed text and a reverence for Jesus which, while not holding him to be divine, reveres him as a prophet.

Christianity and Islam—unlike Judaism—are religions which proselytize.[5] Christians are committed to mission and Muslims to *da'wah*, literally "invitation," to attract new members to the faith. In fact, Christianity and Islam are the two fastest growing religions on the planet. Although accurate figures are difficult to find, Muslims account for some 1.1 billion people while Christians account for almost 2 billion people with Roman Catholics accounting for somewhere between 1.1 and 1.2 billion of the Christian world population. Until very recently the growth of Islam was mostly in Africa. Recently, however, there has been marked growth in the number of Muslims in Europe and North America. While some of this growth is certainly due to immigration, there is also clearly an increased number of conversions—some of them famous such as the boxer Muhammad Ali and the pop singer Cat Stevens.

As we shall see in the coming chapters—"Christian-Muslim Relations: The Seventh Century C.E. Until the Crusades," "Christian-Muslim Relations: The Crusades Until Vatican II," and "Christian-Muslim Relations: Vatican II Until the Present," the history of the relationship between Christianity and Islam has been a very checkered one, a fact which *Nostra Aetate* also recognizes (¶3).Crusades, jihad, conquest, reconquest, colonialism, anti-colonialism, competition for converts, power, trade routes, and so on have often put Christianity and Islam at odds—frequently at violent odds. Until the twentieth century, Roman Catholicism and Protestant Christianity lived in relative isolation from the world of Islam. To be sure there were always contacts between the two religions, but they were for the most part contacts of an individual, scholarly, or commercial nature and as such not on a massive scale. When encounters on a larger scale occurred, they tended to be hostile and certainly not on the level of equals—the possession of dominance and power alternated frequently between Muslims and Christians.

The twentieth century witnessed a major change in relations between Roman Catholics and Muslims. At least two things were responsible for this change. On the purely religious level the Second Vatican Council opened the Roman Catholic Church in a new way to dialogue with Islam. To be sure, scholars and holy people like Louis Massignon and Charles de Foucauld had close relations with Muslims long before the Council. However, with the Council the Roman Catholic Church as an institution not only opened itself to a dialogue with Islam but also actively pursued such a dialogue. In a later chapter we will look at this dialogue in greater detail.

Among Christians it was not only the Roman Catholic Church which actively pursued a dialogue with Islam. The World Council of Churches in Geneva, national councils of churches around the world, and innumerable local interfaith councils set up dialogues and cultivated relationships between Christianity and Islam.

In addition to a strictly religious initiative towards dialogue, another factor which played and continues to play a major role in the increased interaction between Roman Catholics or Protestant Christians and Muslims is the new immigration patterns of the second half of the twentieth century. To be sure there was always a small number of Muslims in Europe, Canada, and the United States. However, the second half of the twentieth century has witnessed a massive immigration of Muslims—and, of course, other believers—into a world that had heretofore understood itself rightly or wrongly as "Christian." Turkish *Gastarbeiter* ("guest workers") in Germany, Algerian immigrants in France and Spain, and sub-continent Muslim immigrants to the United Kingdom have introduced major demographic changes in northern Europe. In the late twentieth century, for example, Islam joined Christianity and Judaism as one of the three officially recognized religions in Belgium. Mosques, some of them large and impressive, can be found in most major European cities, including Rome. This has not been without problems. For example, official French "secularism" conflicted with the wearing of scarves by women students in state-run schools. The French court banned the scarf or veil. In the Netherlands the assassination of a well-known film artist by a Muslim extremist, offended by the artist's film on Muslim women, has caused some to question the open tolerance of the Dutch

Why Now? Islam and Changing Patterns of Immigration in the US

for Islam. In many countries calls for immigration "reform" are a thinly veiled response to a Muslim population that is increasing in numbers and political clout.

Why now? The situation that prevails in Europe is to some extent parallel and to some extent different from that in the United States. Most Americans are understandably unfamiliar with the history of American immigration legislation. In 1882, the Forty-seventh Congress of the United States enacted the Chinese Exclusion Act. Section 14 of the Act fairly well summarizes the entire Act: "That hereafter no State court or court of the United States shall admit Chinese to citizenship and all laws in conflict with this act are hereby repealed." In the early twentieth century Congress and the courts increasingly restricted immigration. The Immigration Act of 1917 and the Immigration Restriction Act of 1924 for all practical purposes cut off immigration not only from China but also from India and Japan. The notorious Supreme Court case *United States vs. Bhagat Singh Thind* was decided in 1923. Mr. Thind, a naturalized American citizen, a veteran of WWI and an Indian, was stripped of his U.S. citizenship. The Court based its decision in great part upon provisions of the Naturalization Act which "shall apply to aliens, being free white persons, and to aliens of African nativity and to persons of African descent." In its decision the Court also noted: "It is not without significance...that Congress by the Act of February 5, 1917, c. 29, &3, 39 Stat. 874, has now excluded from admission to this country all natives of Asia within designated limits of latitude and longitude, including the whole of India. This not only constituted conclusive evidence of the congressional attitude of opposition to Asiatic immigration generally but is persuasive of a similar attitude toward Asiatic naturalization as well, since it is not likely that Congress would be willing to accept as citizens a class of persons which it rejects as immigrants."[6] The situation brought about by the above legislation and court decision obtained until President Johnson signed the 1965 Immigration and Naturalization Act on July 4, 1965, some three months before the promulgation of *Nostra Aetate.*

The 1965 Immigration and Naturalization Act had as profound an effect on the religious atmosphere in the United

States as did *Nostra Aetate*. To be sure there were Muslims living in the United States even before the Chinese Exclusion Act of 1882. Diana Eck notes that Cedar Rapids, IA, is the home of what is called the "Mother Mosque of North America," founded from a community that traces itself back to 1895.[7] However, after 1965, increasingly large numbers of Muslims from the Middle East and India and Pakistan have entered the United States. Together with African-American Muslims, Islam forms the third—or second, depending on who is counting—largest religion in the United States. Although statistics are notoriously hard to come by, the number of Muslims in the United States is estimated between a low of three million and an unrealistic high of twelve million, with the reality being likely somewhere in between. In any case, it has become commonplace to note that there are more Muslims in the United States than there are Episcopalians or Presbyterians.

It is not as if all these Muslims had been here all along and simply went unnoticed. The changes in immigration laws have allowed a large number of people, among whom are Muslims, to enter the United States and become part of the American society. It is a *new* challenge for Roman Catholics and Christians in general. Not only are Muslims our neighbors, they are increasingly visible in our society. The expression "churches and synagogues," used by politicians, has become "churches, synagogues, and mosques." The navy's first Muslim chaplain was commissioned in 1996 and the first mosque was opened at the Norfolk Naval Base in 1998.[8] The United States Post Office issues a stamp to commemorate 'Eid al-Fitr, the feast of the breaking of the Fast of Ramadan. The suspension of alternate side of the street parking for Muslim religious holidays signals a type of "coming of age" in New York City. College and university students are increasingly in contact with Muslim students. This results not only in sharing information about their respective faiths but also the inevitable inter-faith marriages. If in the past, a "mixed marriage" meant a marriage between a Roman Catholic and a Protestant or Orthodox Christian, the field of possibilities has broadened almost infinitely. Once again it is very difficult to get hard data on the number of

Roman Catholic-Muslim marriages. Some, if not many of them, do not take place within the structure of the Roman Catholic Church and so it is difficult to determine the strength of the trend. We do know, however, that it is happening and it is happening with some increased frequency.

Summary

We may summarize the responses to the questions of this chapter in the following way: as to the question, "Why this?"

1) Interreligious dialogue is fundamental to the mission of the Roman Catholic Church;
2) Islam together with Judaism stands in a unique relationship to Roman Catholicism/Christianity among the religions of the planet;
3) Islam is the second largest religion on the planet after Christianity;
4) Relations between Roman Catholicism/Christianity and Islam have often been poor and even violent.

As to the question, "Why now?"

1) Muslims are quickly becoming a major religious presence in the United States;
2) Roman Catholics are increasingly coming into contact with Muslims in the United States in interreligious gatherings, prayer services, and even marriages;
3) Roman Catholic professionals—military, hospital, university prison chaplains, and others—are increasingly encountering Muslim clients and patients;
4) This situation is new and most Roman Catholics are unprepared for it.

Public Perceptions and Misperceptions

Not least among the reasons for "this" and "now" are the tragic events of September 11, 2001, and their aftermath. In understanding Christian-Muslim attitudes towards each other both September 11 and the aftermath are important. On September 11, 2001, a group of Muslim terrorists attacked and destroyed the World Trade Center and destroyed part of the Pentagon. For Americans the events were traumatic.[9] The fact that it was Muslims who were involved in the attacks fed the fears of Islam which many Americans already harbored. September 11 merely "proved" what they had believed all along—Muslims were bloodthirsty terrorists with no other desire than to kill Americans.

Some two years after the events of September 11, 2001, the United States invaded Iraq to overthrow Saddam Hussein, the Iraqi dictator, and to neutralize a perceived threat he posed to the security of the United States with weapons of mass destruction. We now know that those weapons did not exist. Nonetheless, the United States entered into a program of democratizing Iraq. The Bloomberg School of Public Health at Johns Hopkins University, Baltimore, MD, estimated that at the end of October 2004, 100,000 Iraqi civilians had died in the war.[10] This fact, less well known among Americans, is well known among many people in the Middle East and it "proves" what they believed all along—Americans are brutal, anti-Muslim, and willing to impose their will and their democracy at all costs.

Both positions are clearly mistaken but both positions are firm in the minds of some. The time for understanding is now. As the second largest religion in the world, Islam is the religion that we need to understand best.

In the chapters that follow there will be an attempt to introduce Roman Catholics and especially Roman Catholic religious educators to Islam.[11] The operative word here is "introduce." Islam is a way of life for over one billion human beings. Muslims live in almost every country of the world and in almost every culture of the world. Islam is a religion with a complex history spanning almost 1500 years. It would be as easy to describe Islam comprehensively in a work of this size as it would be to describe Roman Catholicism or Christianity comprehensively. In other words, it is impossible. In the chapters that follow I hope to describe the world in which Islam arose—admittedly from a Christian historical and geographical perspective. The basic tenets of Islam, its sacred text, the Qur'an, and the Traditions will be presented to give some indication of the rich diversity of Muslim spiritual experience. Here the reader may discover and deal with some common misunderstandings about Islam. Although comprehensiveness may exceed the limits of this work, every attempt will be made to make a presentation that is accurate, representative and above all fair.

STUDY QUESTIONS

1. What non-Christian religions can be found within my own parish boundaries?
2. Is there a mosque in my neighborhood? Have I ever visited it or wanted to visit it?
3. Who is Allah?
4. Have the events of September 11, 2001, affected my opinions about Islam and Muslims? If yes, how?

SELECT BIBLIOGRAPHY

Eck, Diana. *A New Religious America: How a "Christian Country" Has Now Become the World's Most Religiously Diverse Nation.* San Francisco: Harper Collins, 2001.

Richardson, E. Allen. *Strangers in This Land: Pluralism and the Response to Diversity in the United States.* New York: The Pilgrim Press, 1988.

NOTES

1. A note about terminology is important here. The Roman Catholic Church clearly differentiates between ecumenical and interreligious dialogue. Ecumenical dialogue is that dialogue which is carried on between Christians and which has as its goal the unity which Christ wills for the Church. Since all Christians belong to the same *religion,* ecumenical dialogue is not strictly speaking *between religions.*

   Interreligious dialogue is between Christians and those religious traditions that are *not* Christian. It has as its goal increased understanding and cooperation and the elimination of violence. Interreligious dialogue is, as the term indicates, a dialogue between *religions.* In common speech the word "ecumenical" is often used to refer to *any* dialogue between people of conviction. Roman Catholic usage will be followed in this book.

   In addition, the expressions "interreligious," "interfaith," "multifaith," etc. can also be found. Insofar as these refer to the dialogue between Christians and members of non-Christian religions, they are identical.

2. Cf. John Paul II, *Dialogue and Proclamation*, & 39, 1984. http:www.vatican.va/roman_curia/pontifical_councils/interrelig/documents. Accessed in April 2005.

3. In what follows the expressions "religious traditions," "religious faiths," and "religions" will be used interchangeably. Although it is often difficult, I try to avoid the expression "non-Christian religions" for several reasons. Firstly, it is a negative expression, i.e., it describes what the religion is *not* and not what it is. Secondly, it is reductionist in that the great religions of the world are more than merely "non-Christian." It is interesting to note that Christianity has no neutral term for other religions. In Islam, Christians, Jews and sometimes some other religious traditions are referred to as "People of the Book." In Judaism, the expression *haggoyim* or "Gentiles" is used and not always with a negative connotation.

4. While the term "Abrahamic" is helpful and often used, it should not be taken in an overly literal sense. While some Muslims and Jews have

an almost genetic understanding of their relationship to Abraham, Christianity has traditionally seen the relationship in spiritual terms, e.g. Christians as "spiritual Semites." Although it is clear that the figure of Abraham functions in a similar and often symbolic way in each of the three religions, it does not function in the same way in all three. The fact that Christianity and Islam are worldwide religions embracing many different races and nationalities further militates against a biological or genetic understanding of the term "Abrahamic religions."

5. I am using the word "proselytize" here in its most neutral sense: the attempt to win new members.

6. Cf. Diana Eck, *A New Religious America: How a "Christian Country" Has Now Become the World's Most Religiously Diverse Nation* (San Francisco: Harper Collins, 2001), 6 and *passim.*

7. *Ibid.*, 246.

8. *Ibid.*, 10.

9. The author lives close enough to the World Trade Center to have been able to see people jumping from the burning building.

10. Cf. www.nytimes.com/2004/10/29/international/europe/29causualities. html.

11. Although this book is written primarily for the Roman Catholic religious educator it is not written exclusively for such. It is hoped that the material here will be of some use and value for anyone who is trying to learn and teach about Islam.

Chapter Timeline

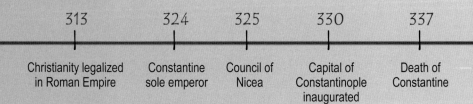

313	324	325	330	337
Christianity legalized in Roman Empire	Constantine sole emperor	Council of Nicea	Capital of Constantinople inaugurated	Death of Constantine

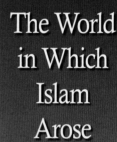

II

The reader is introduced in this chapter to the historical and religious milieu in which Islam arose and broke onto the stage of world history. The chapter will explore how the profound and sometimes traumatic divisions which occurred in Christianity aided the phenomenal spread of Islam in some ways.

The political and religious world of the Mediterranean and Middle East in the centuries before Islam

- *Christianity as the official religion of the Byzantine Empire*

- *Christian attempts to articulate the Faith-Ecumenical Councils*

- *The Council of Chalcedon—cause of major divisions among Christians*

- *The attempts of the Byzantine Empire to foster or impose orthodoxy in the empire*

The Byzantine and Sassanid Empires

In about the year 570 C.E.[1] Muhammad ibn Abdullah,[2] the Prophet of Islam, was born in Mecca in what is known as the Hijaz and is now part of Saudi Arabia. While an important center for incense trade, Mecca lay on the boundaries of the arena of world history of the time. The world into which Muhammad was born was divided between two hostile and warring "superpowers," the Byzantine Empire and the Sassanid or Persian Empire.[3] At the time of Muhammad's birth these two empires had intermittently been at war for over a century, with all the tolls that such a war takes. The Byzantine Empire more or less covered the western Mediterranean world. Technically

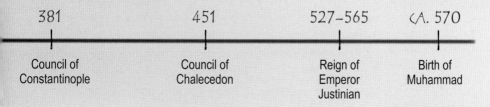

381	451	527–565	CA. 570
Council of Constantinople	Council of Chalecedon	Reign of Emperor Justinian	Birth of Muhammad

divided into the Eastern and Western Empires, at times the Byzantine emperor was only nominally in control of certain areas. The Emperor Justinian, who ruled from 527-565, reasserted the control of Constantinople over the entire Mediterranean basin. However, within thirty years of the death of Muhammad in June of 632, the entire Sassanid Empire had disappeared, fallen to the Muslim armies. The Byzantine Empire fared only slightly better. It lost territory in what is today modern Turkey, Iraq, Jordan and Syria. In addition, large sections of North Africa, such as Egypt and modern Tunisia, had fallen to the Muslim invaders.[4] The "Holy Land" and its shrines were lost to Byzantine control and came under Muslim administration. Christians of the time recognized five patriarchates or ecclesiastical centers: Jerusalem, Antioch, Alexandria in Egypt, Constantinople and Rome. Of the five cities, three, namely Jerusalem, Antioch, and Alexandria, were lost to Christian control within the first half-century of Islam's existence. In the fifteenth century Constantinople itself would fall to the Muslim Ottoman Turks.

Many, if not most, introductions to Islam begin with the birth of Muhammad or with the beginning of Islam as a recognizable religion or movement. The fall of the Sassanid Empire and the major loss of Byzantine and Christian power in the lands of Christianity's birth are often mentioned. Rarely, however, is attention given to the world situation in which Islam arose. Regardless of what one believes about the origins of Islam, it did not arise in a vacuum. Lack of knowledge about the world in which Islam arose can result in a picture of a peaceful, prosperous and united Christianity which was then overrun by an Islam which was "spread by the sword." Such a picture is basically inaccurate. While Muslim armies clearly did attack the Byzantine and Sassanid Empires, as well as other lesser nations, for the most part conversions to Islam were not encouraged in lands with large Christian populations. In addition, and perhaps more importantly, Christians in the eastern half of the Empire were often bitterly divided among themselves over theological questions.[5]

The fourth century was important for Christianity and the Byzantine Empire. In February 313 Christianity became a *religio licita* or a legal religion. For almost three centuries

Christianity had been illegal and its followers subject to prosecution under Roman law. The Roman emperors Constantine and Licinius published the so-called Edict of Milan and Christianity moved out of the catacombs into the full light of Roman history.[6] Slightly over ten years later in 324 Constantine conquered Licinius, took over the eastern half of the empire and began building the new capital of the empire on the straits of the Bosphorus in what is modern Turkey. On May 11, 330, the new capital, Constantinople, was officially inaugurated.[7] With Constantine's move to Constantinople the shift of the empire moved significantly eastward. "Old Rome" remained an important center of Christianity especially in the west, although Milan also played an intermittently important role. "New Rome" became the center of the political power of the empire. However, as we shall see, the lines separating religion and political power in a post-Edict of Milan world were not clear at all. Although Constantine legalized Christianity and gave it a great deal of his attention, it would be a mistake to see him as the "first Christian Roman Emperor." John Meyendorff notes that Constantine put off his baptism until he was dying in 337 and even then he was baptized by an Arian bishop. Meyendorff further notes that before his baptism Constantine's life style was little different from that of his pagan predecessors. He executed his former co-emperor Licinius (324) with whom he signed the Edict of Milan and he also executed his wife Fausta and his son Crispus at the very time he was attending the Council of Nicea.[8]

It is with the Council of Nicea that imperial involvement with theological and ecclesiastical affairs begins to be evident. Doctrinal conflict was not new to Christianity. Within a few decades of the death and resurrection of Jesus, the New Testament gives witness to a conflict among Christians concerning the relationship of the new faith to the Law of Moses. Some Christians, such as, the "Judaizers," were of the opinion that converts to Christianity from paganism should be circumcised and be obliged to follow the Mosaic Law. Other Christians, for example, Paul, held that such converts were neither obliged to be circumcised nor to follow the Law of Moses. Although attempts were made to reconcile

Heresy: Threat to the Stability of the Byzantine Empire

both positions,[9] there is no indication that the question was ever settled to everyone's satisfaction. In the second century Irenaeus of Lyons[10] in Gaul wrote *Adversus haereses* or more accurately, *Detection and Overthrow of the False Knowledge*. Irenaeus' work is directed not against "Judaizers" but against Gnostics, another group which was ultimately rejected by normative Christianity. Likewise in the year 318 or 319 a priest named Arius began preaching in Alexandria in Egypt. Arius' Christology held that the Son of God was a created being and was not "one in being with the Father."[11] This movement, which came to be called Arianism, spread throughout the Empire and at times the majority of those professing Christianity in a given part of the Empire were Arians.

It is not within the scope of this book to deal with the intricacies of the theology that developed in the orthodox response to Arianism and other Christian heresies.[12] What is to be noticed, however, is that after Christianity became a—and finally the only—legal religion in the Empire, the response to heresy changed considerably. In 313, Christianity went from being a persecuted religion to one that was recognized in the Roman legal system. In 325, less than fifteen years later, the Council of Nicea was convoked to respond to Arianism. What is significant is that the Council of Nicea was convoked by the Emperor Constantine, despite that fact that the Emperor was not even a Christian at the time. Not only did Constantine convoke the Council, but he also had considerable influence on its procedures and decisions.[13] Thus within an incredibly short period of time the Roman Emperor went from being a persecutor of Christianity to being its defender. To a great extent this was due to a vision of an empire united by one Emperor, one law code, and one faith. Other faiths were not merely ecclesiastical problems: they quickly became considered as threats to the unity of the Empire. Heresy became tantamount to treason and was often punished accordingly.

Nicea and its response to Arianism was the first of several general or ecumenical councils which met to deal with the burning theological questions of the day. The Councils of Nicea (325) and Constantinople (381) dealt with the basic question of what Christians believe God did in Jesus of Nazareth, the nature of the Son of God as created or uncreated, and the relationship of the Son to the Father. The result of the Councils of Nicea and Constantinople was an articulation of the faith that most Christians profess today, namely, the Son is consubstantial (*homoousios*), which is to say of one substance with the Father, uncreated and begotten from all eternity. While the results of these councils were impressive and expressive of the faith of most Christians today, it would be historically inaccurate to say that they "solved" the problem of Arianism. Arianism survived for a while after these Councils.[14] The Emperor Theodosius was an ardent supporter of the Councils opposing both pagans and heretical Christians. George Ostrogorsky, a historian of the Byzantine state, holds that under Theodosius the orthodox Christianity of the Councils of Nicea and Constantinople "became the state religion...while other religions and beliefs were denied the right to exist."[15] In fact, it is almost the universal history of Christianity that an ecumenical or general council never solved a problem in the sense that all Christians of the time accepted the decisions of the council and became reconciled with each other.

Arianism, however, was not the only problem with which Christianity had to deal. Once Nicea and Constantinople had clarified the relationship between the Son and the Father, a further question arose concerning the relationship between the human and the divine in Jesus Christ. At the risk of considerable simplification the question revolved around whether there were one or two natures in Christ and how the one or two natures were related to his "person." Those who held that there was one nature in Christ were known as Monophysites from the Greek expression "one nature." However, "monophysite" is a term that encompasses different understandings at different periods. A more accurate term might be "anti-Chalcedonians," that is, those people who did not agree with the decrees of the Council of Chalcedon and which would include the Armenians, the Copts of Egypt, and those Christians who are sometimes referred to as "Nestorians." Since most works refer to Monophysites, that is the term which will be used here.

The question of the relationship between the human and the divine in Christ was dealt with by the Ecumenical Council

of Chalcedon that met in 451. However, before looking at
the results and the impact of the Council of Chalcedon it is
important to see what had happened in Christianity between
the Council of Constantinople and the Council of Chalcedon.
In the year 527 Justinian became the Emperor. A skilled
theologian and an energetic politician, Justinian set about
restoring the unity of the Byzantine Empire. This included
reasserting his influence over Italy and the Gothic kingdom
in Ravenna, as well as those areas of North Africa under the
control of the Vandals. Political unity, however, was seen
as unachievable without religious unity. Under Justinian the
Corpus juris civilis was compiled and edited. Under Justinian's
Code, orthodox, that is, Chalcedonian, Christianity became the
religion of the state. Meyendorff notes that "By 451, 'orthodox'
means the faith of Nicea, as understood by the Cappodocian
Fathers, and the faith of Athanasius and Cyril of Alexandria,
as interpreted at Chalcedon. Dissenters were legally excluded
from the Church and from society in general."[16] The problem
is that a large segment of the population of the Empire did not
accept the decrees of Chalcedon. It is important to remember
that Byzantium was the heir and continuation of the Greco-
Roman world and culture. However, that was not the only
culture to be found within the borders of the Empire. Large
segments of the Empire belonged to a culture which was a
mixture of Greek Hellenistic culture and the native Semitic
cultures. While Greek was the language of the Empire and of
the theology of the Ecumenical Councils, Meyendorff notes
that "except in Greece and Western Asia Minor, the vast
majority of the population spoke neither Latin nor Greek. The
largest and most influential ethnic groups within the Eastern
part of the empire were the Syrians, the Armenians, the Arabs
and the Egyptian Copts."[17] Earlier Meyendorff estimates that
"the opponents of Chalcedon...constituted at least half the
population of the East."[18] Thus Justinian was faced with a
huge problem in his attempt to unify the Empire religiously.
Justinian's attempts to solve this problem, while typical, were
bound to fail. Religious oppression became increasingly
common in the eastern parts of the Empire. The civil rights
of Jews were limited and those considered to be Christian
heretics, such as Gnostics, Montanists, and Manichees, were

forbidden to practice their faith openly and were also deprived of many of their civil rights. Some were even executed.[19] Given the extent of anti-Chalcedonian feelings in the eastern parts of the Empire, Justinian's program was almost certainly doomed to failure. Once again it is important to note that resistance to Chalcedon and the imperial attempts to impose its decrees was a "movement of the masses" who were "beginning to identify their religious cause with the cultural non-Greek and non-Roman identity of Syrians, Armenians, Arabs and Copts."[20] Franz Georg Meier sees the tensions between Constantinople and the anti-Chalcedonians as resurrecting resentments that lay deep in the differences between Greece and the Orient, the West and Asia Minor. The heavy-handed measures of Constantinople unleashed or at least strengthened a religious separatism which led to a "de-hellenization" which further led to tendencies towards political separatism.[21]

The Religious and Political Milieu of the Sixth Century

There are a number of theories as to why the Muslim forces enjoyed such spectacular success. Although the Byzantine Empire decisively defeated the Sassanids, it was a Pyrrhic victory in which the victor was exhausted. There is considerable disagreement as to the role religion played. It is important here to recall that Justinian died in 565, less than ten years before the birth of Muhammad. Did anti-Chalcedonian Christians welcome the Muslims as "liberators" or as at least the lesser of two evils? Ostrogorsky holds that "the religious ferment in the eastern provinces [of the Byzantine Empire] which had assisted the Persians was now to do the same in the cause of the Arabs."[22] Meyendorff disagrees. "Recent research does not condone the view the non-Chalcedonian Copts welcomed Muslims as liberators from the Roman rule; even then, and in spite of Chalcedonian persecutions, there was widespread loyalty to the Christian empire."[23] Although Meyendorff and Butler are referring primarily to Coptic Egyptian resistance (or lack of) to the Muslim forces, other facts seem to support this position. For example, Sophronius, the Patriarch of Jerusalem who surrendered the city to the Caliph Omar was an ardent defender of Chalcedon. Nonetheless, at the time that the forces of Islam came out of Arabia, the Byzantine Empire was exhausted militarily and financially. More significantly, it was bitterly divided religiously, with little hope of a reconciliation on the horizon. Whether or not the non-Chalcedonian Christians welcomed the Muslim forces, it is indisputable that Christianity in the Byzantine Empire was incapable of offering a unified resistance to the new religious and political movement coming out of Arabia.

STUDY QUESTIONS

1. What were some of the principal internal and external challenges facing Christians in the time between the Edict of Milan and the advent of Islam?

2. How did the legalization of Christianity in the Roman Empire change it?

3. How did the official, imperial Church of Constantinople look upon dissidence and why?

4. What cultural differences might have existed between Chalcedonian and non-Chalcedonian Christians? What role did Hellenism versus Semitic cultures play?

5. How might the situation of Christianity in the sixth century have affected the spread of Islam?

6. How might the history of Christianity and the role of the Church in that history influence my own role in implementing the Kingdom of God in the twenty-first century?

SELECT BIBLIOGRAPHY

Meyendorff, John. *Imperial Unity: The Church 450-680 AD.* Crestwood, NY: St. Vladimir's Seminary Press, 1989.

Ostrogorsky, George. *History of the Byzantine State.* Translated by Joan Hussey. New Brunswick, NJ: Rutgers University Press, 1969.

NOTES

1. In most scholarly works today the abbreviations used are: C.E., "Common Era," and B.C.E., "Before the Common Era."

2. Arabic is notoriously difficult to transliterate into Roman letters. There are many sounds in Arabic which simply do not exist in western European languages. In order to represent Arabic words, scholars have developed several different systems of transliteration. Probably the most widely accepted method—though by no means the only one—is the one used in the multi-volume *Encyclopedia of Islam* published by Brill. In a work such as this I believe a complicated -if accurate—transliteration of Arabic words would confuse rather than clarify. As a result I am avoiding diacritical marks as much as possible.

3. Since the present work is geared for Christian educators, I will not deal with the Sassanid Empire at the time of the rise of Islam. Although an important actor on the stage of world history, the Sassanid Empire is not really relevant to the topic of this book.

4. "Muslim," literally "one who submits," the participle form whose verbal noun is Islam. Although one sees moslem from time to time, muslim is the correct spelling.

5. Since this work is on Islam and not Christian theological controversies of the first five centuries, I will not treat those controversies in theological detail. They will be dealt with only insofar as they provide an insight into the religious and political world in which Islam arose.

6. Cf. the extremely important work, John Meyendorff, *Imperial Unity and Christian Divisions: The Church 450-680 A.D.* (Crestwood, NY: St. Vladimir's Seminary Press, 1989).

7. Cf. George Ostrogorsky, *History of the Byzantine State*, trans. Joan Hussey (New Brunswick, NJ: Rutgers University Press, 1969).

8. Meyendorff, 6.

9. Cf. Acts 15:5-19 and Galatians 2:1-14.

10. Little is known about the life of Irenaeus. The date of his birth is placed as early as 115 and as late at 142 C.E. He became bishop of Lyons in Gaul sometime after his mission to Rome in 177/178 and died sometime after 191. The details of his death are as cloudy as those of his life, although traditionally it is held that he died a martyr's death.

11. Christology is that section of theology which deals with Christ, the Incarnate Word of God.

12. "Orthodox" is a very slippery word and can change meanings with the context. It can be used to describe the theological position taken by a theologian, a general council, etc., that ultimately became part of the accepted belief of the undivided Church. It can also be used to describe those ancient Churches which are not in communion with the Bishop of Rome, thus, Greek Orthodox, Russian Orthodox, etc. Orthodox can also refer to those who follow the faith of a particular Church. Lastly, it can be used as a slogan by people with little or no understanding of theology, heresy or orthodoxy to separate themselves from fellow believers with whom they disagree. It is the first meaning which obtains here.

13. Ostrogorsky, 47-48.

14. Although Ostrogorsky, 53, speaks of the "final collapse of Arianism" after the defeat of Valens in August of 378, Arianism remained the dominant form of Christianity among the Gothic peoples who were migrating to and conquering large parts of the Western Empire, e.g. Spain and North Africa. In fact, Arian Christians remained in control of much of North Africa until it was reconquered by Justinian in the middle of the sixth century.

15. Ostrogorsky, 53. See also Meyendorff,' 8. "In 391-392, Theodosius issued two decrees banning pagan cults, public or private, altogether. It is at this point that the Empire became constitutionally and legally a Christian state with paganism reduced to the position of a barely tolerated minority."

16. Meyendorff, 16. See also Ostrogorsky, 76.

17. Meyendorff, 95.

18. *Ibid.*, 17.

19. *Ibid.*, 210.

20. *Ibid.*, 230.

21. Franz Georg Meier, *Byzanz. Fischer Weltgeschichte.* Band 13. (Frankfurt: Fischer Taschenbuch Verlag, 1983), 64.

22. Ostrogorsky, 109.

23. Meyendorff, 27. In this opinion he refers to the research done in A.J. Butler, *The Arab Conquests of Egypt and the Last Thirty Years of the Roman Dominion*, ed., F.M. Fraser. Second Edition. (Oxford: Oxford University Press, 1978).

Chapter Timeline

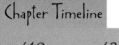

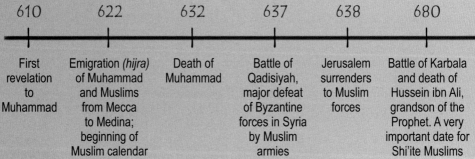

610	622	632	637	638	680
First revelation to Muhammad	Emigration *(hijra)* of Muhammad and Muslims from Mecca to Medina; beginning of Muslim calendar	Death of Muhammad	Battle of Qadisiyah, major defeat of Byzantine forces in Syria by Muslim armies	Jerusalem surrenders to Muslim forces	Battle of Karbala and death of Hussein ibn Ali, grandson of the Prophet. A very important date for Shi'ite Muslims

III

Christian-Muslim Relations: The 7th Century Until the Crusades (1095)

Modern western attitudes and prejudices towards Islam have deep roots. In this chapter the reader encounters the phenomenal spread of Islam in what was the Byzantine Christian Middle East. The Holy Land and three of the five ancient Patriarchates of the Church (Jerusalem, Antioch, and Alexandria) come under Muslim political control. The southern shore of the Mediterranean Sea, the "Byzantine lake," comes under Muslim control and western Europe is threatened and attacked. Western Christianity has its first encounters with Islam which forms western attitudes for centuries to come.

- Stories of positive Christian-Muslim encounters during the life of Muhammad

- Waraqa ibn Nawfal, the refugees to Abyssinia

- Expansion of Islam after the death of Muhammad

- The transfer of the Holy Land from Byzantine to Muslim control

- Muslim conquest of the Middle East, North Africa, and Spain

- Islam as a religious and political threat to Byzantium and Western Christianity

- The Western attitude towards Islam as a religious and political threat

- Events leading to the Crusades

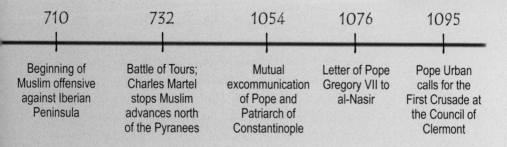

710	732	1054	1076	1095
Beginning of Muslim offensive against Iberian Peninsula	Battle of Tours; Charles Martel stops Muslim advances north of the Pyranees	Mutual excommunication of Pope and Patriarch of Constantinople	Letter of Pope Gregory VII to al-Nasir	Pope Urban calls for the First Crusade at the Council of Clermont

Some Important Distinctions

In treating the relationship between Christianity and Islam over the centuries, several things have to be taken into account. First, the relationship between these two traditions covers a vast area both geographically and chronologically. In the classical period the lands of Islam extended from Morocco on the Atlantic Ocean to Xinjiang (Sinkiang) Province in Western China. Likewise the lands of Christianity included all of Europe, to a great extent Russia, and later the New World. As we shall see, relations between Christians and Muslims differed radically depending upon geography. Christians in Syria and Moorish Spain, for example, had a very different attitude towards Islam than did Medieval Christians living north of the Alps. Christians in Moorish Spain lived in relative peace with their Muslim neighbors and rulers. Christians in Eastern Europe, on the other hand, lived in fear of an imperialistic Ottoman Empire, which expanded from Turkey to the gates of Vienna.

In addition to the vast geographical extent of the two religions, the chronology of Christian-Muslim relations covers almost fourteen centuries. During this period there were times when this or that Muslim group was politically expansive or this or that Christian group was the same. At times Muslims took advantage of Christian political and military weakness and at other times Christians took advantage of Muslim weakness. In an introduction such as this it is almost impossible adequately to outline the extremely complex fabric of relationships that obtained between Christianity and Islam over the past fourteen centuries.

There is also a problem of terminology. Although Islam has several division or sects, for example, Sunni, Shi'ite, Ismaili,[1] it is, for the most part, accurate to speak of "Islam" when speaking of Christian-Muslim relations. For the most part, Christians have encountered Sunni Islam. To be sure, there were and continue to be Christians living among Shi'ite Muslims, but the vast majority of encounters on the personal and institutional level are with Sunni Muslims. While the term "Islam" can fairly be used in speaking of Christian-Muslim relations, the term "Christian" is problematic. Islam came onto the stage of world history in the seventh century C.E.

Although, as we have seen, there were bitter theological divisions between Christians in the eastern half of the Byzantine Empire, those divisions had not yet developed into full-fledged schisms. To be sure, the seeds were present in the seventh century which would develop into full blown divisions and the breaking of communion between orthodox Chalcedonian Christians and non-Chalcedonian Christians. Likewise, the tragic divisions between the western Church in Rome and the eastern Church in Constantinople were several centuries in the future as were the divisions which occurred in western Christianity later still during the Reformation. This means that the term "Christian" can be ambiguous. In the first centuries of the Muslim-Christian encounter, the word "Christian" does not need further clarification. After 1054 and the Reformation, it is necessary to clarify whether we are talking about Eastern Orthodox Christians, Roman Catholics, or Protestant Christians. To some extent, the same applies to the term "Catholic." While in common speech "Catholic" is used to mean Roman Catholic and those churches in communion with the See of Rome, Eastern Orthodox Christians and many Protestants see themselves as "catholic" in the sense that the word is used in the Nicene Creed: we believe in one, holy, catholic, and apostolic Church. Before 1054, all Chalcedonian Christians would have seen themselves as "catholic." After 1054, most western Christians would have seen themselves as "catholic." After the Reformation, however, "catholic" and specifically Roman Catholic, is used precisely for the Roman Catholic Church which is in communion with the Pope in Rome.

It is important to keep these divisions in mind especially as we approach Christian-Muslim relations in the modern era. The Roman Catholic Church, the different Orthodox Churches and the Protestant Churches each have developed a relationship with Islam especially since the middle of the twentieth century.

Dividing the history of Christian or Roman Catholic-Muslim relations into a thirteenth century pre-Vatican II period and a 40-year post-Vatican II period is not arbitrary. As we shall see, it was with the publication of *Nostra Aetate*, or *The Declaration on the Relation of the Church to Non-Christian*

Religions in October 1965 that the Roman Catholic Church officially initiated a systematic and institutionally driven attempt to engage Muslims—as well as members of other world religious traditions—in dialogue. This by no means indicates that there was no dialogue before 1965, because indeed there was. However, those encounters tended to be of a personal or local nature. With Vatican II, the Roman Catholic Church committed itself *institutionally* to pursuing and promoting dialogue with Muslims.

Early Encounters Between Christians and Muslims

The earliest encounters between Islam and Christianity are brief and poorly documented. What is interesting is that they are positive. When Muhammad receives his first revelation, which is traditionally held to be chapter 96:1-5 of the Qur'an, he was overcome by doubt and fear. According to Islamic tradition,[2] his wife Khadijah took him to her cousin Waraqa ibn Nawfal, who is described first as a *hanif*, or a person who was a monotheist before the coming of Islam. However, Waraqa is not merely a *hanif* but is purported to have converted to Christianity. According to the biographer Ibn Ishaq, Muhammad was brought to Waraqa in an attempt to calm his doubts.[3] There is not a great amount of information about Waraqa. While we are told that he was a Christian—and seemingly remained one—we do not know what kind of a Christian he was. According to Ibn Ishaq, Waraqa convinces Muhammad that his revelations are indeed genuine and that he is, in fact, within a long tradition of prophets. Waraqa states, "there has come to him [Muhammad] the greatest law that came to Moses "and that" surely he is the prophet of this people."[4] Much of Waraqa's life before and after the advent of Islam is not clear and there are often contradictory details. However, inconsistencies do not affect the fact that the first encounter between incipient Islam and Christianity was a positive one.

A second encounter between Muslims and Christians took place during the emigration to Abyssinia. It is generally held that Muhammad received his first revelation about the year 610 after which he began to preach and to encourage "submission (to the one God)."[5] Almost from the beginning, the new movement met with opposition from the polytheistic citizens of Mecca. That opposition became violent and in about the year 615, a group of Muslims left Mecca for Abyssinia, a Christian kingdom, in Africa. Some of the Muslims remained there even after the Hijra or Emigration of Muhammad and his followers to Medina in 622. According to Muslim sources the small band of refugees was brought before the Negus, or king of Abyssinia. When asked who they were and what they believed, they read to him the chapter of the Qur'an entitled Maryam, or Mary. The Negus, a Christian, was supposedly so impressed by the Muslim reverence for Mary, the mother of Jesus, that he granted them asylum.

There has been considerable discussion as to the role which Christianity and Judaism may have played in Muhammad's immediate world. It is clear that the people of Arabia had some contact with Christianity and Judaism. Yemen on the southern tip of the Arabian peninsula had briefly been a Jewish kingdom. It is also clear that there was a considerable Jewish population in Yathrib.[6] We have already mentioned the Christian kingdom of Abyssinia. Lastly, the Byzantine Empire, one of the two "superpowers" of the day, was Christian and included Egypt, which would have had regular contacts with the Arab world at the time of Muhammad. Arabians and especially Meccans were engaged in trade with the Byzantine and Sassanid Empires and clearly came in contact with Christianity, Judaism, and Zoroastrianism. Perhaps Marshall G. S. Hodgson summarizes the religious situation best. He notes that all the Irano-Semitic monotheistic religions were represented in the area around Arabia. Reflecting the divisions between Christians mentioned in the previous chapter, Hodgson states "Most widespread was Christianity, which in a variety of mutually hostile forms prevailed in the Mesopotamian plain." However, he writes that the region around Mecca had shown itself fairly impervious to the surrounding religions. While Muhammad would have used a vocabulary of heaven, hell, judgment, and other terms which would have been familiar to even pagan Arabs, Hodgson posits that Muhammad "may have been in the one place where paganism was still most vital."[7] Thus although Muhammad and Islam did have some, mostly positive, contact with Christianity, it does not seem to have been a very profound encounter and certainly did not provide the opportunity for direct Christian influence on Islam, which has been asserted at times in the past.

If the initial encounters between Islam and Christianity were positive, it was not to set a pattern for the fourteen and a half centuries which have followed. Almost immediately after the death of Muhammad in June of 632, Islam entered into a state of conflict and competition with Christianity. To say, as it often is said, that Islam was spread by the sword, is misleading and historically inaccurate. However, to imply that the spread of Islam was totally disconnected from military endeavors is also historically inaccurate. Beginning in the seventh century, Islam and Christianity began a series of conflicts which would continue with different agents, different geographies, and different outcomes right into modern times. Often it was Muslim armies which were the aggressor. However, Christianity was by no means always the victim. In point of fact, aggressions were initiated by both sides with great frequency.

The closing lines of Robert Burns's poem *To a Louse* (in "translation" from the Scottish) are instructive for a Christian understanding of Islam: "Would some Power give us the gift to see ourselves as others see us; it would from many a blunder free us." The ability to see oneself through the eyes of others is indeed a rare gift. In these circumstances it is a crucial one. While both Muslims and Christians alternately engaged in aggression against each other, religious adherents of both groups tend to be blind to their own aggression. Thus, Muslims will remember the Christian Crusades, the Reconquista in Spain, and Colonialism whereas Christians will remember the attacks of early Muslims against the Byzantine Empire, the military expansionism of the Ottoman Empire, and the ghazi tradition. Although both Muslims and Christians have been at one time aggressor and at another time victim, popular memory within both groups tends to remember victimhood and forget aggression. Thus, the image of the other is often colored, if not determined, by a very selective reading of history. In what follows, I will—given the limits of this work—briefly set out broad lines of conflict which have existed between Islam and at least parts of Christianity over the past fourteen and a half centuries. As indicated above, this is not an attempt to write a detailed history of Christian-Muslim encounter. For the most part, the focus of what follows will be on Europe. Although Christians encountered Muslims and *vice versa* in other parts of the world, the encounters which took place in the Middle East and Europe seem to have worked their ways into the respective collective consciousness of Christians and Muslims, strongly coloring the image that each has of the other. In briefly looking at Christian-Muslim encounter the result will be to show that neither Christians nor Muslims were always the victim or always the aggressor. At times, Christians oppressed Muslims; at other times, Muslims oppressed Christians. On the level of politics and institutions, relations between Christians and Muslims do not enjoy a friendly history. *Nostra Aetate* is well aware of this. However, that is not to say that the picture is irredeemably bleak. Even before Vatican II there were positive, though limited, encounters between open-spirited Christians and Muslims over the centuries.

Expansion of Islam in the 7th Century

Muhammad died on June 8, 632, in Medina. Before his death he had engaged in military activities. To some extent these were defensive and then later offensive tactics against the enemies of Islam in Mecca. However, there were other campaigns against Arab tribes elsewhere on the Arabian peninsula. After triumphantly entering Mecca in 630, destroying the idols and symbols of polytheism, and setting up Islam as the religion of Mecca, Muhammad turned his attention back to other non-Muslim Arabs on the peninsula. In 631, messengers were sent to tribes in the area requiring submission to Islam. However, it should be noted that in dealing with the people of Najran, a part of Yemen, a different policy prevailed. Since the people of Najran were Christians and, hence, monotheists, they were not required to accept Islam. Acceptance of the political leadership of Muhammad sufficed and they were able to continue practicing their Christianity. While Islam spread politically through military means, it did not spread religiously in formerly Byzantine Christian lands through coercion.

Taking advantage of the loss of Sassanid control over Iraq and the military and financial exhaustion of Byzantine forces, Muhammad sent military excursions into Byzantine and Sassanid territories to bring Arab tribes living there into Islam. In 631, a year before Muhammad's death, an army of some 30,000 men were sent against the (Christian) Arab defenders on the Byzantine Syrian frontier. This excursion does not seem to have had any permanent or notable effect on the situation in Syria, but it was certainly a portent of things to come.

When Muhammad died in June of 632, there had been no provision made for any type of succession. A true succession was impossible, since Muhammad was the "Seal of the Prophets," that is, the last of the prophets. After Muhammad there could be no more prophets. Nonetheless, Muhammad was also the political and military leader of the Muslim community or *umma*. If the community were to survive, indeed, if Islam itself were to survive, some kind of political and military leadership had to arise. When Muhammad died, leaders in the community chose Abu Bakr, one of Muhammad's first converts to Islam and his faithful companion, to be Caliph, a word meaning "replacement, vicar, representative." While the Caliph was in no way a prophet, he did exercise considerable power in issuing religious decisions and interpretations. Abu Bakr had to deal with Arab tribes who, having recognized the authority of Muhammad, refused to recognize the authority of any successor to the Prophet. The so-called *Riddah* ("apostasy") Wars succeeded in quelling the rebellion and solidifying the power of Abu Bakr. However, Abu Bakr was to live only two years after Muhammad's death. He died in 634 and was succeeded in the Caliphate by Umar[8] ibn Khattab. With the Caliphate of Umar (634-644), the great period of Islam's initial expansion began.

In 635, Muslim forces moved into Byzantine Syria and temporarily captured the city of Damascus. The following year Muslim forces met a large contingent of the Byzantine army in the Battle of Yarmuk in modern day Jordan. The Byzantine army, led by the brother of the Byzantine emperor, was soundly defeated. The emperor's brother was killed in the battle and Damascus was decisively captured at this time, leaving Syria vulnerable to further attacks by Muslim forces. At the same time in the east, Muslim forces were conquering lands which had been under Sassanid rule in Iraq. A large Sassanid army was defeated in the Battle of Qadisiyah in 637 with the ensuing loss of Ctesiphon, the Sassanid capital, and by 641, the Sassanid empire had been totally defeated and disappeared from the pages of history.

In the west, Muslim forces continued to enjoy success. In 638, Jerusalem surrendered without a fight to the Muslims. Sophronius, the Christian Patriarch of Jerusalem, met the Caliph Umar on the Mount of Olives to surrender the city. It is said that Sophronius was impressed by the simple way in which Umar was dressed and offered him better clothing. When Umar was invited to pray at the Church of the Holy Sepulchre, he refused. It is said that he feared that if he prayed in the church, Muslims would think that it belonged to them. Even to this day across the square from the Church of the Holy Sepulchre one can see the small Mosque of Umar, where the Caliph chose to pray after accepting the surrender of Jerusalem. With the fall of Caesarea in 640, Byzantine control of Syria came to an end. The birthplace of Christianity would now be under Muslim political control.

Between 639 and 646, Muslim forces conquered Egypt. Alexandria, the center of Hellenism since the fourth century B.C.E., was now under Muslim and Arab control. At this time Muslim forces began using a navy which became increasingly powerful and which would ultimately control the Mediterranean. In 649, Cyprus was conquered by the Muslims and Sicily was attacked in 652, although at this time it was not conquered. Finally, in 655, the Muslim navy almost completely destroyed the Byzantine fleet off the southern coast of modern Turkey.

It is scarcely possible to overestimate the magnitude of what happened in an extraordinarily short period of time. In the period of less than 25 years between the death of Muhammad in 632 and the defeat of the Byzantine navy in 655, one of the great powers of the day, the Sassanid Empire, had totally disappeared, its territories coming under Muslim control. At the same time, huge sections of the Byzantine

Empire were also lost, although the empire itself survived. Syria, Armenia, Egypt, part of Anatolia (modern Turkey), and North Africa were lost to Byzantine control forever. Some of the territory lost was of tremendous historical and cultural significance. The loss of Alexandria, the heart of the Hellenistic world, was tremendous. Most traumatic, however, was the loss of the "Holy Land," the birthplace of Christianity, where Jesus had been born, taught, was crucified, and raised from the dead. The unthinkable had not only happened, it had happened with incredible speed and ease. The loss of Christian control of the "holy places" would impress an indelible stamp on Christianity's attitude towards Islam.

Recognizing the tremendous military successes of the Muslim forces and the tremendous threat which they were to pose to the Byzantine Empire and Western Europe for centuries to come still leaves many questions unanswered. For one thing, the lack of popular resistance to the Muslim invaders is significant. Neither Damascus nor Jerusalem, for example, offered significant resistance to the Muslims. While it is often difficult enough to ascertain *what* happened in the past, it is infinitely more difficult to ascertain adequately *why* something happened. Meyendorff is of the opinion that at least non-Chalcedonian Copts (Egyptians) did not welcome Muslims as liberators but rather there was a "wide loyalty to the Christian empire."[9] However, one wonders how widespread this loyalty was—did it extend beyond Egypt?— and how deep it was. Meyendorff himself lists several instances of Byzantine brutality against non-Chalcedonian Christians. A century and a half before the arrival of Islam, the Byzantine Emperor Leo I (457-474) put down a popular revolt against the Chalcedonians at the cost of 10,000 Egyptian Christian lives. After the time of the Emperor Justinian, non-Chalcedonian Christians were vigorously persecuted and Meyendorff speaks of a "radical repression of religious dissidents."[10] Jews also found their civil rights severely curtailed under Justinian and there was an attempt to force them to use the Septuagint, the Greek translation of the Hebrew Bible, instead of the original Hebrew, in synagogue services. Nor was resistance to the orthodoxy of Constantinople limited to a small segment of the population.

Meyendorff estimates that half of the population of the east opposed Chalcedon, while Meier holds that almost the entire eastern and southeastern parts of the Empire were in opposition to the imperial orthodoxy.[11] Scholars recognize that while resistance to Constantinople was religious in origin and nature, it began to take on nationalist, cultural, and political overtones. At the risk of oversimplification, the resistance went from being Chalcedonian vs. Monophysite to being Hellenistic vs. Semitic.

The advancing Muslim armies did not attempt to convert local Christian populations. Hodgson notes that Christian Arab tribes were not required to accept Islam and were even allowed to join the Muslim forces.[12] Nonetheless, after the *Riddah* Wars, there was a movement to unify the faith of the Arabian peninsula under Islam.[13] However, non-Arab Christians in the newly conquered lands were allowed to continue to practice their faith. To be sure, Christians and Jews were considered by the Muslims to be *dhimmi*, or a protected minority, whose rights were limited *vis-à-vis* Muslims. In later centuries some *dhimmis* were severely restricted in their civil rights and in the practice of their religion. However, in the first centuries of Islamic rule, Christians formed the majority of the population in the former Byzantine lands and their condition was often considerably better than it had been under the Empire. The scholar John Joseph notes that a few centuries after the Muslim conquest a Nestorian[14] chronicler wrote, "The hearts of the [non-Chalcedonian] Christians rejoiced over the domination of the Arabs—may God strengthen it and prosper it...."[15] Jews fared much better under Muslim rule than they had under an increasingly hostile Byzantine state. For the most part as long as the local populations recognized the authority of the Muslim conquerors, the Muslims "left the internal life of the conquered Christian, Jewish, Mazdean, and Buddhist communities to proceed on its own...."[16]

In addition to the improvement which Islam brought to the civil lives of non-Chalcedonian Christians and to Jews in the Empire, another element was also at work. To be sure Judaism, Christianity and Islam have a great deal in common, as we shall see in Chapter 7. While it is very clear now that

Islam is not a Jewish or a Christian sect, that distinction was not as clear to people when Muslims first appeared on the historical stage. In some of the polemic literature against Islam in the first two centuries, some Christians believed that Islam was another Christian heresy or a peculiar form of Judaism. There are indications that St. John Damascene, (John of Damascus ca. 650-754) whose family had worked at the court of the Umayid Caliphs in Damascus, was of the former opinion. Reasons for this opinion included the facts that Muslims worshiped the same one God as Christians and Jews, believed in God's judgment, and held Jesus and Mary in high regard.

Among the vast majority of contemporary Christians, the stories, indeed the history, of the initial conquests of Islam have been mediated through Byzantine and western Christian (Chalcedonian) historians. For the Byzantine Empire, and later for Western Europe, Muslim conquests were an unmitigated disaster and presented a powerful threat which would last for centuries. Nevertheless, it is important to realize that there were other groups of Christians who held a different—and sometimes radically different—attitude towards the presence of Muslim rule in the former lands of the Byzantine Empire. If Byzantium and the West looked upon the "loss of the Holy Land" as a tragedy, that was not an opinion necessarily shared by every Christian of the time. Recall that almost all of Egypt and much of the Semitic world consisted of non-Chalcedonian Christians. For these non-Chalcedonian Christians life was often better under Islam.

While the loss of Syria, Iraq, and Egypt profoundly affected the eastern half of the Mediterranean, it was not long before Islam was having a major impact on the western half. The Muslim conquest of the southern shore of the Mediterranean is not well-documented. North Africa had been lost to the Arian Christian Vandals in the fifth century only to be re-conquered by the Byzantine Emperor Justinian. The culture, language, and religion of North Africa was superficially Byzantine Christian. Berbers, the local population, seem for the most part to have resisted being assimilated to Greco-Roman customs. By the end of the seventh century there was a Muslim presence in the western part of North Africa, the Maghrib. In 663, a Muslim general, Uqbah ibn Nafi al-Fihri, had established an important military base at Kairouan. However, Muslim presence in North Africa was precarious and it was not until about 710 that Muslims under Musa ibn Nusair were sufficiently entrenched to begin a campaign against Spain.

Musa sent a force to Spain under the Berber Muslim Tariq. The place where Tariq landed was later called Tariq's Mountain, *Jebel Tariq* in Arabic, which is now known as Gibraltar. At the time, Spain was ruled by the Goths who were sharply divided among themselves. Tariq and his forces were able to defeat and kill King Roderick, plunder Toledo, and reach almost to the northern coast of Spain. From Spain, Muslim forces were able to initiate campaigns into southern France. The very heart of France was threatened by the Muslim army's advance into the Rhone Valley. It was only in 732 that Charles Martell in the Battle of Tours and Poitiers was able to stop the Muslim advance north of the Pyrenees in Europe. Nonetheless, most of Spain, except for the northernmost sections, was to remain under Muslim control for several centuries. It was not until the *Reconquista* under King Ferdinand and Queen Isabella that Muslim forces were driven from Spain in 1492. In the intervening centuries, however, an extraordinary civilization blossomed in Muslim Spain. Muslims, Christians, and Jews lived in relative peace and prosperity. Philosophy, theology, the arts, and science all flourished in Spain. Al-Andalus, Andalusia, was a center of learning, art, and culture during a time when the rest of Europe was in the so-called "Dark Ages." It is estimated that in the thirteenth century, Cordoba had almost a quarter of a million inhabitants. In the same period it is estimated that Paris, Florence, Venice, and Milan had roughly 100,000 inhabitants, making Cordoba the largest city in Europe at the time.[17] Roswithe, a Catholic nun visiting Cordoba during Muslim rule, wrote that it was the cleanest, most beautiful city that she had seen in Europe.

For most Europeans, however, Islam was an unrelenting threat. By the end of the ninth century, the eastern and southern flanks of Christianity were in Muslim hands. The

Expansion of Islam from the Eighth Century to the Tenth Century

Mediterranean, which had been a "Roman lake" and then a Byzantine, that is to say Christian, lake, was effectively under Muslim control. While Christians in the Middle East had considerable firsthand knowledge of Islam and Muslims, that was not the case in western Europe until the time of the Crusades. Knowledge about Islam in the west derived from stories and polemic that revolved around the incredible military successes of Islam and the demonic forces which Europeans believed drove those successes.

Strange events in Egypt would lead to a radical and detrimental change in Christian-Muslim relations. In 969, the Fatimids, a smaller Shi'ite sect of Islam, took over Egypt. For the most part the Fatimids were extraordinarily tolerant of Christians and Jews even by Muslim standards. However, al-Hakim V (996-1021) proved to be one of the strangest and most mysterious characters in Muslim history. He attempted to impose his puritanical views of Islam on the people of Egypt through a series of draconian laws. For a time men were forbidden to go out at night and women were forbidden to go out at all. Yet at another time merchants were only allowed to open their shops at night to show that Cairo was totally safe under al-Hakim's rule. The manufacture of women's shoes was forbidden; violations were punished by death. It was al-Hakim's treatment of Christians and Jews, however, that was most fateful. Jews and Christians were forced to wear distinctive clothing—Jews were forced to wear bells around their necks—and a persecution of Christian and Jews went on from 1008-1013. During this period, several churches and synagogues were destroyed. One of the churches that was burned was the Church of the Holy Sepulchre in Jerusalem. Although later Fatimids helped Christians rebuild the church, the story of its burning and of the persecution of Christians was brought back to Europe by Christian pilgrims and provided major propaganda and motivation for the Crusades.[18] Finally, one night al-Hakim rode into the desert and disappeared.

Until this point our emphasis has been on Muslim military activity. Of course over the entire period Christians— Byzantines, Spanish Goths, Franks, Sicilians, and others— were also engaged in military activity against the Muslim forces. Christian military activities were for the most part, however, defensive and at least initially not overly successful. However, a new era of Christian-Muslim relations was about to begin with the Crusades.

STUDY QUESTIONS

1. It is often stated that Islam was "spread by the sword." How accurate is that description? How might the phrase have arisen?

2. How might the expression "crusader" impact a Christian and a Muslim differently?

3. What was the attitude of Muslims towards Christians and Jews in Muslim lands?

4. What was the attitude of Christians towards Muslims? How much did Christians know about Muslims and where did they learn it?

SELECT BIBLIOGRAPHY

Armstrong, Karen. *Holy War: The Crusades and Their Impact on Today's World*. New York: Anchor Books, 2001.

Maallouf, Amin. *The Crusades Through Arab Eyes*. New York: Schocken Books, 1984.

Nicolle, David. *The Crusades*. Oxford: Osprey Publishing, 2001.

Riley-Smith, Jonathan. *The Crusades*. New Haven: Yale University Press, 1987.

NOTES

1. The different sects of Islam will be treated briefly in the chapter on Islam as a religious system.

2. An important religious literary genre among Muslims is the *s'rah* or biography of the Prophet. For the most part these biographies, while not lacking in legend, are fairly sober compared with the often fantastic details outlined in the hagiographic (lives of holy people/saints) texts of other religious traditions.

3. The details are not clear. In some accounts Khadijah, Muhammad's wife, brings him to Waraqa. In other accounts she goes alone to her cousin and tells him what happened and in still other accounts she goes to her cousin in the company of Abu Bakr, later to be the first Caliph.

4. See *The Encyclopedia of Islam* (hereafter *EI*), (Leiden; Brill): XI, 142-143 and W. Montgomery Watt, *Muhammad Prophet and Statesman,* (Oxford: Oxford University Press, 1961), 22. Watt's work, however, should be read with some caution.

5. *Islam* is the verbal noun in the IV form of the Arabic root *slm*. It means "submission," originally to God and his Messenger. In its earliest stages, Muhammad's call is precisely that, a call for his hearers to submit to God. The "generic" use of the verb can be found in the Qu'ran 2:131

in the account of Abraham's faith. "When his Lord said to him 'Submit,' (*aslim*) he said, 'I have submitted (*aslamtu*) to the Lord of the Worlds.'" Here submission is not strictly to a "religion" with a developed code and cult but to God's will.

6. Yathrib, the name of the city about 250 miles to the north of Mecca, to which Muhammad and the Muslims emigrated in the Hijra. Yathrib then became known as *madinat u-nabi*, "the City of the Prophet," hence Medina.

7. Marshall G. S. Hodgson, *The Venture of Islam: The Classical Age of Islam*, vol 1. (Chicago: University of Chicago Press, 1974), 157.

8. Often transliterated as Omar.

9. Meyendorff, 27.

10. *Ibid.*, 210.

11. Meyendorff, 17; Meier, 64.

12. Hodgson, 199.

13. Hodgson, 199; Claude Cahen, *Der Islam I: Vom Ursprung bis zu den Anfängen des Osmanischen Reiches. Fischer Weltgeschicthe.* (Frankfurt: Fischer Taschenbuch Verlag, 1982), 25. Cahen notes that after the *Riddah* Wars Christians and Jews were no longer permitted to live in the Arabian peninsula.

14. "Nestorian" or better "Church of the East." The term "Nestorian" is seen as derogatory. It was used to describe a group of Christians who were followers of Nestorius. The theological position of Nestorius on the persons of Christ was declared heretical by the Council of Chalcedon.

15. John Joseph, *Muslim-Christian Relations and Inter-Christian Rivalries in the Middle East: The Case of the Jacobites in an Age of Transition.* (Albany, NY: State University of New York Press, 1983), 11.

16. Hodgson, 227.

17. Albert Hourani, *A History of the Arab Peoples*, (Cambridge, MA: Harvard University Press, 1991), 111.

18. Cahen, 261-167

Chapter Timeline

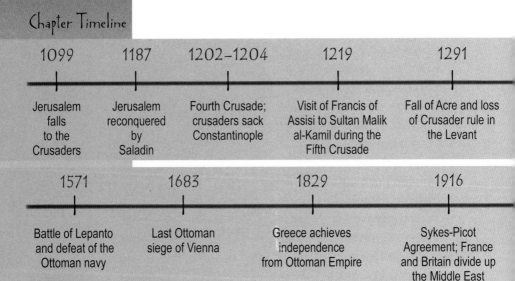

1099	1187	1202–1204	1219	1291
Jerusalem falls to the Crusaders	Jerusalem reconquered by Saladin	Fourth Crusade; crusaders sack Constantinople	Visit of Francis of Assisi to Sultan Malik al-Kamil during the Fifth Crusade	Fall of Acre and loss of Crusader rule in the Levant

1571	1683	1829	1916
Battle of Lepanto and defeat of the Ottoman navy	Last Ottoman siege of Vienna	Greece achieves independence from Ottoman Empire	Sykes-Picot Agreement; France and Britain divide up the Middle East

IV

Christian-Muslim Relations: The Crusades Until Vatican II (1962)

The reader encounters some of the roots of Muslim attitudes and prejudices towards Christianity and the West in this chapter. The Crusades have a very different image in Islam. The excesses of the Crusaders and even the term "Crusader" still strongly color Muslim images of Christianity. The reader is introduced to the history of recurring victory and humiliation which both Christians and Muslims have experienced at each other's hands.

- *Pope Urban II calls for the First Crusade in 1095*
- *The Crusades as a religious and military phenomenon*
- *Victories and excesses of the Crusades*
- *Muslim reconquest of the Holy Land*
- *The Ottoman Empire as a threat to Western Christian Europe*
- *The gradual ascendance of the West*
- *Western Colonialism*

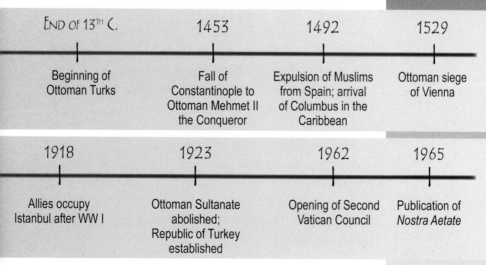

END OF 13TH C.	1453	1492	1529
Beginning of Ottoman Turks	Fall of Constantinople to Ottoman Mehmet II the Conqueror	Expulsion of Muslims from Spain; arrival of Columbus in the Caribbean	Ottoman siege of Vienna

1918	1923	1962	1965
Allies occupy Istanbul after WW I	Ottoman Sultanate abolished; Republic of Turkey established	Opening of Second Vatican Council	Publication of *Nostra Aetate*

- *Muslim attitudes towards the West as a religious and political threat*
- *Positive and non-violent encounters between Christians and Muslims*

The Crusades

By the eleventh century, Muslim power in the Middle East and the Mediterranean basin was becoming increasingly fragmented. Although the Abbasid Caliph in Baghdad was nominally the "Commander of the Faithful," in point of fact the Caliphate was becoming increasingly unable to exercise any real, independent power. Turkic[1] tribes were exerting more and more influence at the court in Baghdad and Seljuk Turks were conquering territories in Syria and Anatolia. The Seljuk victory over the Byzantines at the Manzikert in 1071 put almost all of Asia Minor out of Byzantine control. Muslim Spain was for all practical purposes independent of Baghdad, and the Fatimids, a Shi'ite dynasty which many Sunni Muslims considered heretical, ruled in Egypt.

The First Crusade

On November 27, 1095, at the Council of Clermont in France, Pope Urban II called for the First Crusade. The question of holy war, crusade, and the relationship of the pope to warfare did not begin with the Council of Clermont. In fact, there had been considerable discussion with some thinkers like Peter Damian (ca.1007-1072) and others who believed that the Church and the pope should have nothing to do with war; these thinkers held that war was basically the role of the state. Peter Damian's position, however, was not to win the day. Relying on the thinking of St. Augustine of Hippo (354-430), Anselm of Lucca (1036-1086) developed the theological basis for allowing wars of defense, providing that certain moral conditions were met. From this position, he derived that the Church had a right to persecute heretics. This position was later further developed into the Church's right to use armed force.[2] Earlier under Pope Gregory VII (1085) there had even been discussion of raising an international *militia sancti Petri*, "army of St. Peter." However, once the

Crusade had been called, other forces besides the papacy came into play. One of the more powerful and fateful forces was Peter the Hermit, whose band of "crusaders" murdered Jews in Prague and German imperial cities, sacked Christian towns and killed their inhabitants, and made themselves so feared and hated that most of them were killed in Hungary.

The Crusades were an oddity when they began. Pilgrimages to Jerusalem had long been a part of Christian piety and especially penitential piety. On a pilgrimage, there were several rules which one had to observe. A pilgrim was in a type of temporary clerical state with certain rights and obligations. While pilgrims were allowed to be accompanied by guards to protect them, they themselves were not permitted to bear arms during their pilgrimage. This radically changed in the eleventh century. The First Crusade was basically an "armed pilgrimage." The connection between crusade and pilgrimage, the religious symbolism connected with knighthood, and the indulgences involved with taking the Crusader vow gave the Crusades a distinctly religious character which was new in Christianity.[3] The infirm, elderly, and women could not become Crusaders. In addition, Pope Urban explicitly forbad monks from taking part in Crusades.[d]

The First Crusade was not a single military event but rather a series of "waves" of Crusaders arriving in the east. Some arrived at Constantinople where relations with the Byzantine Emperor Alexius were at best strained. The Byzantines clearly wanted to recover lands which they had recently lost to the Muslim Seljuk Turks. However, some of the Christian knights had plans of colonizing the conquered lands and establishing themselves as rulers. This was certainly the case in Edessa with Baldwin of Bourgogne (†1118), who set up the first Latin government in the Middle East, a practice which would be followed for almost two hundred years.

Supplying the Crusader entourage with sufficient food and other necessities of life was a major difficulty. In addition to the normal supplies needed by an army, the Christian knights required a tremendous amount of equipment together with servants and pack animals to transport the equipment. Famine stalked the Crusaders almost every step of the way.

Those who stayed for a while in Constantinople to purchase supplies rioted when those supplies were withheld. As the army of the Crusaders moved through what is now modern Turkey on the way to Syria, they often plundered conquered cities and lands to supply the needs of the Crusaders. Their numbers also increased as more Crusaders arrived, despite the fact that many who took the Crusader vow never left their home countries. On the way to Syria and Palestine they enjoyed considerable success militarily, despite the hardships they endured. Hardships were looked upon as a part of the penitential experience of the pilgrim. The Crusaders who conquered Nicea, Antioch on the Orontes (Antakya in modern Turkey), Edessa, and cities on the way to Palestine generally encountered little resistance, because the Seljuk Turks were often bitterly divided among themselves.

Conquest of Jerusalem

The high point of the First Crusade was the "liberation" of Jerusalem. The Crusader army arrived at Jerusalem on June 7, 1099. The city was defended by Iftikhar al-Dawla, a Muslim Egyptian general, who had made all the necessary preparations for what he thought would be a normal siege and attack. The Crusaders, however, did not attack as expected. Rather, under the leadership of Peter the Hermit, they processed barefoot around the outside of the city walls, stopping at the various holy place such as the Garden of Gethsemane to listen to sermons by Peter. Finally, in what can only be called a religious frenzy—a foreboding of what was to come—they hurled themselves at the walls of Jerusalem without equipment, discipline, or tactics. Needless to say, this first "attack" was not successful. However, more successful tactics were to follow and on July 15, 1099, the Crusaders breached the defenses and entered Jerusalem. What then occurred is best described in the eyewitness account of Raymund of Aguiles:

> "Wonderful sights were to be seen. Some of our men (and this was more merciful) cut off the heads of their enemies; others shot them with arrows, so that they fell from the towers; others tortured them longer by casting them into the flames. Piles of heads, hands and feet were to be seen in the streets of the city. It was

*necessary to pick one's way over the bodies of men
and horses. But these were small matters compared
to what happened at the Temple of Solomon, a place
where religious services are normally chanted. What
happened there? If I tell the truth it will exceed your
powers of belief. So let it suffice to say this much, at
least, that in the Temple and porch of Solomon, men
rode in blood up to their knees and bridle reins. Indeed
it was a just and splendid judgment of God that this
place should be filled with the blood of the unbelievers
since it had suffered so long from their blasphemies.*[5"]

K. Armstrong states that with the fall of Jerusalem some 40,000 Muslims died in two days. Nor were the Crusaders discriminating, since many Jews and non-Latin Christians were also killed. Godfrey of Bouillon was then declared the King of Jerusalem and the First Crusade was seen as having accomplished one of its major goals. Stories of the "liberation" of Jerusalem and the ensuing massacre, rather than filling European Christians with horror and revulsion, actually stoked the crusading fervor. Christians often are unaware that the events of July 15-17, 1099, have burned themselves into the collective memory of Muslims to this very day.

For a very important insight into how the Crusades have colored Muslim perceptions of the west even into contemporary times one may look to an important book by Amin Maalouf, *The Crusades through Arab Eyes*.[6] In some of the taped messages which have been shown on Al-Jezirah television, Osama bin Laden refers to Americans and Europeans as *salibiyun*, "Crusaders." It is a metaphor which is alive, well, and powerful among Muslims, especially Muslims in the Middle East. For many in the west, the Crusades are "ancient history." These events still offend the sensibilities of modern day Muslims who have a deep and abiding memory of the sack of Jerusalem in 1099. Nor is it only Muslims who have bitter memories of the Crusades. During the Fourth Crusade (1202-1204), western Christian knights attacked and plundered Constantinople. Latin Crusader states were established in Greece on the pattern of those established in the Middle East. Greek Orthodox Christians have never forgotten the sack of Constantinople and when Pope John Paul II visited Athens he apologized to the Greek Orthodox Metropolitan of Athens and the Greek Orthodox people for the brutality of the Crusaders. Although some 900 years in the past, the reality of the Crusades are still very much alive and color the mindset of Muslims and Christians in many parts of today's world.

Jerusalem remained under Crusader control until the summer of 1187. Salah al-Din, known in the west as Saladin, decisively conquered Crusader forces at the Battle of Hittim in Galilee on July 3, 1187. He then proceeded to Jerusalem. Saladin was famous for his magnanimity to those whom he conquered and to his enemies. As prescribed by the Qur'an, Saladin made an offer of peace to the defenders of Jerusalem. If they surrendered the city unconditionally there would be no massacre. The Christians refused and began to fight. Saladin swore an oath that he would treat the city as it had been treated by the Crusaders in 1099. When it became clear that the Christian situation was hopeless and that there would be a massacre, there were further negotiations with Saladin. The Christian representative, Balian of Ibelin, told Saladin that once the Christian defenders of the city saw that death was inevitable they would destroy everything in the city including the Al-Aqsar Mosque and the Dome of the Rock. Saladin was in a quandary. He had sworn an oath to destroy the Christians but he had no desire to see the Muslim holy places destroyed. Upon consultation with Muslim jurists, Saladin agreed to take the city peacefully but demanded a ransom for Christian prisoners. He took Jerusalem on October 2, 1187, without further bloodshed or plunder. Those Christians who were too poor to pay a ransom were released. When the Crusaders had conquered Jerusalem in 1099, Jews and Muslims were forbidden access to the holy places. When Saladin retook the city in 1187, "Frankish," that is, western European Christians, were no longer granted access to Jerusalem. However, Jews and both Greek and Orthodox Christians were given free access to the shrines.[7]

The Crusaders were able to occupy Syria and Palestine with varying degrees of success for almost two centuries. By the beginning of the fourteenth century the Crusaders had been driven out and their Latin Kingdoms disappeared, leaving only scattered fortresses which can be seen even today in Syria. The Crusader period had as profound an effect on Muslim consciousness as did the spectacular early military successes of the Muslims on Christian consciousness. The incredibly fast spread of Muslim political and military power deeply impressed on Christian consciousness an image of Islam as having been "spread by the sword," an impression which exists among some Christians even today. The Crusades impressed on Muslim consciousness an image of Christians as violent, brutal, land-grabbing, but ultimately conquerable, an impression which exists among some Muslims even today.

The initial and spectacular military successes of Islam and the Crusades tragically set a pattern which has continued to play itself out in history. Whether in reality or in perception there has been an alternating pattern of victory and humiliation. If initially the Muslim armies were successful and humiliated the power of Byzantium, the role was reversed during the Crusades. The Crusades, the invasion of Turkic tribes into the traditional Arabic and Persian lands of Islam, and, most importantly, the devastating attacks of the Mongols seriously weakened Islam in the Middle East and ultimately brought the Abbasid Caliphate to an end in 1258.

The actual power of the Baghdad Caliphate had been weakening under pressure from migrations of Turkic tribes for several generations before the catastrophic arrival of the Mongols. One of the main Turkic groups was the Seljuk Turks who maintained power for a while in the Middle East. By the end of the thirteenth century a new Turkic group appeared on the scene and, at least according to legend, helped the Seljuks in a battle against the Mongols.

The Rise and Decline of the Ottoman Empire

With Ertoghrul[7] and his son Osman the history of the Ottoman Empire began. Osman and the Osmanlis began rather cautiously in central Anatolia and it was several years before there was an armed conflict with Byzantine forces. When that did occur, it was the Osmanlis who were victorious. Osman was extremely cautious in expanding his holdings. Among the Osmanlis the tradition of the ghazi, a border raider who fought on the boundaries of the Muslim state, was decisive and was to remain a powerful force through most of Ottoman history. Initially the ghazis were more interested in booty than empire but that was to change as the Ottoman leadership first under Osman, then under Orkhan, his son, and finally under Murad I, his grandson, became more and more imperialistic. Step by step the Ottomans extended their power first through what is modern Turkey and then into the Balkans. The Ottoman leader did not take the title Caliph but rather Sultan. Through clever negotiations with and intrigues against the weakened Byzantine Empire, the Ottoman forces under Sultan Mehmet II the Conqueror (reigned 1451-1481) set themselves up in siege of Constantinople on April 2, 1453, Easter Monday. The Ottoman forces relied heavily on technology such as cannons and the brilliant strategy of moving ships overland to outflank the Byzantine navy. After seven weeks of bombarding Constantinople without great success, the Ottomans made a concerted attack on the city walls early in the morning of May 29, 1453. After intense fighting, the defenses of the city were breached and the Ottoman forces entered the city. Constantine XI (reigned 1449-1453), the last emperor of Byzantium, is reputed to have removed his royal insignia and gone into battle on foot as it became clear that the day was lost. He was killed in the battle and his body never found. Over a thousand years of Byzantium and almost two thousand years of the Roman Empire came to an end on May 29, 1453. For the modern reader the year 1453 may have little meaning other than being "long ago." In order to put it in some context, the following events took place within less than fifty years of the fall of Constantinople to the Ottomans: the births of Queen Isabella (1451), King Ferdinand (1452), Copernicus (1473), Michelangelo (1475), Martin Luther (1483), and King Henry VIII (1491). Of course, the best-known event to have taken place in this period was the arrival of Christopher Columbus into the Western Hemisphere. L. Kinross notes that "...May 29, 1453, has been enshrined among the myths of history as the turning point between the Middle Ages and the modern age."[8] Although Byzantium had ceased to be a major player on the stage of world history before that fateful day in 1453, one can hardly overestimate the psychological and symbolic impact which the fall of the Byzantine Empire had on western Europe.

In fact, the trauma of the Fall of Constantinople was only the beginning of the problems which Europe would experience. The Balkans, modern Bulgaria, Hungary, Poland, Austria, Romania, and the Ukraine would soon experience the power of Ottoman expansionism. In 1520, while Henry VIII was king of England and Charles V the Holy Roman Emperor, Suleiman, called the Magnificent, became Sultan in Istanbul. Suleiman attacked the weakest part of the Holy Roman Empire, captured the city of Belgrade, and in 1522 brought about the capitulation of the city.[9] Suleiman did not hesitate to use terror as one of his military tactics. In his war against the Hungarians, massacres were commonplace. At the battle at Mohacs the carnage was frightful. Kinross, citing notes out of Suleiman's diaries, records the entry for August 31, 1526: "...massacre of 2,000 prisoners;" on September 2 "20,000 Hungarian infantry and 4,000 of their cavalry buried;" on September 4 on the march to Buda "order to massacre all peasants in the camp." Kinross also notes "to this day, when disaster overtakes him a Hungarian will say: 'No matter, more was lost on Mohacs field.'"[10] On September 27, 1529, Suleiman and the Ottoman army were at the walls of Vienna. Suleiman threatened to destroy the city entirely and massacre the entire population. The defenders, however, proved to be stronger than expected and on October 14 inflicted a serious defeat on the Turkish forces. Unprepared for winter and disheartened by the lack of success, the Ottomans withdrew from Vienna. Internal Christian politics and rivalries between Protestants and Catholics and France and the Holy Roman Empire all worked together to create shifting alliances between Christians in Europe and the Ottoman Empire. These rivalries made a unified response to the Ottoman threat virtually impossible. Throughout the sixteenth and seventeenth centuries, Ottoman Turkish armies continued to harass central Europe. The conquest of Vienna was a constant but unattainable goal for the Ottomans. In 1683, the Ottomans laid siege to Vienna for the last time. Once again the Habsburg defenders kept the Turks in check and ultimately the winter forced them to withdraw back to Istanbul. The lifting of this last siege of Vienna by the Ottomans is recalled in the Feast of the Name of Mary on September 9th. Nor was it only central Europe which suffered from Ottoman attacks. The Turkish navy for all practical purposes controlled, at the very least, the eastern half of the Mediterranean. The coasts of Italy and even Nice (May 23, 1543) were attacked and plundered by Turkish forces. It was not until October 7, 1571, with the Battle of Lepanto that the European naval forces were able to defeat a major Ottoman fleet.[12] However, the beginnings of decline were becoming evident. Since the time of Mehmet II and earlier, the Ottoman Turks had been known for their openness to new military technologies. The extensive use of cannons in the siege of Constantinople would be an example of this. Nonetheless, by the middle of the seventeenth century, European armies began to outclass the Ottomans in military technology.

The ultimate decline of the Ottoman Empire took several centuries. The rise of European powers such as the Austro-Hungarian, British, French and Russian empires conspired to make the Ottoman Empire the "sick man of Europe" by the end of the nineteenth century. Step by step, the Ottoman conquests in central Europe were pushed back as local independence movements freed these conquered lands from Ottoman domination. Greece won its independence from the Ottomans in 1829 and other independence movements sprung up in the Balkans. By the time of World War I, the Ottoman Empire was in its death throes and western European colonialism was on the rise. Nonetheless, the Ottoman Empire had left an indelible mark on European history and consciousness. The often-brutal successes of the Ottoman armies were burned into the collective memories of the Christians of central Europe. The pendulum had swung in the direction of European Christian humiliation for almost four centuries and it was now beginning to swing in the opposite direction.

Shift of Political Power to Europe

European colonialism is not something which began in the nineteenth century. The "discovery of the New World" and the opening of new trade routes to the markets of Asia show the origins of colonialism already in the sixteenth century.

The British, Dutch, and French extended their influence and power over large sections of Asia. Although the French and British had been involved in attempting to control Egypt since the time of Napoleon, it was with the end of World War I and the fall of the Ottoman Empire that European colonialism in the Middle East accelerated. In 1918, the Allies occupied Istanbul and at the Paris Peace Conference presided over the dissolution of the Ottoman Empire with the intention of dividing Anatolia (modern Turkey) among France, Italy, and Greece. The efforts and struggle of Mustafa Kamal Atatürk prevented the dismemberment of the Turkish homeland. The Sultanate was abolished and the last Sultan, Mehmet VI was sent into exile. On October 29, 1923, the Republic of Turkey was declared. While the heartland of the Ottomans was saved and became modern Turkey, the lands in the Middle East dominated by the Ottomans were vast. Modern Iraq, Syria, Lebanon, Palestine, Israel, Jordan, Saudi Arabia, Egypt and the Gulf States were all *vilayets* or provinces of the Ottoman Empire. The British were concerned with keeping trade routes open to India, which it had made a part of the British Empire. The French were eager to keep the British in check and to assure their own interests in the region and both were eager to keep the Russians in check. The history of the Middle East in the period after World War I until the present is one which is complicated and not well known by most Americans.[13] Even before the end of World War I and the subsequent collapse of the Ottoman Empire, the Allies were planning to divide the Middle East up into "spheres of influence." The English and French, and to a lesser extent the Russians, seem to have believed that the Middle East would be theirs to divide up with little or no reference to the people living there. On January 3, 1916, the Sykes-Picot Agreement was reached between France and Great Britain which effectively provided the blueprint for the dismantling of the Ottoman Empire. In effect France was granted what is modern Syria and Lebanon as well as the Turkish *vilayet* of Mosul (the northern, Kurdish section of modern Iraq). Great Britain was to keep Egypt, Palestine, Transjordan (modern Jordan), and the *vilayets* of Baghdad and Basra, comprising the central and southern parts of modern Iraq and the country of Kuwait.[14] With the fall of the Ottoman Empire, countries were literally created in the Middle East which suited the interests of the colonialists but rarely reflected the needs, histories, and cultures of the locals involved. The result is two countries which are named after a family or a clan, viz., Saudi Arabia, named after the family of ibn Saud, an ally of the British, and the Hashemite Kingdom of Jordan, named after the family of Amir Hussein of Mecca, a member of the clan of Hashem. British machinations in Arabia, popularized and romanticized by Thomas Edward Lawrence of *Lawrence of Arabia* fame, were to influence the politics of modern Jordan, Israel, and Iraq up to the present day. Amir Hussein ibn Ali was the Sharif of Mecca. Although Hussein tended to play both sides, the British through him hoped to instigate an Arab revolt against the Ottoman Turks, who were technically responsible for the holy shrines of Islam in Mecca and Medina.[15] Although the Ottoman Sultan had been generally accepted as the Caliph, there were sporadic discussions by the British about making Amir Hussein, an Arab of the Prophet's family, Caliph. In the end Hussein was made King of the Hijaz. At the same time, Ibn Saud was the *de facto* ruler of the Najd, the central and eastern part of the Arabian peninsula. Ibn Saud, a member of the arch-conservative Wahhabi movement in Islam, was an avowed enemy of Hussein. Ultimately ibn Saud was to invade the Hijaz and drive King Hussein into exile in 1924. Not accepted by either of his two sons, the kings of Jordan and Iraq, Hussein died in Cyprus in 1931.

Britain managed to set up Amir Hussein's two sons as kings in the territory which had broken off from the Ottoman Empire after World War I. In 1946, Transjordan was given independence by the British and became the Hashemite Kingdom of Jordan under King Abdullah, the son of Amir Hussein. Abdullah was assassinated in 1951 and was briefly succeeded by his son Talal ibn Abdullah who abdicated in favor of his son Hussein ibn Talal, who died on February 7, 1999.

The British set up Feisal, another son of Amir Hussein, as king of Iraq from 1921-1933. He was also king of Syria for one year until driven out by the French. Feisal was succeeded by his inexperienced son, Ghazi, who was overthrown in a coup in 1936. The history of Iraq has been one of coup and countercoup leading up to the ultimate emergence of the Baathist Party in 1968 and of Saddam Hussein.

The parceling out of the Middle East brought the pendulum back to the point where Muslims were the ones experiencing powerlessness and humiliation. The disdain in which some of the architects of the modern Middle East held the local Arabs is nothing less than shocking. David Fromkin notes that Sir Mark Sykes, one of the architects of the Sykes-Picot Agreement, wrote that urban Arabs were "cowardly," "insolent yet dispicable (sic)," "vicious as far as their feeble bodies will admit," while Bedouin Arabs were "rapacious, greedy...animals."[16] The European division of the Middle East, however, was only a small part of the impact which European colonialism had on Muslims throughout the world. British India, which included what is today also Pakistan and Bangladesh as well as India, had one of the largest concentrations of Muslims in the world. With the withdrawal of the British, India became independent on August 15, 1947. Pakistan had achieved its independence as a Muslim state distinct from India, to which it had belonged under the British, on the previous day. Pakistan itself was divided into Pakistan in the west and Bangladesh in the east on March 26, 1971. Indonesia, presently the largest Muslim country in the world, was declared independent from the Netherlands on August 17, 1945, and became legally independent on December 27, 1949. Thus, by the beginning of World War II, almost the entire Muslim world was not in control of its own fate. The countries in the Middle East had been artificially created by European superpowers and countries with huge Muslim populations such as Indonesia and pre-independence India were under the direct control of Europeans. By the middle of the twentieth century, colonialism had politically been dismantled but its effects remain to this day. Muslims remember the days of glory during the Caliphate in Baghdad, the great Muslim Persian Empires, the Moghul Empire in India, and the great Muslim cultures of central Asia. Yet even after independence, no Muslim country has achieved the same level of power and culture as the great cultures of the past. Many Muslims find themselves living in underdeveloped countries with high levels of unemployment and governments that at best are non-responsive and at worst are despotic. While it would not be accurate to attribute all these difficulties to colonialism, local perceptions are, nonetheless, important and there is a great reservoir of resentment against the colonial past in many Muslim countries.

History is rarely clear or universally agreed upon. If it is difficult enough to ascertain *what* happened in the past, it is almost impossible to ascertain *why* something occurred and *what it meant*. Nonetheless, scientific objectivity in understanding the history of Christian-Muslim encounters is less important than understanding the perceptions, fears, and attitudes that have arisen on both sides as a result of those encounters. In the past fourteen centuries, Christians and Muslims have alternately been victim and victimizer, the ones who were humiliated and the ones who did the humiliating, the aggressor and the aggrieved. It is easy to pick out the faults of the other while ignoring one's own faults. The faults of the other may be real but that does not present a true, accurate, or fair picture. If any approach is to be made between Christians and Muslims and if any dialogue is to be successful, it is important to understand why mutual stereotypes exist.

Non-Violent and Positive Encounters between Christians and Muslims

If relations between Muslims and Christians were mostly characterized by hostility, it would, nonetheless, be a mistake to believe that the history is one of unmitigated hostility. Throughout the centuries, some open-minded and broad-spirited individuals—both Christian and Muslim—have encountered each other with respect and at times even affection. What follows highlights these encounters in an attempt to show that an alternative has always existed to the conflict which all too often occurred between Christians and Muslims.

There were many encounters between Christians and Muslims in those lands of the Middle East in which large numbers of Christians had lived before the Muslim conquests. The encounters, while not violent, were often apologetic, taking the form of a quasi-debate on the validity of Christian over against Muslim claims. Over the centuries, apologetics would be replaced by polemics on both sides. Nonetheless, there were those Christians and Muslims who did attempt to understand the faith of the other.

As early as 1076 we find an extraordinary piece of correspondence between Pope Gregory VII (1020-1085) and al-Nasir (1062-1088), a Muslim ruler in North Africa. Al-Nasir had sent a priest from his realm to Rome to be ordained a bishop to take care of the Christians living under his rule. Pope Gregory's letter to al-Nasir is quite amazing. Speaking of the love which al-Nasir has shown for him by releasing Christian captives, Gregory wrote, "God Almighty who wants all men to be saved and none to perish, likes nothing more in each one of us than the love of the neighbor after the love of God and to avoid doing to others what we would not like them to do to us."[17] Gregory states that he and al-Nasir owe each other charity in a special way since "we confess and acknowledge—in different ways, it is true—one God whom we praise...He who has made the two into one." Gregory speaks of "the grace that God has conferred upon you." Gregory closes his letter stating "we ask with our lips and from our heart that He [God] himself may receive you, after a long stay here below, into the bosom of the most holy patriarch Abraham's beatitude."[18] The tone and vocabulary of the letter are extraordinary and one does not find anything comparable to it institutionally until Vatican II. While it is only one example of how Christians and Muslims have interacted positively, it is nonetheless, an important one.

One of the more famous Christian-Muslim encounters took place during the Fifth Crusade. In 1219, St. Francis of Assisi accompanied the Crusaders to Damietta, Egypt. Although details are extremely sketchy and to some extent also surrounded by legend, it seems that Francis was appalled by the violence and immorality of some of the Crusaders. Francis was able to meet with Sultan al-Kamil, the Muslim leader. According to all accounts, Francis was courteously received and was able to address the Sultan. Although *The Little Flowers of St. Francis*, a pious and often legendary life of the saint, has the Sultan converting to Christianity, there is no historical record or indication that such happened.[19]

Raymond Lull (ca. 1233-1315), a prolific writer on Islam, a layman and member of the Third Order of St. Francis, wrote in Arabic as well as Catalan and Latin. Lull's approaches to encounters with Islam run the gamut of friendly preaching to warfare. Nonetheless, Lull writes in a prayer that the violence of the Crusades has not been successful but that the conquest of the Holy Land should be done "in the manner in which You [Jesus] and Your apostles have conquered it: by love and prayers and the shedding of tears and blood."[20]

Ricoldo de Monte Croce, a Dominican friar, spent some twenty years traveling through the Middle East, experiencing Islam first hand and becoming personally acquainted with Muslims. Ricoldo's extensive personal experiences of Islam and Muslims are unique among Christians of the Middle Ages. In his *Refutation of the Law Set Down by Muhammad for the Saracens*, Ricoldo uses all the traditional insults usually hurled at Muhammad by European Christian polemicists. Nonetheless, Ricoldo has a high regard for Muslims in his *Itinerarium* or travel diary. He writes, "Who will not be astounded...how great is the concern of these very Muslims for study, their devotion in prayer, their pity for the poor, their reverence for the name of God and the prophets and the Holy Places, their sobriety in manners, their hospitality to strangers and love for each other."[21]

Another interesting encounter between Christianity and Islam took place in the monastery of Cluny in France. Peter the Venerable (1094-1156) was abbot of the monastery at Cluny, a monastery which had shown interest in Islam. An earlier abbot, Majolus, had lived among Muslims as a captive; a monk of Cluny, Anastasius, had been sent on a (unsuccessful) mission to Muslims in Spain; and monks of the Cluniac reform were to be found in Arabic-speaking Spain. Some Arabic-speaking monks were probably also to be found at the monastery of Cluny itself. Peter initiated a translation project of religious works from Arabic into Latin. Although Christian translators had previously worked on scientific or philosophical texts in Arabic, concentration on religious texts was something of a novelty. The project which produced what is known as the Toledan Collection included translations of some of the *hadith,*[22] *sirat* or lives of the Prophet, and the

Qur'an. What is interesting to note is that the Qur'an was translated by Robert of Ketton, a Christian, and Muhammad, a Muslim whom Peter had personally requested to work on the project so that the translation be done "with the fullest fidelity, without anything left out by deceit."[23]

It is clear from Peter's own works, *Summa totius haeresis Saracenorum* (Summa of the Entire Heresy of the Saracens) and *Liber contra sectum sive haeresim Saracenorum* (Book against the Sect or Heresy of the Saracens), that the translation project was not merely to increase understanding between Christians and Muslims. The purpose was to provide Christian preachers with an apologetic that would be built on a fair and accurate understanding of Islam. Peter hoped that his works, written in Latin, would eventually be translated into Arabic and hence available to the Muslim reader. With this in mind he wrote: "I do not attack you—Muslims—as our people often do, by arms, but by words; not by force, but by reason; not in hatred, but in love."[24]

As we come to the end of the period we are investigating and approach the decades preceding Vatican II, two figures and one movement in Roman Catholicism signal a change in the way Roman Catholics approached Islam both theoretically and practically.[25] The first of these is Charles de Foucauld (1858-1916).[26] A soldier in the French army and quite indifferent to his faith, he spent a year traveling through North Africa experiencing the people, the culture, and Islam firsthand. He returned to the practice of Catholicism in 1886 and joined the Cistercian Order (the Trappists), living in different monasteries in the Middle East, most notably in Nazareth and later as a hermit in Algeria. Ordained a priest in 1901, Foucauld was killed in Tamanrassat by raiders in 1916.

The importance of Foucauld is his understanding of the "life of Jesus at Nazareth," a quiet, unspectacular life before Jesus began his public ministry. Foucauld's emphases are on a life of poverty, on quietly living among the native people whom one loves and appreciates, on having a daily occupation, and of becoming as inculturated into the native situation as possible.[27] Two groups of Foucauld's followers, viz., the Little Brothers of Jesus and the Little Sisters of Jesus, do not engage in any organized apostolate but rather give witness by their lives among the Muslims with whom they live and share life. Foucauld's approach not only takes Islam seriously but also takes Islam as a lifestyle, which to some extent should be imitated and as far as possible incorporated into the Christian's witness. There is a major shift here. At most levels in the history of Christian-Muslim interaction, there was little or no knowledge of Islam. When such knowledge existed or was sought, it was mainly to insure that the Christian apologetic or polemic was accurate and effective. There was little or no positive good seen in Islam as a religious, spiritual, and cultural phenomenon. With Foucauld, a change was introduced to the approach of *some* Roman Catholics both towards Islam and towards ministry among Muslims.

The second figure in this change of attitude towards Islam is Louis Massignon (1883-1962). Massignon, also a French Roman Catholic originally indifferent to his faith, underwent a conversion experience during a serious illness in Baghdad in 1908. Massignon's life work was dedicated to Islamic mysticism with special emphasis on the mystic al-Hallaj, who was executed for heresy in 922. Like al-Hallaj and many other mystics, Massignon experienced an overwhelming awareness of the transforming love of God. For Massignon, who, like Foucauld, was also ordained a priest, the overwhelming love of God transformed him, allowing him to enter not only into a state of communion with the Triune God and the Church but also with Islam. The study of Islamic mysticism was never a "merely academic" exercise for Massignon. A man of deep prayer, it seems that Massignon was able to incorporate Islamic mysticism deeply into his Christian, Roman Catholic life. Massignon believed that God was able to draw Muslims to the Divine not through Christian influence or Christian doctrine but through the very Spirit of the invisible Christ using Islam to draw people to himself "beyond the limits set by dogmas and orthodoxies."[28]

During his illness in Baghdad Massignon had been cared for by a Muslim family. The experience of their care, hospitality and love remained with him his entire life. The arrogance and triumphalism prevalent in so many of Massignon's contemporaries was totally lacking in him.

Like Foucauld, Massignon proposed that the Christian live as totally as possible within the Muslim culture, leaving his or her home, language, and prejudices behind in order to assimilate as far as possible into the new culture. Drawing on his experience of Muslim hospitality, Massignon saw it to be a primary duty of a Christian living in a Muslim culture to welcome that culture, its religion, its spirituality, and its people into the Christian's life. He even advocated adopting Muslim forms into Christian prayer as long as the adoption did not do violence to either the Christian or the Muslim faith. While Massignon experienced considerable resistance to his ideas from some of his fellow Christians, his scholarship and indeed his overall attitude towards Muslims and Islam would profoundly affect Christian-Muslim relations in the years to follow.

As France was extending its colonial empire into North Africa, a religious order known as the Missionaries of Africa was founded in 1868.[29] The Missionaries of Africa were founded by Charles Lavigerie (1825-1892), a brilliant Frenchman who became Archbishop of Algiers on March 27, 1867. Lavigerie, later to become a cardinal (1881) and Archbishop of Carthage (1884), was intensely concerned about the Catholic mission to the Muslims of North Africa. Much like Foucauld and Massignon, Lavigerie insisted that the missionary assume as far as possible the culture of the people whom he or she was serving. He was profoundly convinced that the Christian mission was the transformation not only of individuals but of cultures and entire societies. He realized that the transformation of an entire culture and society is not something which takes place overnight but can take centuries to accomplish. Lavigerie was of the opinion that preaching Christian dogmas was to be reserved for those who had opted to become Christians. Those dogmas which are peculiar to the Christian faith did not provide a proper topic for the initial stages of evangelization. Stress should be placed rather on themes held commonly between the Christian missionary and his or her (Muslim) hearer: the oneness of God, the importance of revelation, God's graciousness and mercy, human sinfulness, and so forth. The details of Christian dogma should be reserved for the catechumenate. As such, therefore, Lavigerie believed that Christian dogmas were not to be preached initially to Muslims.[30]

Lavigerie's theology was developed and put into practical application by Henri Marchal (1875-1957) who was the Assistant to the Superior General of the Missionaries of Africa from 1912-1947. Marchal developed Lavigerie's theology and applied it to the missionary activities of his Order in Africa. First and foremost, Marchal was convinced that it was God who converts the human heart. Arguments, power, pressure—to say nothing of force—are unable of themselves to change the human heart. The missionary was called not to convert but to discern the working of God's Spirit in everyone and to help make the call and working of the Spirit clearer in each person's life. Marchal's Christian anthropology provided a critique of those things which rendered a person resistant to God's Spirit and grace: arrogance (including the arrogance of religious supremacy), legalism, external pressures, and spiritual indifference arising from a sense of religious superiority. Marchal had a theory of three meanings of conversion. The first sense is conversion to God. As Jean-Marie Gaudeul notes, Marchal's understanding of conversion to God is very similar to the original sense of *islam*, obedient submission to God's will. It is that "attitude made up of adoration, humble thankfulness, repentance, acceptance of God's will for our lives, prayer and love."[31] For Marchal this is the faith that is the basic requirement for salvation.

The second meaning of conversion is conversion to Jesus. This involves a personal relationship with Jesus, an acceptance of Jesus, and the progressive personal revelation of the role of Jesus in one's salvation. The third and last sense of conversion is conversion to Christianity. It is conversion in the popular understanding of the word: the changing of religious loyalties, the moving from one religion to another, the adoption of new beliefs and ways of worship, communal interaction, and so on. Although he is clearly a Christian missionary, it is interesting to see that Marchal separates the three meanings of conversion and at least recognizes that it is theoretically possible for one to be converted to God and even to Jesus without being converted to Christianity.[32]

This made for an extraordinary missionary program for Marchal. All people must be called to conversion to God. With dependence on the Spirit of God, the missionary calls all people to surrender themselves to God. What is extraordinary is that the person addressed by the missionary may also feel drawn to Jesus. Marchal realized that the missionary can build on Islam's reverence for Jesus and the traditions that have developed about him, in spite of the reality that many traditions are different from or even in conflict with Christian traditions and beliefs about Jesus. Nonetheless, the Muslim can find him- or herself bound to Jesus in bonds of love. This is possible for Marchal even without the Muslim ever taking the final step of conversion to Christianity. Marchal realized from experience that—for any number of reasons—conversions from Islam to Christianity were rare. However, his theology of a three part conversion allowed for the possibility of a non-Christian Muslim being in a salvific relationship with God and even, to some extent, with Jesus, without formally becoming a Christian. Marchal's theology has had a discernable impact on Vatican II and its attitude towards missionary activity and non-Christians. Gaudeul is of the opinion that several of the themes which Marchal developed have played a major role up to the present: "that the Church has to speak to human groups and not just to individuals; that the Church has a ministry towards those who do not think of joining her ranks; that foremost in that ministry is the proclamation of the Kingdom of God, the help given to a whole milieu to enable it to become receptive to God's invitation and guidance."[33]

Conclusion

Relations between Catholics and Muslims over the centuries have been very complicated and for the most part troublesome and challenging, difficult and problematic. On the "macro" level of institutions, politics, and countries there has been an almost unbroken struggle. At one time Muslims were victorious and Christians were humiliated; at another time the roles were reversed. The brutality of the Crusades were matched by the brutality of the Ottomans. The loss of Muslim Spain was paralleled in the loss of Christian Constantinople.[34] Yet it would be a mistake to impose too-orderly a pattern on the alternating victories and humiliations of Christianity and Islam. Individual encounters between Christians and Muslims often transcended the prevailing attitudes. Pope Gregory VII's friendly letter to al-Nasir in 1076 was written less than 25 years before the massacre of Muslims (and Jews) in Jerusalem in 1099.[35] While Christians were attacking Muslims in the Fifth Crusade, Francis of Assisi had a courteous encounter with Malik al-Kamil in Damietta, Egypt. While French colonialism and imperialism were overrunning Muslim countries, French Catholics such as Marchal, Lavigerie, de Foucauld, and Massignon were exhibiting extraordinary appreciation for Muslims and Islam, paving the way for a new type of interaction between the two communities in the latter half of the twentieth century.

In this extremely brief survey of Catholic-Muslim relations from the sixth century until the beginning of the Second Vatican Council, what is important is to understand how Muslims have developed an understanding of Catholics and Christians which is often very different, even at odds, with the understanding we have of ourselves. Likewise, it is important for Catholics and Christians to understand the historical events which have led up to our understanding of Islam and Muslims, an understanding which is mediated through Christian historical experience in Europe and the Middle East. At the risk of repetition, knowledge of the history of Catholic-Muslim relations will show that there is no single innocent victim. Both sides have been aggressor and victim; both sides have used religion to perpetrate violence. Both sides have sinned against the best in their respective traditions. Knowledge of the history of Catholic-Muslim relations will not justify either side. However, it can clarify the origins of the alienation which has existed between Catholics and Muslims and by clarifying the origins of the alienation help to overcome it.

Study Questions

1. How might Christians and Muslims look on their own history to form a negative opinion of the other? How might such an opinion be justified?
2. Faced with a history of mutual hostility and humiliation, is

"forgetting the past," a viable way of improving relations between Muslims and Christians?

3. How aware are American Catholics of the history and effects of Colonialism?

4. How can an attitude of "God is on our side" impact relations between Christians and Muslims?

5. How can Muslims and Christians be faithful to their belief that God loves them without assuming that God does not care for the other?

SELECT BIBLIOGRAPHY

Fromkin, David. *A Peace to End All Peace: The Fall of the Ottoman Empire and the Creation of the Modern Middle East*. New York: Harry Holt and Company, 1989.

Kinross, Lord. *The Ottoman Centuries: The Rise and Fall of the Turkish Empire*. New York: Morrow Quill Paperbacks, 1977.

NOTES

1. Turkic refers to those peoples from central Asia, originally nomadic, who spoke Turkic languages. Turkish strictly refers to Turkey and the particular Turkic language spoken there. There were several Turkic groups, the most important of which were the Seljuks and Ottomans.

2. Friedrich Kemp, et al editors, *Handbuch der Kirchergeschichte, III/1* (Freiburg: Herder Verlag, 1985) 509.

3. Jonathan Riley-Smith, *The Crusades* (New Haven, CT: Yale University Press, 1987), 2-10.

4. Ibid., 8.

5. Karen Armstrong, *Holy War: The Crusades and their Impact on Today's World* (New York: Anchor Books, 2001), 178-179. Also David Nicolle, *The Crusades: Essential Histories* (Oxford: Osprey Publishing, 2001).

6. Amin Maalouf, *The Crusades through Muslim Eyes* (New York: Shocken Books, 1984).

7. See Armstrong, 255-259.

8. Ertoghrul is the traditional founder of the Ottoman dynasty. Very little is known about him historically and he has been the subject of a great deal of legendary material.

9. Lord Kinross, *The Ottoman Centuries: The Rise and Fall of the Turkish Empire* (New York: Morrow Quill, 1977), 111.

10. It would be inaccurate to say that Suleiman actually conquered Rhodes. It was more like a draw in which the Knights, who had inflicted terrible losses on the Turkish army, chose a truce which allowed them to withdraw from the island. See Kinross, 178-179.

11. Kinross, 187.

12. The defeat of the Ottoman navy at Lepanto is recalled in the Feast of the Holy Rosary on October 7th.

13. Without doubt one of the best books on this topic is David Fromkin, *A Peace to End All Peace: The Fall of the Ottoman Empire and the Creation of the Modern Middle East* (New York: Henry Holt and Company, 1989).

14. Fromkin, 192.

15. Saudi Arabia as a geographical entity did not exist until after World War I. The Hijaz is the coastal region on the west central coast of the Arabian peninsula. Mecca and Medina are in the Hijaz.

16. Fromkin, 181.

17. Jean-Marie Gaudeul, *Encounters and Clashes: II Texts* (Rome: Pontificio Istituto di Studi Arabi e Islamici, 1984), p. 75.

18. Ibid.

19. Rollin Armour, Sr., *Islam, Christianity and the West: A Troubled History* (Maryknoll, NY: Orbis Press, 2002), 88-89. Jean-Marie Gaudeul, *Encounters and Clashes: I- A Survey* (Rome: Pontificio Istituto di Studi Arabi e Islamici, 1984), 151-154.

20. Armour, 92.

21. Armour, 91.

22. *Hadith* are traditions about Muhammad, his saying, decisions, and practices.

23. Gaudeul, 116-117.

24. Gaudeul, 119.

25. In what follows, I am highlighting several Roman Catholics notable for their openness to Islam. At the same time Protestant and Anglican scholars such as Montgomery Watt, Kenneth Cragg, and a host of others have made major contributions to the overall encounter between Christianity and Islam. While this book is geared for Catholic educators, the ecumenical dimension of the Christian-Muslim dialogue must not be overlooked. In the dialogue with Islam, Christians of every denomination are dependent on the work of all those Christians of any Church or denomination who have labored to increase understanding between Christians and Muslims.

26. The Vatican announced the beatification of Foucauld in 2005.

27. Gaudeul, 308-309.

28. Ibid., 319-320.

29. The Missionaries of Africa are also known popularly—and less felicitously—as the White Fathers from the habit they wear which is basically the traditional clothing of Muslims in North Africa.

30. Gaudeul, 313.

31. Ibid., 316.

32. I experienced a similar phenomenon when at a Catholic-Muslim dialogue one of the Muslim participants described himself as "LaSallian." When questioned as to what he meant, he replied that he was a good and faithful Muslim and had no intention of becoming a Christian. However, he had been educated by the "De LaSalle Brothers," i.e. the Christian Brothers, and had appropriated enough of their spirituality and values to consider himself a "LaSallian" Muslim.

33. Ibid., 320.

34. Christians who visit Cordoba in Spain are often saddened at how Christians literally inserted a Gothic type cathedral right in the center of a mosque of incredible architectural beauty. One has only to visit the former Hagia Sofia in Istanbul, however, to see that Christians were not the only ones who took over and changed the worship places of the other. The Christian cathedral of Hagia Sofia was turned into a mosque, its mosaics plastered over, and its Christian symbols removed. Today it is a museum.

35. In fact, Gregory VII had offered to lead troops personally against the Turks in 1074. See Jonathan Riley-Smith, The Crusades: A Short History (New Haven, CT: Yale University Press, 1987), 2.

Maps & Photos

Index of Maps

Index of Photos

THE WORLD ON THE EVE OF THE MUSLIM CONQUESTS CIRCA 600 AD
(Reprinted with permission from *An Historical Atlas of Islam*, Second, revised edition, Hugh Kennedy, ed. Boston: Brill, 2002, p. 6)

EARLY MUSLIM CONQUESTS
(Reprinted with permission from *An Historical Atlas of Islam*, Second, revised edition, Hugh Kennedy, ed. Boston: Brill, 2002, p. 7)

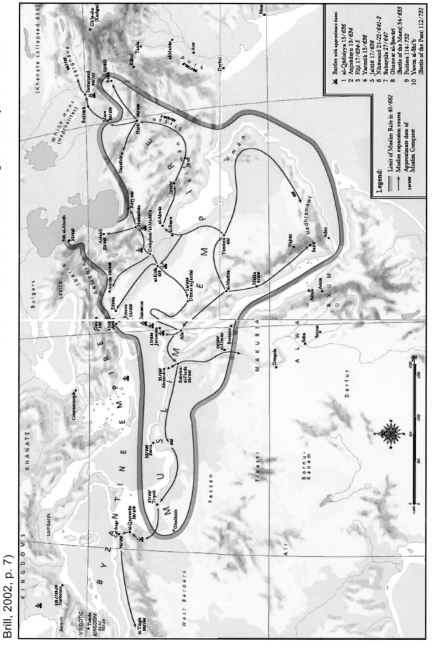

Pope Paul VI and delegation from Saudi Arabia, 1976.

Pope John Paul II received at the Royal Palace in Casablanca, 1985.

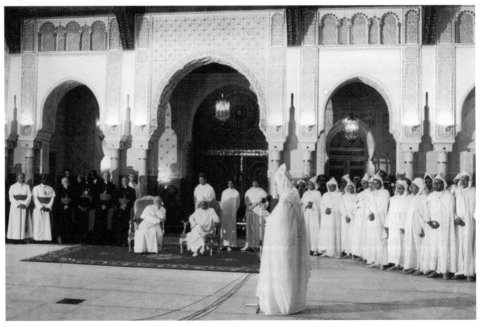

Above photos reprinted with permission from *Recognize the Spiritual Bonds Which Unite Us,* Vatican City: Pontifical Council for Interreligious Dialogue, 1994.

Pope John Paul II and King Hassan II of Morocco, 1985.

Day of Prayer for Peace, Assisi, 1986.

Reprinted with permission from *Recognize the Spiritual Bonds Which Unite Us,* Vatican City: Pontifical Council for Interreligious Dialogue, 1994.

Istanbul with the Blue Mosque and the Mosque of Suleyman.

Photo by Elias D. Mallon

The Blue Mosque in Istanbul.

The mosque in the Citadel, Cairo.

The former Byzantine Church of Hagia Sofia, now a mosque, in Istanbul.

Above photos by Elias D. Mallon

Statue of the Jewish philosopher Maimonides in Cordoba, Spain. Maimonides lived and worked in Muslim Moorish Spain.

Photo by Elias D. Mallon

A poster on a wall in Luxor, Egypt 1995. The Arabic reads: *Religion is for God and the Nation is for everyone. No to Terrorism.* Note the crescent and the cross on the poster.

Fountain in the Court of the Lions in the Alhambra, a magnificent Moorish palace in Granada, Spain.

Islamic Center in Washington, D.C.

Pattani's new central mosque.

As-Siddiq elementary school, Al-khobar prayer.

Muslims from all over the world gather in the plaza before Mecca's Grand Mosque.

The ihram, the dress worn by the hajj pilgrims to Mecca, is a symbol of their equality.

Muslims arrive in Mecca.

S. M. Amin/Saudi Aramco World/PADIA

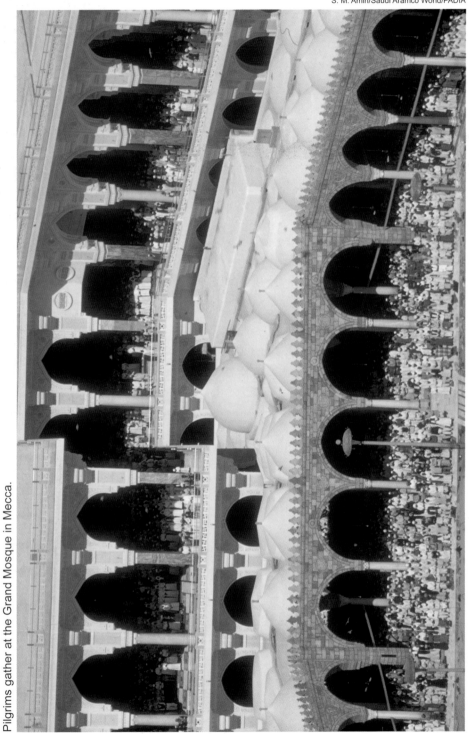

Pilgrims gather at the Grand Mosque in Mecca.

V

Christian-Muslim Relations: Vatican II Until the Present

Vatican II introduced epochal changes in the Catholic Church's relations with non-Christian religions. In its attempt to foster dialogue with peoples of other religions, the Catholic Church has given special place to its relationship with Islam. The reader will learn of these efforts in the world and in the United States. The reader will also be introduced to some resources helpful for engaging in local dialogue.

- *Vatican II and the decree Nostra Aetate dealing with the relation of the Catholic Church to non-Christians*

- *Initial attempts at dialogue with Muslims*

- *The Secretariat for Non-Christians and the later Pontifical Council for Interreligious Dialogue*

- *Resources for Dialogue*

- *A brief overview of the Catholic-Muslim Dialogue in the United States*

- *African-American Muslims and Dialogue*

Groundbreaking Movement

The Second Vatican Council (1962-1965) introduced many changes into the way Roman Catholics look at things. For those who are familiar with what had been going on in the years and decades before the Council, many of the changes were not surprising. Rather, they were the results of long and careful scholarship. Theological reflection on the experience of living in an ever-smaller world in which the great religions of the world came in contact with each other increasingly stirred reflection about how the Catholic Church looked at these religions and how it was to interact with them. It was clear that the Church had little choice as to *whether* it would interact with the great religious traditions of the world. The question was *how* it was to interact. To some extent this is a question that is still being asked.

On October 28, 1965, the Council published *Nostra Aetate*[1] or *The Declaration on the Relation of the Church to Non-Christian Religions*. With *Nostra Aetate*, the Roman Catholic Church officially and institutionally took a positive stance towards the great religious traditions of the world. Although it is often erroneously called the Church's "Decree on the Jews," *Nostra Aetate* attempts to present the stance of the Roman Catholic Church *vis-à-vis* all the great religions of the world. To be sure, Judaism holds a special place for all Christians and *Nostra Aetate* mentions the "spiritual ties" which connect Christians and Jews and encourages "mutual understanding and appreciation" (¶4). Nonetheless, it is not Judaism which is the first religion mentioned in the *Declaration*; it is Islam. After two introductory paragraphs, the Council states: "The Church has also a high regard for the Muslims" (¶3). The Council notes the points of agreement between Christians and Muslims: "they worship God, who is one...who has also spoken to man (*sic*)...Although not acknowledging him as God, they venerate Jesus as a prophet, his virgin Mother they also honor...Further, they await the day of judgement and the reward of God following the resurrection of the dead. For this reason they highly esteem an upright life and worship God, especially by way of prayer, alms-deeds and fasting" (¶3). The Council recognizes that Christians and Muslims have not enjoyed a happy history and that there were "many quarrels and dissensions." Nonetheless, the Council "pleads with all to forget the past, and urges that a sincere effort be made to achieve mutual understanding..." (¶3).

In a matter of a few words the Church has shown an appreciation of Islam as a monotheistic religion which worships the same God as do Christians and Jews. Likewise the mention of prayer, alms-deeds, and fasting is a reference to three of the five Pillars of Islam[2] which we will see later.

Not only the openness of the Council but also the familiarity shown in *Nostra Aetate* is a tribute to people like Foucauld, Massignon, the Missionaries of Africa, and others who had been working with Muslims in the decades preceding the Council. The courage, openness, and scholarship of these people provided the initial theological framework with which the Council could approach the topic of Islam. Although the Council is optimistic about relations with Islam, it is by no means naïve. It recognizes that any relationship between Catholics and Muslims has a long history to overcome. It is highly improbable that the Council intended its call to "forget the past" to be taken literally. Pasts which are forgotten have a way of resurfacing in surprising and unsettling ways. I believe that the Council is calling Catholics and Muslims to face our history together, both the mutual humiliations and the mutual aggressions and to overcome them for the glory of God and the benefit of humanity.

As important and ground breaking as *Nostra Aetate* undoubtedly was, it was only the beginning. The Roman Catholic Church had officially announced its regard for Islam and its desire to engage Muslims in dialogue. The task of implementing the brief remarks of *Nostra Aetate* was daunting. The previous year on Pentecost Sunday (May 19, 1964), Pope Paul VI founded the Secretariat for Non-Christians with the task of initiating and maintaining dialogues between the Roman Catholic Church and the major religions of the world.[3] While visiting the Middle East earlier in 1964, Pope Paul VI had visited King Hussein of Jordan and the Mufti in Jerusalem. In 1967, on a visit to Athenagoras, the Greek Orthodox Patriarch of Constantinople (Istanbul), the pope had the opportunity to meet with the Mufti of Istanbul. At that meeting Paul VI stated: "We want to declare to you our esteem for Muslims...as was well expressed by the recent Council, which exhorted us to promote together, on the basis of common truths, social justice, moral values, peace and liberty. All those who adore the One and Unique God are called to establish an order of justice and peace on the earth."[4]

In the years following the Council, many encounters, local and national, took place between Christians and Muslims.

At this time the World Council of Churches in Geneva initiated a sub-unit for dialogue with "peoples of living faiths and ideologies." At its first plenary session, the Secretariat had observers from the World Council of Churches and the Greek Orthodox Church. Other meetings took place in countries such as Switzerland, Lebanon, Jordan, and Spain, in which Christians and Muslims discussed areas of common interest and concern, such as profession of faith, evangelization, da'wah,[5] and freedom of religion. Much was to be learned in this period and not all of it was happy. The Secretariat was involved in a conference with the Libyan Socialist Party. At the end of the conference the "General Conclusions" were published. Unfortunately, unknown to the Catholic participants, paragraphs 20-21 of the "General Conclusions" dealt with Israel and were an embarrassment to the Secretariat.[6] During the pontificate of Pope Paul VI, diplomatic relations were established between the Holy See and at least seventeen Muslim countries. On one level, at least, Muslims were responding to the call of Nostra Aetate.

In the general reorganization of the Roman Curia, the Secretariat for Non-Christians became the Pontifical Council for Interreligious Dialogue in 1988. Although its mission remained the same, the name change was a happy one. The negation "non-Christian" was replaced by a more positive term, "interreligious dialogue." In the early years of the Secretariat, Cardinal Pignedoli was its president. With his unexpected death on June 15, 1980, he was replaced by Archbishop Jean Jadot, who had previously been Apostolic Delegate to the United States of America. In 1984, Archbishop Jadot was succeeded by Francis Arinze, the Archbishop of Onitsha in Nigeria. Archbishop (and later Cardinal) Arinze came from the largest Muslim country in Africa, which is also one of the largest Muslim countries in the world. As such he was eminently prepared for encounters with Muslims. Bishop Michael Fitzgerald, a member of the Missionaries of Africa, was Secretary of the Pontifical Council and a person well informed about Islam. Archbishop Michael Fitzgerald was appointed to lead the Pontifical Council for Interreligious Dialogue on October 1, 2002.[7]

On the official website for the Pontifical Council for

"Should Muslims be forbidden the desire to see their Christian friends become Muslims, or, similarly, do Christians not have the right to wish that their Muslim friends become Christians? They should not be denied such a desire, for otherwise there would be an undue limitation to their desire for sharing with others. Muslims will know that a famous hadith[1] says, 'No one is truly a believer who does not love for others that which he loves for himself.' Christians have heard from Jesus himself as a commandment that is ancient, but also ever new: 'You shall love your neighbor as yourself' (Matthew 22:39), 'Love one another as I have loved you...' (John 13:34). So there is no reason why Christians and Muslims should not wish that they meet someday in the same faith, and in identical worship, whenever God wills it, and however He wills it. Such desires are legitimate even if practically speaking they effectively exclude each other. This is what is meant by undertaking the impossible. And yet it should be ventured, in the name of God: to practice mutual acceptance to the limit and to acknowledge that full concurrence is as yet unachievable. Such is the inherent contradiction in dialogue when it is seriously pursued." *The Guidelines for Dialogue between Christians and Muslims*, 41-42.

Interreligious Dialogue (PCID), several very important things are noted. In explaining the "Methodology of the PCID," it is stated, "Although the PCID is the central office for dialogue in the Catholic Church, dialogue is mainly carried out through the Local Churches...The PCID works in close collaboration with these, and encourages their (i.e. local dialogues) formation where they do not exist." An oft-overlooked aspect of interreligious dialogue is also clearly stated: "The ecumenical dimension of interreligious dialogue is kept in mind. The PCID has an ongoing relationship with the corresponding office in the World Council of Churches."[8]

In the time since the first appearance of *Islam: What Catholics Need to Know* the relationship between the Catholic Church and Islam has experienced several ups and downs. On September 12, 2006, Pope Benedict XVI delivered an address at the University of Regensburg in Germany where he had been a professor. In his address the pope showed some lack of familiarity with Islam by, for example, stating the Qur'an sura/chaper "The Cow" was one of the earliest chapters, whereas in fact it is one of the latest. More tragically, the pope cited a statement of the Byzantine Emperor Emmanuel II Paleologus (1350-1425): "Show me just what Muhammad brought that was new and there you will find things only evil and inhuman, such as his command to spread by the sword the faith he preached." Although the pope was citing what someone else had said, Muslims around the world were incensed and relations between the Catholic Church and the Muslim world became strained.

While the citation was certainly ill-advised, Pope Benedict went out of his way to apologize for any offense he might have given. Shortly after the talk he visited Turkey and made a point of visiting the Blue Mosque in Istanbul. Several years later he convoked the first Catholic-Muslim Forum in Rome November 4-6, 2008.

Although genuinely committed to the Catholic-Muslim dialogue, Pope Benedict was never able to generate the trust and affection with the Muslim community as was his predecessor Pope John Paul II or his successor Pope Francis. Finally on January 20, 2011, the Islamic Research Academy of al-Azhar University in Cairo suspended its dialogue with the Vatican. Earlier in the month there had been attacks on Christian churches in Egypt and in his address to the Vatican's diplomatic corps on January 10, 2011, Benedict mentioned this and called on the Egyptian government to do more to protect Christians. The next day Egypt recalled its ambassador to the Holy See and this was followed by Al-Azhar's suspension of dialogue. Benedict's relations with the Muslim world highlighted both the fragility and the strength of the dialogue. It underlined its brittleness by showing how easily dialogue can be disrupted by real, unintended or perceived insults and by showing how difficult it can be to restore trust. On the other hand, it showed that despite the difficulties and even the suspension of dialogue, the Catholic-Muslim dialogue can survive crises.

Pope Benedict XVI stepped down from office on February 28, 2013. Two weeks later on March 13 the Argentinian Cardinal Jorge Bergoglio was elected as Pope Francis. The new pope brought a different atmosphere to the Vatican. If Benedict was retiring, shy and academic, Francis was outgoing and comfortable in a world broader than that of academia. As Archbishop of Buenos Aires, Francis not only engaged in dialogue with Protestants, Jews and Muslims, he befriended them. Rabbi Abraham Sorka and Imam Omar Abboud are not only long-standing friends of Francis since his days in Argentina, he invited them to be part of the "official delegation" when he visited the Holy Land. One often hears of the three levels of ecumenism: theology, life and witness. Francis has added the ecumenism of friendship.

Relations between the Vatican and al-Azhar began to improve and on May 23, 2016, Sheikh Ahmed al-Tayeb, Grand Imam of the Al-Azhar Mosque and former president of al-Azhar University, visited the pope at the Vatican. Within a year Pope Francis repaid the visit and spoke at al-Azhar University on April 28, 2017. Relations between the Vatican al-Azhar, the oldest Muslim university in the world, were once again under way.

By his visits to Muslim majority countries, through his speeches and meetings Pope Francis has moved the Catholic-Muslim dialogue forward and strengthened it.

Although the Pontifical Council for Interreligious Dialogue is responsible for dialogue with all the great religious traditions of the world, it is significant that Islam holds a special place for the Roman Catholic Church. There is the Commission for Religious Relations with Muslims within the Pontifical Council. The Commission is composed of a President, Vice-President, Secretary, and eight Consultors. Once again it is clear that in the vast world of interreligious relations, Islam holds a special place in relationship to the Roman Catholic Church.

One of the most valuable tools to have been produced by the PCID, *The Guidelines for Dialogue between Christians and Muslims*,[9] was originally written in French in 1969 and was revised in 1974. The *Guidelines* appeared in any number of different translations before they appeared in English in 1990. However, in one of those marvelous accidents of history, the French document was translated by R. Marston Speight, one of the giants in the Christian-Muslim Dialogue in the United States. Speight, now a retired minister in the United Methodist Church, lived in Muslim North Africa from 1951-1979 when he returned to direct the Office on Christian-

Important Resources For Christian-Muslim Dialogue

Muslim Relations of the National Council of Churches of Christ USA from 1979-1992. His book, *God Is One*,[10] remains a sensitive and classical introduction to Islam. His participation in the English version of *The Guidelines* (1990) highlights the ecumenical nature of interreligious dialogue mentioned above.

The Guidelines for Dialogue between Christians and Muslims is an extremely important milestone in the history of Catholic-Muslim relations because in a manner that is both theological and practical *The Guidelines* provides the rationale and method for engaging Muslims in a meaningful and fruitful dialogue. While it also presents a very brief but helpful introduction to Muslims,[11] the text gives practical advice on places and times to engage in dialogue, how to behave, and what to expect. There is an honest awareness of the feelings which Muslims and Christians may have when they encounter each other. Both Christianity and Islam are missionary religions that seek converts. The document recognizes that dialogue partners may hope for the "conversion" of the other even in the most open and honest dialogue. An acknowledgment of these hopes and feelings is an important part of Christian-Muslim encounter.

Note that *The Guidelines* do not merely try to provide the Christian partner with an excuse for wishing that the Muslim becomes a Christian. It is recognized as real and legitimate that the Muslim partner may very well entertain the same wish for the Christian partner in dialogue. It is also recognized that such wishes are mutually exclusive. However, recognizing the presence of such wishes and their exclusivity does not invalidate the dialogue. Such wishes render the dialogue neither dishonest nor undesirable. The call to "undertake the impossible" is a brave and honest attempt to recognize dynamics which can and do occur in the encounters between Christians and Muslims.

Although written before Desert Storm,[12] the attack on the World Trade Center in NYC and the Pentagon on September 11, 2001, and the Iraq War,[13] *The Guidelines* provide great help in dealing with religious and cultural misunderstandings and stereotypes. There is no naïve attempt to whitewash serious differences and difficulties which exist between the two communities. However, the overarching rationale for *The*

Guidelines is that dialogue between Catholics and Muslims is difficult. However difficult it may be, it is, however, neither impossible nor optional. Christians and Muslims can and must engage each other in dialogue. The conclusion, written in 1969, states, "Christian-Muslim dialogue should be seen as one of the principal dimensions of life for men and women of faith in those many countries where believers in the two religions live, work, love, suffer and die together."[14] One wonders if in 1969 the author could have realized that by 2001 Islam would become the second largest religion in places like the United States and France.

The 1994 publication of the Pontifical Council for Interreligious Dialogue, *Recognize the Spiritual Bonds Which Unite Us*[15], is also significant. It provides a history of sixteen years of Catholic-Muslim dialogue. Extremely beautifully printed with many color photographs, the book recounts the history of Catholic-Muslim dialogue under the pontificate of Pope Paul VI and the first 14 years of that of Pope John Paul II. The very sumptuousness of the book underlines the importance with which the Vatican approaches Catholic-Muslim dialogue. It is not, however, merely a *tour de force* of visual beauty. A popular history of 16 years of Roman Catholic dialogue, it recounts conferences, dialogues, and encounters, often giving citations from the pope or different Muslim dialogue partners. This publication is a good introduction to the multi-national nature of Islam and Catholicism and how they interact in different places of the world.

Another resource coming from the Pontifical Council is entitled *Interreligious Dialogue*.[16] A massive, scholarly work dedicated to collecting official statements of Vatican II and Popes Paul VI, John Paul I, and John Paul II, the book does not limit itself to statements about dialogue with Islam but includes all the non-Christian religions with whom the Vatican holds dialogue. Having said that, it must be noted that the vast majority of material in the book deals with Islam. *Interreligious Dialogue* is at the opposite end of the spectrum from *Recognizing the Spiritual Bonds.* It is primarily a reference book for scholars and is not a book which one would normally read from cover to cover. It, too, is a witness to the importance of the Catholic-Muslim dialogue for the post-Vatican II Church.

The concern of the Pontifical Council for Interreligious Dialogue with Catholic-Muslim relations was made clear in a May 14, 2004, interview with Archbishop Fitzgerald.[17] In the interview, John L. Allen of *The National Catholic Reporter* asked Archbishop Fitzgerald about bilateral relationships which the Holy See has with other religions. In response, the archbishop listed a liaison committee with Muslims, with international Islamic organizations, with al-Azhar,[18] with Turkey, and with the World Islamic Call Society of Libya. Archbishop Fitzgerald added, "But with other religions, with Hindus or with Buddhists, we haven't any formal agreement we have signed." When asked if the initiative for these agreements came from the Muslim side, the archbishop responded, "In a number of cases, yes. We have responded to that." He then added, "One of our concerns, of course, is that when we respond as an office of the Holy See, the dialogue should not just be at the top level. The local church in that particular area should be implicated, should be concerned with the dialogue, and should be brought in so far as it is possible."[19] It seems clear that within the vast world of interreligious dialogues, the Catholic-Muslim dialogue enjoys a privileged place.

The above material has dealt to a great extent with the work of the Pontifical Council for Interreligious Dialogue and the very useful and important resources which it has produced. However, as Archbishop Fitzgerald indicated and as the website for the Council states, Catholic-Muslim dialogue occurs on the local level. It is the every-day encounters between Catholics and Muslims and the dialogues which take place in parishes and dioceses which is the dialogue at work.

It is almost impossible to report adequately on the work of local Catholic-Muslim dialogues. The field is simply too vast. Many dioceses have engaged in dialogue with Muslims for many years. The Archdiocese of New York observed the 20th anniversary of its Roman Catholic dialogue in 2005. Although the demographics of a particular location have greatly determined the presence or lack of a Catholic-Muslim dialogue, it is becoming increasingly the case that Muslims are found in almost all parts of the country and no longer just in large coastal metropolitan areas. The Diocese of Dodge City, KS, had an educational program for its clergy and workers on Islam in 2002 and the Diocese of Wichita, KS, is planning a similar one. Around the United States, dioceses are responding to the need to educate Catholic clergy and laity about Islam. Islam and Muslims can be found in the so-called American heartland and many bishops and dioceses are responding to the new situation by setting up dialogue groups. In addition, even in dioceses where there is no formal Catholic-Muslim dialogue, there are often to be found active interfaith groups where Catholics interact with people of other religious traditions, including Muslims. While these interfaith groups are not a formal bilateral dialogue, they nonetheless provide a rich opportunity for Catholics and Muslims to share concerns, explain their faith and understand the faith of the other, and to build friendships.

Institutional Obstacles to Dialogue

The radically different institutional structure of the two faiths is one of the obstacles which Catholics face when attempting to establish a dialogue with Muslims. The Roman Catholic Church has a very clear structure on the global, national, and diocesan levels. While Protestant Churches may not have a strictly hierarchical structure like Catholics, there are, nonetheless, parallel institutions to set up dialogue and to speak for a particular Christian church. While Judaism is far less structured without a generally recognized central organization, there are often agencies which can act as quasi-official partners in a Catholic-Jewish dialogue. Until recently, this has not at all been the case with Islam in America. Muslims are quick to point out that Islam does not have a clergy. However, it is not true to say that Islam in America is totally without an internally recognized leadership. Likewise, while American Muslims do not have organizations and agencies to the degree that Jews have, one does notice that Muslims are adapting to the American religious scene. Over the past 20 years or more, several Muslim organizations have arisen. Nonetheless, the Secretariat for Ecumenical and Interreligious Affairs of the United States Conference of Catholic Bishops found it difficult to find an Islamic organization with whom it could dialogue on a *national* basis, as it does with the Episcopal Church in America, the Presbyterian Church (USA), the Evangelical Lutheran Church in America, and so forth. After attempting a Catholic-Muslim dialogue on the national level, it was decided that it would be more fruitful and more representative of the institutional situation of Islam in America to have three regional dialogues, viz., East Coast, Central, and West Coast. These dialogues invite ecumenical and interreligious officers from the Catholic dioceses in the region together with their Muslim dialogue partners and any Islamic organization in the area which might be appropriate.

Since the first publication of this book, the Catholic Muslim dialogue has continued to mature in the United States. Continuing to build on the regional dialogue under the guidance of the Secretariat for Ecumenical and Interreligious Affairs of the United States Conference of Catholic Bishops (USCCB), each of the groups produced study papers — some for internal, others for external consumption — on topics such as marriage and education. The spring 2011 edition of *Chicago Studies* published the collected papers of the Catholic-Muslim dialogue of that region.

The first joint meeting of the regional dialogues was held in 2012 in Chicago. At this meeting the seeds were planted for the ultimate restoration of the dialogue on a national scale. In 2015 all the regional groups met once again at The Catholic University of America in Washington, D.C., to celebrate the fiftieth anniversary of the decree *Nostra Ætate* of the Second Vatican Council. It was at this meeting that the decision was made to set up a National Catholic-Muslim Dialogue, under the chairmanship of Cardinal Blase Cupich, the archbishop of Chicago.

In addition to the dialogues, several important interreligious events involving Muslims (and other religious traditions) have taken place. When Pope Francis came to New York to address the United Nations on September 25, 2015, the USCCB hosted an interfaith prayer service at the September 11 Memorial, commonly known as "Ground Zero," in New York. The prayer service involved leaders from most of the religious traditions in the New York Metropolitan Area.

More recently in 2016 the USCCB, in partnership with the Kroc Institute for International Peace Studies, held a public event in San Diego at which Bishop Robert McElroy, bishop of San Diego, spoke on the problem of Islamophobia.

Both locally and on the national level the Catholic Church in the United States is actively and creatively engaged in dialogue with Islam. Given the ethnic and structural diversity of Islam as a religion in the US and elsewhere, the dialogue takes different forms in different times and places. The National Catholic-Muslim Dialogue of the USCCB coordinates the results of the dialogues and provides, when possible, resources for Catholics around the country.

As mentioned above, however, the number of Islamic organizations in the United States has burgeoned in the last 20 years.[21] Many of these are actively engaged in dialogue with Christians and some Jewish groups. While some of the newer organizations, such as the Islamic Shura Council, maintain close relations with other Islamic organizations, in many cases the organizations are quite independent of each other. In footnote 17 above, the reader can find several important Islamic American organizations listed with their website addresses. The reader is advised to visit the websites to get a clearer idea of how Muslims in America are beginning to organize themselves. In addition there are many important and interesting links.

Thus, the official dialogue between Catholics and Muslims in the United States is quite active. It is not unusual for parishes and local communities to engage in less formal dialogues with a parish, offering a lecture on Islam or inviting the imam of the local mosque to address parishioners about Islam. Many, if not most, Roman Catholic High Schools include world religions and interreligious dialogue in their curricula that includes a specific component on Islam in which a Muslim is invited to speak to the students on Islam and the students then visit a mosque.

Dialogue with African American Muslims

Another important aspect of Catholic-Muslim dialogue which is unique to the Unites States has to do with people often referred to as "black Muslims." Originally begun as the Nation of Islam by W. D. Fard in the early 20th century, the movement had a superficial relationship to Islam as most Muslims would recognize it. On February 26, 1975, Wallace Delaney Muhammad succeeded his father, Elijah Muhammad, to leadership in the Nation of Islam. Over the years W.D. Muhammad worked to bring the Nation of Islam closer to a normative Sunni Islam.[22] W. D. Muhammad's relationship with the Nation of Islam was a stormy one and he was suspended twice (1969 and 1971) for his "dissident views." Elected Supreme Minister of the Nation of Islam in 1975, W. D. Muhammad openly resumed his attempts to reformulate the theology of the Nation of Islam, finally bringing it more into conformity with "orthodox" Sunni Islam. In 1977, Louis Farrakhan broke with W. D. Muhammad and formed a separate group, following the older teachings of black separatism and nationalism. In 1976, W. D. Muhammad changed his title from Supreme Minister to the more Islamic title, Imam. He also adopted the name Warith Deen Mohammed.[23] In 1978, he changed the name of the organization to the American Muslim Mission from which he resigned soon after. In 1985, each of the mosques of the organization became independent although most remained connected with the Muslim American Society, the successor of the American Muslim Mission. The Muslim American Society, also known as the Ministry of W. Deen Mohammad, still exists and is centered in Calumet City, IL. The vast majority of those Muslims affiliated with the Ministry of W. Deen Mohammad are African-American. It is estimated that there are several million Muslims in the United States affiliated in one way or another with W. Deen Mohammad.[24]

In the years after Vatican II as the Catholic-Muslim dialogue began to develop in the United States African American Muslims were under-represented at the dialogues, if represented at all. One reason for this is clearly the confusion that exists in many people's minds between Louis Farrakhan's Nation of Islam with its often racist and anti-Semitic rhetoric and the Ministry of W. Deen Mohammad. "Black Muslims" has become a catchall term which is not only inaccurate but also misleading. "Black Muslims" are not a group that is separate from Muslims. Nor do they form a sect within Islam. Since the 1970's, African-American Muslims have moved to the center of Sunni Islam. Many African-American imams are quite learned in Islam and represent a genuine and indigenous form of Islam in America. Nonetheless, they are not commonly present at many Catholic-Muslim dialogues.

The efforts of Cardinal Keeler of Baltimore, the efforts of the Secretariat for Ecumenical and Interreligious Affairs and the efforts of the members of the Focolare Movement have been very successful in integrating African-American Muslims into the Catholic-Muslim dialogue in the United States. In 1996, W. D. Muhammad visited Rome where he visited the Pontifical Council for Interreligious Dialogue, the Pontifical Institute for the Study of Arabic and Islam, the Community of San Egidio and the members of the Focolare Movement. On May 18, 1997, Chiara Lubich, the founder of the Focolare Movement, addressed 3000 people at the Malcolm X Mosque in Harlem, NY. She was later to address the Muslim American Society on "Faith Communities Together" at its annual convention in Washington, DC, on November 12, 2000. Lastly, W. Deen Mohammad was part of an interreligious conference which took place at the Vatican in October 1999. Through the work of the Catholics mentioned above, African-American Muslims have become a valued part of the Catholic-Muslim dialogue in the United States. Although they are often prejudiced against because they are African-American and then because they are Muslims, the African American Muslims affiliated with the Ministry of W. Deen Mohammad make a valued contribution to understanding between Catholics and Muslims in the United States.

Dialogue between Catholics and Muslims has become an important element in the lives of Roman Catholics. It is not always an easy undertaking. Since September 11, 2001, and the Iraq War with its tragedies and atrocities, old fears have surfaced again and again. It would be naïve to think that all Muslims are well inclined to having friendly relations with Christians. We shall see that even the Qur'an has an ambiguous attitude on how Muslims should relate to Christians. There have been attacks on Christians in Pakistan, Algeria, and most recently Iraq. While some of these attacks have been against foreign Christians living in the country, that is not always the case and has certainly not been the case in Iraq where the attacks have been against an ancient Iraqi Christian community. It is very easy for fear to become anger, anger to become rage and rage to become violence. An example of violence against Catholics was also the opportunity for one of the most beautiful witnesses to Christian love and the importance of mutual love and respect between Christians and Muslims.

Crossing the Threshold of Crucified Love

On March 27, 1996, seven Trappist monks of the Monastery of Our Lady of Atlas in the remote town of Tibhirine in Algeria were kidnaped by members of the Armed Islamic Group which was engaging in a guerrilla war of terrorism against the Algerian government. In the 1990's, several Christian missionaries had been killed but the monks of Our Lady of Atlas were spared until that night in 1996. After much negotiations the Armed Islamic Group announced on May 23, 1996, that the seven monks had had their throats cut. The heads of the monks were found but never their bodies. One of the monks, Dom Christian de Chergé, long aware of the dangers facing him and his fellow monks, wrote a "testament" two years before his death. The testament is an extraordinary witness to Christian love and commitment to interreligious dialogue and understanding in a world that seems torn apart by violence and rage. Below is Dom de Chergé's testament in its entirety because of its relevance not only for Algeria in 1996 but also for 21st century America.

> *Facing a goodbye. If it should happen—and it could be today—that I become a victim of the terrorism which now seems ready to engulf all the foreigners living in Algeria, I would like my community, my Church and my family to remember that my life was GIVEN to God and this country. I ask them to accept the fact that the One Master of all life was not a stranger to this brutal departure. I would ask them to pray for me: for how could I be found worthy of such an offering? I ask them to associate this death with so many other equally violent ones which are forgotten through indifference or anonymity. My life has no more value than any other. Nor any less value. In any case, it has not the innocence of childhood. I have lived long enough to*

*know that I am an accomplice in the evil which seems
to prevail so terribly in the world, even in the evil which
might blindly strike me down. I should like, when the
time comes, to have a moment of spiritual clarity which
would allow me to beg forgiveness of God and of my
fellow human beings, and at the same time forgive with
all my heart the one who would strike me down. I could
not desire such a death. It seems to me important to
state this. I do not see, in fact, how I could rejoice if
the people I love were indiscriminately accused of my
murder. It would be too high a price to pay for what will
perhaps be called the "grace of martyrdom" to owe it
to an Algerian, whoever he might be, especially if he
says he is acting in fidelity to what he believes to be
Islam. I am aware of the scorn which can be heaped on
the Algerians indiscriminately. I am also aware of the
caricatures of Islam which a certain Islamism fosters.
It is too easy to soothe one's conscience by identifying
this religious way with the fundamentalist ideology of
its extremists. For me, Algeria and Islam are something
different: it is a body and a soul. I have proclaimed this
often enough, I think, in the light of what I have received
from it. I so often find there that true strand of the
Gospel which I learned at my mother's knee, my very
first Church, precisely in Algeria, and already inspired
with respect for Muslim believers. Obviously my death
will appear to confirm those who hastily judged me
naïve or idealistic: "Let him tell us now what he thinks
about his ideals!" But these persons should know that
finally my most avid curiosity will be set free. That is
what I shall be able to do, God willing: immerse my
gaze in that of the Father to contemplate with him His
children of Islam just as He sees them, all shining with
the glory of Christ, the fruit of His Passion, filled with
the Gift of the Spirit whose secret joy will always be to
establish communion and restore the likeness, playing
with the differences. For this life lost, totally mine and
totally theirs, I thank God, who seems to have willed
it entirely for the sake of that joy in everything and in
spite of everything. In this thank you, which is said for*

*everything in my life from now on, I certainly include
you, friends of yesterday and today, and you, my
friends in this place, along with my mother and father,
my sisters and brothers and their families. You are the
hundredfold granted as was promised. And also you,
my last-minute friend, who will not have known what
you were doing: Yes, I want this thank you and this
goodbye to be a "God bless" for you too, because in
God's face I see yours. May we meet again as happy
thieves in Paradise, if it please God, the Father of us
both.*[25]

Any commentary on Dom de Chergé's testament seems
not only superfluous but also disrespectful. The history of
Catholic-Muslim relations from the inception of Islam in
the seventh century until Vatican II is long, checkered, and
needs much more research. However, it is the past. Catholic-
Muslim relations after Vatican II are open ended; we do not
know where they will go. We can be certain that there will
be further difficulties and misunderstandings together with
rapprochements and successes. What is certain is that the
courage, the love, and the example of Dom de Chergé and
his Trappist companions will be a constant beacon for all who
work to improve relations between all Christians and Muslims.

STUDY QUESTIONS

1. How did *Nostra Aetate* articulate a change or development
   of the attitude of the Catholic Church to Islam?
2. For Catholics where does the Catholic-Muslim dialogue fit in
   the overall constellation of interreligious dialogues?
3. What are some of the difficulties which a Catholic faces in
   the Catholic-Muslim dialogue?
4. What are some of the difficulties which a Muslim faces in
   the Catholic-Muslim dialogue?
5. How might a local Catholic-Muslim dialogue benefit from,
   interact with, and even contribute to the work of the
   Pontifical Council for Interreligious Dialogue and the
   Secretariat for Ecumenical and Interreligious Affairs of the
   United States Conference of Catholic Bishops?
6. As the Body of Christ on earth—individually, as a Catholic
   Christian, and collectively as the Church—in what ways

do I see the Spirit of God at work in me and the Church, transforming the world in Christ? How might the *Guidelines* facilitate a deeper understanding of the work of the Spirit in me?

SELECT BIBLIOGRAPHY

Guidelines for Dialogue between Christians and Muslims. Maurice Borrmans, ed. Mahwah, NJ: Paulist Press, 1990.

Interreligious Dialogue: The Official Teaching of the Roman Catholic Church (1963-1995). Francesco Gioia, ed. Boston: Pauline Books and Media, 1997.

Marsh, Clifton E. *From Black Muslims to Muslims: The Transition from Separatism to Islam, 1930-1980.* Metuchen, NJ: Scarecrow Press, 1984.

Speight, Marston. *God Is One.* Second Edition. New York: Friendship Press, 2001.

Recognize the Spiritual Bonds Which Unite Us: 16 Years of Christian-Muslim Dialogue. Vatican City: Pontifical Council for Interreligious Dialogue, 1994.

NOTES

1. The title *Nostra Aetate,* "in this age of ours" in Latin, is taken from the opening words of the Declaration.

2. The Five Pillars of Islam, Creed, Prayer, Almsgiving, Fasting and Pilgrimage, will be treated in detail in the chapter on Islam as a Religious System.

3. It is interesting to note that the Secretariat for Non-Christians was not responsible for Roman Catholic-Jewish relations. That responsibility was given to the then-Secretariat for Promoting Christian Unity. The reason given for what might initially seem an odd placing of this dialogue was the special nature of the relationship between Christianity and Judaism, a relationship Christianity did not enjoy with other non-Christian religions.

4. *Cf. Recognize the Spiritual Bonds Which Unite Us.* Vatican City: Pontifical Council for Interreligious Dialogue, 1994, p. 8.

5. *Da'wah,* "invitation" in Arabic, is the word used for the missionary endeavor of Islam. Although Muslims will often react negatively to the word "missionary" because of the history of colonial proselytism, *da'wah* is almost identical to mission.

6. *Cf.* Maurice Borrmans, "Le séminaire du dialogue islamo-chrétien de Tripoli (Libye)," *Islamochristiana* 2 (1976), 135-170.

7. If one does an Internet search for "Pontifical Council for Interreligious Dialogue," it will state that Archbishop Fitzgerald "resigned" on April 2, 2005. That is the day on which Pope John Paul II died. Upon the death of a pope, all heads of dicasteries in the Roman Curia with two exceptions automatically "resign. At this writing, the new pope, Benedict XVI, has not made a decision about the leadership of the Pontifical Council for Interreligious Dialogue. See http://www.vatican.va/roman_curia/pontifical_councils/interelg. Accessed July 2005.

8. *Cf.* www.vatican.va... above.

9. *Guidelines for Dialogue between Christians and Muslims.* Maurice Borrmans, ed., Mahwah, NJ: Paulist Press, 1990.

10. R. Marston Speight, *God Is One,* Second Edition, New York: Friendship Press, 2001.

11. This is an area where *The Guidelines* shows its concern for person-to-person encounter. The first chapter, entitled "The Partners in Dialogue" is an introduction to Muslims, *i.e.* the people who follow the way of Islam, rather than an introduction to Islam, the religion.

12. A *hadith* is a saying or account of an action of the Prophet. They will be dealt with more fully in the chapter on Islam as a Religious System.

13. Operation Desert Storm began on January 16, 1991 and ended with the capitulation of the Iraqis on March 3, 1991. Its purpose was the liberation of Kuwait which had been attacked and occupied by Iraq the previous year.

14. Operation Iraqi Freedom began on March 19, 2003.

15. Borrmans, *op. cit.,* p. 112.

16. *Recognize the Spiritual Bonds Which Unite Us,* Vatican City: Pontifical Council for Interreligious Dialogue, 1994.

17. Francesco Goia (ed.), *Interreligious Dialogue: The Official Teaching of the Catholic Church (1963-1995).* Boston: Pauline Books and Media, 1997.

18. "Interview with Archbishop Michael Fitzgerald," *National Catholic Reporter*, May 7, 2004, from http://ncronline.org/mainpage/specialdocuments/fitzgerald.htm. Accessed July 2005.

19. The ancient Muslim university in Cairo.

20. http://chicagostudies.org/issue/2011-1.asp

21. Some of the more prominent American Islamic organizations are: The Muslim World League www.muslimworldleague.org; The Council on American Islamic Relations (CAIR) www.cair-net.org; The Islamic Society of North America (ISNA) www.isna.net; The American Islamic Congress www.aicongress.org; The International Institute of Islamic Thought (IIIT) www.iiit.org; The Islamic Circle of North America (ICNA) www.icna.com; The Muslim American Society www.musnet.org; The American Muslim Association of North America (AMANA) www.al-amana.org; The American Sufi Muslim Association (ASTHMA) www.asmasociety.org; and The Islamic Shura Council. This list makes no attempt whatever at being comprehensive, much less exhaustive. In fact, there is no Shi'ite organization listed here. Nonetheless, the organizations listed are among the major Islamic organizations in the United States at present. It must be assumed that the list will keep growing.

22. Sunni Islam is the majority "sect" in Islam. By speaking of normative Sunni Islam I am speaking of the larger phenomenon and not including the Wahabi tradition of Saudi Arabia, which, although Sunni, is not representative of the majority of sunni Muslims.

23. W.D. Muhammad differentiates his name from his father, Elijah Muhammad, by using the spelling Mohammed or Mohammad. This, however, is not always followed consistently in the literature. Likewise Warith Deen, an Arabic name, often appears in different forms some closer to Arabic and some closer to English. I have opted to use Muhammad here, since it is used in the literature and is closer to the English spelling of the name of the Prophet of Islam.

24. The Nation of Islam with Louis Farrakhan is considerably smaller though it tends to be much more visible in the media. It was Farrakhan's Nation of Islam that sponsored the Million Man March in 1995. Some of Farrakhan's followers have caused considerable disturbance by rather incendiary speeches which many consider anti-Semitic or anti-Jewish.

24. "Testament of Dom Christian de Chergé, December 1993-January 1994, from http://www.ocso.org/testc-vv.htm. Accessed July 2005.

VI

The "Arab Spring"

I n 2010 Pope Benedict XVI convened a Special Assembly of the Synod of Bishops on the Middle East. The Synod met from October 10-24 and discussed important problems and issues facing Catholic Christians in the Middle East. To be sure, the Middle East had been a center for conflict and problems for a long time. In 2010 the occupation of Palestine had been going on for over 40 years, and there did not seem to be any solution to the Israeli-Palestinian conflict on the horizon. The Oslo Agreement (December 13, 1993) was approaching its 20th anniversary without having engendered a just peace between Israel and Palestine.

During the Synod Iraq was a major concern. The American invasion of the country under George W. Bush on March 20, 2003, unleashed centrifugal forces which the United States had naively overlooked or dangerously underestimated. Never a united country, Iraq was created after World War I by the Sykes-Picot Treaty (May 1916), which with astounding hubris divided up the Middle East according to French and British interests with no regard for the history, culture, ethnicity or religion of the people involved. The three *vilayets* of the Ottoman Empire— Kurdish, Muslim and Christian Mosul; Sunni Arab Baghdad; and Shi'ite Arab Bosra—were simply combined to form Iraq. After several revolutions, the dictator Saddam Hussein was able to hold these three together through terror and brutality. The Kurds in the north and the Shi'ite in the south suffered terribly under Saddam Hussein. The Second Gulf War of 2003[1]unleashed forces that would tear Iraq apart and open up a window of opportunity for monsters to appear. At the time of the Synod, those monsters were in the background and some as yet unborn.

At the end of the Synod, the Middle East had areas of conflict—Iraq, Israel-Palestine—and was, due to the Sykes-

Picot Treaty, inherently unstable. However, it was predictable, and there were forces which more or less kept the instability under control. Strong men/dictators held together countries with deep divisions and kept—often brutally—any opposition in check. In fact, to the casual observer, the region might have appeared deceptively stable. In 2010 Hosni Mubarak had been in control of Egypt for 30 years (1981-2011), and he had been preceded by two other strong men, Gamel Abdel Nasser, who came to power in 1956, and Anwar Sadat. Thus, Egypt had been "stable" for over 50 years. In Syria the al-Asad family came into power in 1971. When Hafiz al-Asad died in 2000, he was replaced by his son Bashar. Although the Islamic Brotherhood had attempted a revolt against Hafiz al-Asad from 1976-82, it was brutally put down, and Asad's forces shelled Hama, a city of 250,000. Casualty estimates ran between one and twenty-five thousand. The Islamic Brotherhood was finished as a force in Syria, which returned to "stability." In other places in the region similar situations existed. From 1955-2011 two strong men held power in Tunisia, Habib Bourguiba (1956-1987) and Zine al-Abdine Ben Ali (1987-2011)—a period of over 50 years. Muamar Gaddafi[2] ruled over Libya with an iron hand from 1969-2011. At the end of the Synod in October 2010, the Middle East was a troubled and troubling entity. Perhaps the worst thing about the situation was that to many the Middle East seemed to be a stable and known entity. To some extent that perception was understandable. Within weeks of the end of the Synod, however, it was going to be proved tragically mistaken.

On December 16, 2010, in Sidi Bouzid, a town in central Tunisia, Mohamed Bouazizi, a poor street merchant, was harassed by the local police. It seems that it was not the first time this had happened to him. Bouazizi's cart containing vegetables for sale was overturned by the police; his electric scale was confiscated, and he was mistreated by the police. His attempts to get his case heard by the local government not only failed but were apparently met by more abuse and humiliation. On December 17, Mohamed Bouazizi set himself on fire in the town square. He died of his wounds a month later on January 14, 2011.

The death of an "insignificant" man in an out-of-the-way

town was in no way insignificant. Bouazizi's death ignited what was to be called the "Arab Spring." The Middle East would never be the same again. Within six months of Bouazizi's death the political structure of the Middle East was thrown into upheaval. In Tunisia, Bouazizi's home country, Zine al-Abidine Ben Ali, the country's leader for 24 years, was forced to step down. Protests quickly spread to neighboring Egypt and Libya.

In Egypt, the most populous Arab country, Tahrir (Arabic for "independence, liberation") Square became the epicenter for demonstrations against the reign of Hosni Mubarak. By February 11, 2011, Mubarak was forced to step down after governing for 30 years.

Libya was also the scene of demonstrations against the government. Libya is a very different country than Egypt. Egypt is estimated to have over 94 million people; Libya has about 6.5 million spread over a vast, thinly populated area. Egypt is urban and agricultural; Libya is to a great extent tribal. The revolt in Libya also differed from those in other Arab countries in that foreign involvement was open and public. The United States and its allies were involved in bombing locations in Libya. Ultimately, on October 20, 2011, Muamar Gaddafi was captured and killed. Libya then descended into a chaos which continues to this writing. Some see two civil wars as having taken place in Libya, the first of which began in 2011 and the second of which began in 2014 and is continuing.

The wave of revolts rolling across the Middle East and North Africa reached Syria early in March 2011. In the city of Deraa, a 13-year-old boy was tortured and beaten to death by government forces for carrying a placard which said, "The Syrian people want the fall of the government." By March 15, 2011, there were anti-government demonstrations in the capital city of Damascus, and by April 8 there were calls for Bashar al-Asad to step down. Demonstrations spread quickly, especially in the western part of Syria, and by April 22 there were demonstrations in 22 Syrian cities. Initially the demonstrations were peaceful. When, however, government forces and hired thugs started attacking the demonstrators, the situation quickly deteriorated to one of outright civil war.

By the end of May 2011 over a thousand civilians had been killed, a portent of things to come.

Six years later at this writing almost a half million Syrian civilians have been killed, and millions have been displaced internally or have become refugees in other countries. In 2011 Syria estimated its population to be about 23 million. It now estimates it to be 17 million. Homs, Raqqa and Aleppo are partially or totally in ruins. Aleppo was the largest city in Syria with an estimated population of 4.6 million. It was one of the oldest continuously inhabited cities in the world with archaeological evidence of habitation dating back to the sixth millennium BC. Half of the city is now in ruins.

Other places in the Middle East also experienced upheavals of differing intensities. Bahrain is a country in which a Shi'ite majority is ruled by a Sunni dynasty. For the most part, the Shi'ites are disadvantaged at best and disenfranchised at worse. The populace rose up in demonstrations early in 2011. It was not long, however, before the government, with the help of Saudi Arabia and other Sunni Gulf States, put down the protests and reinforced the rule of the Sunni al-Khalifa royal family. The Saudis built a bridge connecting the island nation to the mainland to facilitate movement of goods as well as military aid.

The situation in Yemen is not much better. Modern-day Yemen was formed after two countries in the southern Arabian Peninsula united. Ali Abdullah Saleh was elected president in 1990. The Zaidis, a Shi'ite sect, not to be confused with the Yazidis in Iraq, under the leadership of Hussein Badreddin al Houthi,[3] had been restive since 2004 in an attempt to "preserve their rights." In 2011 President Saleh tried to amend the constitution to make himself president for life. Demonstrations broke out almost immediately. Saleh had to leave the country in 2012, and he was replaced by the vice president Abd Rabbuh Mansor Hadi. The Zaidi opposition strengthened and invaded the capital city of Sanaa in September 2014 with the help of the former president Saleh. There were mass resignations of the existing government in January 2015. Saudi Arabia, considering the Houthis illegitimate and terrorists, has become militarily involved in Yemen in an effort to defeat the Houthis. Never a wealthy or particularly stable country, Yemen is now engaged in what is, for all practical purposes, a war with its northern neighbor. This has precipitated a humanitarian crisis in an already impoverished country.

At the close of the Synod of Bishops Assembly in October 2010, not even the most perceptive participant or observer could have foreseen the tectonic changes that would take place in the Middle East in the months ahead. One year after the Synod the governments had fallen in Libya, Tunisia and Egypt; Syria became involved in a civil war, and Iraq moved closer to disintegrating into three distinct, independent entities.

Nature and politics abhor a vacuum. The turmoil in the Middle East and North Africa provided a vacuum which allowed many non-state agents to play significant roles in the region. Different al-Qaeda affiliates appeared in many countries, and the Islamic Brotherhood gained control in Egypt. Mohamed Morsi, a member of the Islamic Brotherhood, was democratically elected the fifth President of Egypt and took office June 30, 2012. He was extremely inept at governing and was removed by a coup on July 3, 2013. He was replaced by General Abdel Fattah al-Sisi, returning Egypt to an autocratic government. Perhaps the most infamous of the non-state agents that arose in the ensuing vacuum was the Islamic State in Iraq and Syria (ISIS). The organization goes by other names: the Islamic State of Iraq and the Levant[4] (ISIL), *dā'ish,* the Islamic acronym for the Islamic State of Iraq and Sham[5],[6]. ISIS is the most spectacular and, at least initially, successful of the non-state agents which have arisen in the region. We will treat ISIS below.

In the Western media, the upheavals that began with the death of Mohamed Bouazizi were quickly referred to as the "Arab Spring." It appeared to me that parallels were being drawn (or wished for) between what was going on in the Middle East and North Africa with what had gone on in Prague starting in January 1968, when the people of what was then Czechoslovakia revolted against the Soviet occupiers of the country. Despite the fact that the Prague Spring was not successful, and the invasion of Soviet tanks on August 21, 1968, brought it to a quick end, it nevertheless captured the imagination of many in the West.

Another thing I found curious was the expression "Arab Spring" itself. In most of Europe spring is the season of rebirth. European literature abounds in references to spring, references to new life and love. In Europe and North America spring is a good time. I did not think that spring was quite so wonderful in parts of the Arabic speaking world. Spring (*rabî'* in Arabic) is the time when the rains stop and the searing heat begins. Psalm 103:15 describes what the heat can do: "man lasts no longer than grass, no longer than a wild flower he lives, one gust of wind and he is gone...." Jesus uses the springtime "lilies of the field" (Matthew 6:28-30) as an image of something that is literally here today and gone tomorrow. Spring in the Middle East is not when things spring up; it is the time when they wither. Even in Egypt, the fruitful season of rebirth was not in the spring but after the flooding of the Nile from July to October. In fact, ancient Egyptians had only three seasons: Inundation, Sowing and Harvest. Clearly, the expression "Arab Spring" would be less likely to evoke pleasant thoughts in the Arab imagination than in that of a European.

While the expression "Arab Spring" did occur in the Arab press, the preferred expression was *nahḍah*, "awakening, renaissance." The choice of the word *nahḍah* in the Arab media was significant in that it hearkened back to a period corresponding to the last third of the 19th and first half of the 20th centuries. During this time in Egypt, Syria, Lebanon and Iraq an intellectual reform movement took place. Originating in the field of literature, the *nahḍa* moved soon into philosophy, political science and even religion. Interestingly, Christians played an important role in this renaissance. World War II, the founding of the state of Israel and the rise of the strong men/dictators all together brought the *nahḍa* to an end. Some Arab thinkers compared the "Arab Spring" to the original *nahḍa* and found significant differences. The former originated as a literary movement and evolved into a political one. The "Arab Spring," on the other hand, started as a political movement. The *nahḍa* was in origin an intellectual and, to some extent, elitist movement, using publications and the press; the "Arab Spring" was a deeply populist movement, using instantaneous social media. To some extent, the *nahḍa* had a unified, articulated goal; the "Arab Spring" did not.

Islam and Democracy

One of the topics that the "Arab Spring" brought to the forefront was democracy. In many, if not most, of the demonstrations throughout the region the word "democracy" (Arabic: *dîmuqrāṭîa*) was commonly in evidence. This engendered much discussion in academia and in the press about the possibility of democracy in the Arab world. Connected with that discussion, if not dominating it, was the question of whether Islam and democracy were even compatible. Subsequent events made that question somewhat moot. Except for perhaps Tunisia, democracy did not "bloom" in any of the countries touched by the "Arab Spring." Democracy may have "sprouted" in Egypt with Mohamed Morsi, who was democratically elected. It was, however, literally "nipped in the bud," when he was removed by a military coup after 13 months in office.

However, the discussions about democracy are still important, if not more so, with its widespread failure in the region. Many of the discussions about the possibility of democracy in the Middle East were, in fact, quite unhelpful. The outcome of an inquiry is often influenced, if not determined, by the way the question is posed. Posing the question "Is Islam compatible with democracy?" had from the outset two major flaws. The terms of the question, *viz.,* Islam and democracy, were treated as univocal terms, that is, as words with one and only one meaning. This is simply not true. In reading discussions about Islam, democracy and the "Arab Spring," one often had the feeling that the meaning of democracy in the discussion was basically "just like us." There are more than a few difficulties with this. Looking at democracy synchronically (at one given point of time) and diachronically (through different periods of time), it becomes clear that democracy is a very complicated reality.

Synchronically we can see that throughout the world at present there are many different types of democracy. There are constitutional monarchies like the United Kingdom, the Scandinavian countries and others. There are democracies like Israel and Iran which are denominationally self-described.[7] Thus, Israel describes itself as a Jewish state, and Iran as the Islamic Republic of Iran. There are also democracies like France which reject all forms of religious self-identification in favor of *laïcité*[8] and others which have constitutional separation of religion and countries like the United States, where religion nevertheless plays a visible and important role in the body politic. There are parliamentary democracies like Canada, Germany, the United Kingdom and others in which the head of government (prime minister) is not directly elected by the people; rather, the people vote for basically a party. The leader of the victorious party then becomes prime minister. Democracy in Switzerland is one person (until recently in some cantons one *male* person), one vote, simulating somewhat the original democracy of ancient Greece. So, when asking about Islam and democracy, the first question should be "what kind of democracy?"

Diachronically we can see that no democracy in the world came into being like Athena in Greek mythology, according to which the goddess was born fully grown and armed from the head of Zeus. Democracies are in almost constant states of development or decay. The *Magna Carta,* signed on June 15, 1215, is seen as an early step in democracy with the English barons limiting the power of King John. It was not, however, until almost 500 years later that the English Parliament passed the English Bill of Rights, which limited further the powers of the monarch and gave considerable rights to citizens, but not to Catholic citizens. The Parliamentary Acts of 1911 and 1949 gave supremacy to the House of Commons (the people) and limited the power of the Lords. Thus, the road to democracy in England took 734 years from the *Magna Carta* to the present parliamentary system.

Even in the United States, which often sees its democracy as exceptional, there has been significant development. Article 1, Section 2, Clause 3 of the U.S. Constitution (1787), speaking about taxation and representation in the legislature, counts "the whole number of free persons…and three-fifths of all other persons." The "other persons," five of whom counted for three persons, were the slaves. It was not until December 6, 1865—78 years later—that slavery was abolished and July 9, 1868, that citizenship was defined by the U.S.

Constitution. Even after that it was not until August 18, 1920, that all the rights of a citizen in a democracy were granted to women. Thus, the American democracy of the "Three-fifths Compromise" was very different from the American democracy which has developed and continues to develop in the 21st century.

Many of the countries in Europe have had several different republics (France, Italy) or democracies of fairly recent vintage (Germany). In many countries there were revolutions, civil wars or setbacks in which authoritarian regimes replaced democracy. Thus, it is fairly safe to say that nowhere at this point in human history has democracy achieved its perfect, ideal form. In inquiring about democracy and Islam, therefore, one must not only define *what kind* of democracy but also *what stage of development* in that democracy, unless one is asking about Islam and some form of democracy which does not exist anywhere at this juncture.

In terms of questioning whether Islam is compatible with democracy, the question is understandable since it has risen in the context of the Middle East. However, it can be too easily overlooked that compatibility with democracy is not a question that is by any means limited to Islam, even if we are talking in the present context about Islam. The same question must be asked about the compatibility of all the world's major faith traditions with democracy.

None of the great religions of the world—Hinduism, Judaism, Buddhism, Taoism, Islam, Christianity, etc.—arose and achieved their classical/normative(?) form at a time when democracy existed. While all religions attempt to answer the deepest questions about human existence, democracy was just not one of the questions available at the time. In addition, most, though not all, of the religions in the world achieved their classical state under conditions in a society which was fairly developed. This also means that governments or at least ways of hierarchically ordering society were often in place as a religion arose and developed. In this context, it is interesting to see how Judaism developed. The Bible sees the origins of its faith in the nomadic patriarchs, Moses and the Israelite slaves in Egypt. When Israel becomes more settled in the period of the Judges, there are clearly opposing attitudes about kings. Although the kingship and the Dynasty of David play an extremely important role in the Bible, and the king, the "anointed one" becomes central to God's plan of salvation in the Bible, the notion of a king is not without powerful opponents. When the Israelites demand a king from the Prophet Samuel, he strongly rejects the idea. When finally convinced by God to give in to the people, Samuel still says, "Consider then and see what a very wicked thing you have done in the sight of Yahweh by asking to have a king" (I Samuel 12:17).

Almost all the major religions of the planet evolved in hierarchically structured societies. Democracy was just not one of the options available. Thus, no religion has a stance towards democracy traceable back to its formative period. To expect or claim such a stance is simply anachronistic. When we speak of "hierarchically ordered" societies, it is important to remember that the word hierarchy is derived from the Greek word *hieros,* "relating to the gods, protected by the gods, priest." In some cases, religion and governing power were one and the same. In no case was there the modern separation of "church and state." Religions developed in a relationship (often close) to governmental systems that existed at the time. Democracy was not one of those systems. Asking if Islam or any other religion is compatible, to say nothing of incompatible, is akin to asking if Islam is compatible with quantum physics.

One of the characteristics of every religion which is relevant to notions of democracy is that almost every religion has a clear understanding of who is "in" and who is "out." Many, if not most, of the great religions of the world were successful enough to include the majority of the population in their region, with the "ins" outnumbering, often vastly, the "outs" or, perhaps better here, the Other. Religions like Hinduism can have very fluid "boundaries" within the tradition, but it is almost always clear who belongs to the overall tradition and who does not. A related and perhaps more important question is how any given religion *considers and treats* the Other.

With some simplification, most religions treat the Other as either a target for conversion, damnation or simply beyond the pale. There are some very harsh statements in the Qur'an concerning *mušrikūn,* "idolaters," and *kāfirūn,* "infidels." Surah 9:5 calls on Muslims to "kill the idolaters wherever you find them and take them prisoner...." This verse of the Qur'an, however, is often quoted without what follows: "And if any one of the idolaters asks protection from you, grant it so that he may hear the word of Allah; then convey him to his place of security. That is because they are a people without knowledge." (9:6)

In Christianity for centuries non-Christians were considered damned, with *extra ecclesia nulla salus,* "outside the church there is no salvation," being a rather clear and simple way of dealing with the Other. Sometimes this was understood literally but with time became interpreted more openly. Likewise, the principle that "error has no rights" made the position of the Other rather precarious in "Christendom."

Islam is perhaps the only religion that had some consideration of the other. In Islam the *ahl-ulkitāb,* "People of the Book," *i.e.* primarily Jews and Christians but also Sabians[9] and Zoroastrians and much less frequently Buddhists and Hindus in later Islam, can become *ḏimmî,* which are protected minorities with obligations and limited rights. There is no doubt that the situation of the *ḏimmî* in Islam was much better than that of, for example, the Jew in Medieval Europe. There is also no doubt, however, that the *ḏimmî* was also a second-class citizen. What is often called *"ḏimmîtude"* has only a tenuous connection to what we would call pluralism and cannot be a substitute for it in the modern world.

One of the most important elements of democracy is that of citizenship. Closely connected with the understanding of contemporary citizenship is pluralism. Thus, many would see citizenship as "having rights and obligations and enjoying the protection of a particular nation by birth or naturalization." Often—but not always—citizenship is seen as disconnected from ethnicity, religion, financial status, gender, etc. We must not forget that this is a very modern, post-French Revolution concept that is not shared in many parts of the world where citizenship and ethnicity are almost identical. While some religions are blind to ethnic differences, the notion of citizenship—the equal rights and obligations of the Other independent of ethnicity, religion, gender, etc.—was something that did not arise until relatively recently in human history. Whether any religion *in its classical form* was compatible with democracy is, I believe, a false question, since pluralistic—to say nothing of secular—democracy was not part of any religion's possible world-view and hence not an option to be considered. A better, more helpful question is how capable is any given religion of dealing with the rights of the Other as an equal in society. It seems to me that this is not a question that can be definitively answered once and for all. In countries where a given religion enjoys an overwhelming hegemony, there is less motivation to deal with this, whereas for co-religionists living in a very pluralistic society the motivation is extremely high, even if only for reasons of survival and self-advantage. It would seem to me that no religion has a monopoly on democratic theories and practices; rather, every religion finds itself in the unusual—and often uncomfortable—situation of being the learner when it comes to pluralistic democracy with, I suspect, no religion having an inherent advantage over any other in this learning experience.

Recently there has been an upsurge of sectarian violence in the world. There have been sectarian conflicts between Hindus and Christians and Hindus and Muslims in India. Muslim Rohingyas in Burma are often brutally discriminated against by the Buddhist majority. The Pew Research Center studies the state of religious people all over the world and measures the difficulties which they are experiencing. In studying the situation of believers, Pew uses two categories: government restriction on religion and social hostilities towards religions. In 2015, in dealing with 198 countries, Pew found that 25% (50 countries) had high levels of restriction on religion and 27% (53 countries) experienced high levels of social hostility towards religion.[10] While there are clearly Muslim majority countries among both categories, they are by no means the only countries. In fact, Pew released a recent study, "Christians faced widespread harassment in 2015, but mostly in Christian-majority countries."[11] Thus, Pew found that Christian minority denominations were targeted by the majority Christian denomination in some countries. In Nicaragua, which is estimated as 59% Catholic, the Catholic Church reported restrictions by the government in 2015.

The Pew research shows several important things. As the largest religion in the world in terms of membership and geographic spread, numerically Christians are the most persecuted religion in the world. However, looking at Christianity and Islam, Pew notes "…despite being one of the most geographically dispersed religious groups 97% of Muslims lived in countries where harassment of Muslims occurred in 2015. (By comparison, 78% of Christians lived in places where Christians were harassed.)[12] Citing this study is not intended to absolve or demonize any particular religion. Indeed, the study shows that would be impossible. It is, however, most clearly to show that when it comes to being victimized or victimizer, no religion has a monopoly.

Islamic countries are often newly created nation states, with many of them less than a hundred years old in their present configuration. Many of these countries have Christian minorities. Among Muslim majority countries, only in Egypt (10%), Indonesia (9.9%) and Nigeria (40%) does the Christian population approach 10 percent or more. Traditional Islamic law does not deal with the notion of citizenship in a pluralistic state any more than does the religious law of most traditions. Admittedly, many Muslim countries have not had to deal with this until recently. Muslim scholars are struggling with how to deal with non-Muslim citizens in a majority Muslim country.

Muslim scholars from around the world gathered in Marrakesh, Morocco on January 25-27, 2016 to study this issue. The specific issues involved were:

1. Grounding the discussion surrounding religious minorities in Muslim lands in Sacred Law utilizing its general principles, objectives and adjudicative methodology.
2. Exploring the historical dimensions and contexts related to the issue.
3. Examining the impact of domestic and international rights.[13]

The scholars began their study with the so-called *Charter*

of Medina which was the agreement which Muhammad made with the Jews of Medina before he and the young community emigrated (the *Hijra*) there in the year 622. The Declaration expressly states that the conference was "... to reaffirm the principles of the *Charter of Medina*...," the objectives of which "provide a suitable framework for national constitutions in countries with Muslim majorities...." The Declaration makes several resolutions, among which is to "establish a constitutional contractual relationship among its citizens," "to rebuild the past by reviving this tradition of conviviality," and lastly declaring it "unconscionable to employ religion for the purpose of aggressing upon (*sic*) the rights of religious minorities...." The Declaration also significantly calls for a legal development of the concept of citizenship "... rooted in Islamic tradition and principles and mindful of global changes."

Given the extremely important fact that democracy is never born fully formed but rather develops in stages— sometimes over a long period of time—the Marrakesh Declaration is to be welcomed. However, I think it should be welcomed as a good start. The Declaration uses the *Charter of Medina* (622) as its beginning point. This is positive in that it attempts to ground citizenship in the Islamic tradition, but historically and methodologically there are problems. For one thing, the state of religious pluralism in Medina did not last very long. For varied reasons and in varied ways—some, like the Banu Qurayza violently—one Jewish tribe after another was removed from the city. All non-Muslims were forbidden—ultimately in all of what is now Saudi Arabia— shortly after the Prophet's death in 632. Methodologically it cannot be overlooked that at the time of the *Charter of Medina*, the notion of citizenship was barely developed, if at all, and certainly not in the Middle East. Thus, the connection between the *Charter of Medina* and modern, pluralistic citizenship still needs to be made.

Likewise, although again understandably, the viewpoint of the document is that of the majority. Citizenship is granted or recognized seemingly from the top down. That is not to say the Declaration denies peoples' inalienable right or denies that government flows from the consent of the governed,[14] but that is not clearly within its purview. Nevertheless, there is a weakness in the approach in that what is granted by the majority can be taken away by the majority.

It would be unrealistic and indeed unfair to expect a conference like the one that met in Marrakesh, composed of many nations, cultures and varieties of Islamic expression, to come forth with a fully researched and fully developed theology of citizenship in a religiously pluralistic society. The Roman Catholic Church did not enter into that discussion officially until the promulgation of *Dignitatis Humanæ,* "The Declaration on Religious Freedom: On the Right of the Person and of Communities to Social and Civil Freedom in Matters Religious" on December 7, 1965. Catholics, especially in the West, should not forget that this important document of the Vatican II was not passed unanimously. Without a doubt, therefore, the Marrakesh Declaration provides Muslims and outside observers with a very important initial attempt by an ancient faith to deal with a very contemporary problem.

Later in 2016 another declaration appeared, the Erbil Declaration. While both declarations are attempts to articulate what is necessary for a religiously pluralistic society, each of the declarations comes out of a very different context. The Marrakesh Declaration came from a gathering of primarily Sunni Muslim scholars meeting in Morocco, a politically stable country not deeply disturbed by the upheavals of the "Arab Spring." The conference was under the patronage of King Mohammed VI and the Ministry of Endowment and Islamic Affairs in the Kingdom of Morocco and the Forum for Promoting Peace in Muslim Societies, based in the United Arab Emirates. The Erbil Declaration was held in Erbil, the capital of Iraqi Kurdistan. Iraq is a country which has been torn apart for 15 years by sectarian conflicts and the terrorism of ISIS.

The Erbil conference was held under the auspices of the Peace Research Institute Oslo (PRIO), the Hikmah Center for Dialogue and Cooperation (HCDC) in Najaf, Iraq, and the Center for the Study of Islam and the Middle East (CSIME) in Washington, DC. PRIO is a Norwegian, non-denominational, non-governmental organization founded in 1959 with the purpose of education about peace and non-violent conflict resolution. The Hikmah Center, founded in 2007, is a Shi'ite foundation which describes itself as "working according to inclusive dialogue vision that has universal, regional, and national dimension that is sponsored by the office of religious Margie Grand Ayatollah Al-Sayyed Mohammed Said Al-Hakeem.[15]"[16] The Center for the Study of Islam and the Middle East, founded in 2010, is "a Washington-based nonpartisan, nonprofit organization committed to interfaith dialogue and the study of Islam and the Middle East."[17] Though not specifically denominational in its mission, much of the staff consists of Shi'ite scholars. Thus, broadly speaking, the Erbil Declaration comes from a conference consisting of European scholars and two institutes connected in different ways with Shi'ite Islam.

Another difference between the two declarations is that the Marrakesh Declaration is dealing globally with countries with Muslim majorities. The Erbil Declaration is dealing primarily with the situation in Iraq. These differences between the two declarations must be kept in mind when comparing them.

The Erbil Declaration consists of nine very concise points. The first point states that "the solution for Iraq is to enhance the status of citizenship, so all have equal rights and duties under the law." This includes guaranteeing "for all Iraqis the fundamental freedoms of belief and expression."[18] Regarding the Declaration itself, the authors do not attempt to connect it with any of the documents—sacred or scholarly—of the Islamic tradition. If the starting point for the Marrakesh Declaration is the *Charter of Medina*, the starting point for the Erbil Declaration is the contemporary situation in Iraq. Thus, the Erbil Declaration is more immediate and less theoretical than the Marrakesh Declaration.

At the conference in Erbil, Ayatollah Dr. Ahmad Iravani, founder of CSIME, delivered a paper entitled "Inclusive Citizenship amid Cultural and Religious Diversity,"[19] which provides significant insight into some of the thinking behind the Erbil Declaration. Although Dr. Iravani is clearly and expressly writing about the specific situation in Iraq, what he has to say is extremely important in that it presents what a prominent Muslim scholar is thinking and writing about pluralistic democracy.

Dr. Iravani notes that "the development of the modern nation-state in the West, although in a unique historical experience and probably not entirely…replicable, gave rise to the notion of civic engagement and citizenship and simultaneously the concept of state accountability." The goal which Iravani holds for Iraq is "to build a state that is accountable to the public and values the notion of citizenship with all its legal and political aspects." The prerequisites for building a democracy with responsible citizenship and accountable government is social cohesion and trust in public institutions. For Iravani this trust comes only "when the government treats its citizens equally regardless of their religious and ethnic identities or economic class positions."

Dr. Iravani's methodology draws heavily on political science. While he most emphatically does not deny Islamic history and theology, his starting point is different from that of the Marrakesh Declaration. He begins with the situation as he finds it in contemporary Iraq. His approach is not deductive, *i.e.* starting from some ideal form of society, which may or may not have ever existed, and then applying it to modern Iraq. Rather he analyzes the characteristics of democracy over time to distill what he considers the "essential ingredients" necessary for a multi-religious, multi-ethnic, egalitarian civil society in Iraq. Although Dr. Iravani makes no pretense of doing so or even intending to do so, he is moving the conversation among Muslim thinkers on pluralism and democracy to a new level.

Iravani ends his paper by speculating that "Building a harmonious social compact that include(s) all Iraqi citizens is achievable perhaps only through the notion of citizenship." What makes this important is that in the discussions at the 2010 Special Assembly of the Synod of Bishops on the Middle East and in the discussions at several synods of different Orthodox churches the crucial importance of a citizenship, independent of ethnic, religious, etc. limitations, plays a recurring role.

One of the most striking results of the "Arab Spring" has been the civil war in Syria. Originally a country of 23 million people, Syria now counts its population as 17 million. Since the start of the civil war, almost a half million Syrians—many, if not most, of them civilians—have been killed. Aleppo, the second and perhaps most populous city in Syria, has had its western half totally destroyed. Other cities such as Homs have been badly damaged, and millions of Syrians have either left the country as refugees or are internally displaced in their own country. Some analysts believe that it will take Syria a generation or more to return to the state of development it had achieved when the conflict began in 2011. Very broadly speaking, Syria is divided into areas which are under the control of the government of Bashir al-Asad, areas under the control of a kaleidoscope of fragmented opposition groups whose alliances, conflicts and leaders are constantly changing, and areas under the control of ISIS.

The aftermath of the "Arab Spring" is not at all what people had hoped/wished for. The Middle East is in turmoil. The futures of Iraq and Syria are not at all certain. Iraq may not survive at all in its post-Sykes-Picot form. Egypt has basically returned to the *status quo ante* with different players. How sustainable this will be in Egypt remains to be seen. In the demonstrations during the early days of the "Arab Spring," democracy was a very visible demand of the demonstrators. For any number of reasons, it is a demand which has not been met in any meaningful way except, perhaps, in Tunisia.

We have seen that democracy is not a univocal concept—there are different types of democracy. We have seen that democracies need time—sometimes a very long time—to develop. Whether truly pluralistic, participatory democracies with transparent, accountable governments can rise in the Middle East is something that remains to be seen. Nevertheless, there are important signs that Muslim philosophers and religious thinkers are beginning to look seriously at the conditions for such democracies in the Islamic world.

STUDY QUESTIONS

1. What is the "Arab Spring?" What were it causes and goals? Were those goals achieved and, if so, where and how?
2. Why is "democracy" not a univocal term?
3. How does democracy differ in the United States, United Kingdom, Canada, Turkey?
4. When did the Roman Catholic Church officially commit itself to freedom of religion and conscience?
5. What work is being done in the Muslim world to promote tolerance and pluralism?

SELECT BIBLIOGRAPHY

An-Na`im, Abdullahi Ahmed, *Islam and the Secular State.* Cambridge, MA: Harvard University Press, 2008.

Anthony Shadid, *Legacy of the Prophet: Despots, Democrats and the New Politics of Islam.* Colorado: Westview Press, 2002.

Tariq Ramadan. *Islam and the Arab Awakening.* Oxford: Oxford University Press, 2012.

Elias D. Mallon, "Will Democracy Bloom? A Closer Look at the Arab Spring." *America Magazine* October 10, 2011.

_____. "Democracy Is Not Enough," *America Magazine,* December 9-13, 2013.

_____. "Contesting the Caliphate," *America Magazine,* July 17, 2014.

_____. "Who Speaks for Islam," *America Magazine, March 16, 2015.*

_____. "The State of Religious Freedom Today," *America Magazine,* February 29, 2016.

_____. "Colonial Creations: Sykes-Picot and the making of the modern Middle East," *America Magazine,* May 17, 2016.

NOTES

1. While the United States and others often refer to the 2003 invasion of Iraq as the Second Gulf War, people in the Middle East refer to it as the Third Gulf War. For people in the Middle East, the First Gulf War was between Iraq and Iran (1980-88); the Second Gulf War was the war to liberate Kuwait (August 2, 1990-February 28, 1991) under the leadership of George H.W. Bush.

2. There are many different spellings for this name. In Arabic it is *al-qaḏāfī,* which allows several different transliterations.

3. Often in the media the Zaidis are referred to as Houthis.

4. The Levant is the eastern coastal region of the Mediterranean.

5. *Dā ͑īš* for *al-dawla al-islāmîya fî al- ͑īrāq wa al-šām* "The Islamic State in Iraq and Sham."

6. Sham is an alternative Arabic name for Syria but which would conceptually include modern day Lebanon.

7. While some might be surprised by Iran being listed as a democracy, that is the case. Although Iran has many problems with its democracy, and there are elements of a theocracy in the government, Iran is now the only country in the region that has a regular exchange of presidential power and a functioning parliament. Iran has had seven presidents. The first president, Abolhassen Banisadr, was impeached in 1981. His successor, Mohammed Ali Rajai was assassinated on August 30, 1981, after four weeks in office. Since 1981, there has been an orderly transfer of power between popularly elected presidents with different political platforms.

8. *Laïcité,* sometimes translated as secularism, according to Wikipedia, "encourages the absence of religious involvement in government affairs, especially the prohibition of religious influence in the determination of state policies; it is also the absence of government involvement in religious affairs, especially the prohibition of government influence in the determination of religion."

9. It is not clear who the Sabians mentioned as People of the Book might be. Conjectures have been made but none which solves the question.

10. http://www.pewforum.org/2017/04/11/global-restrictions-on-religion-rise-modestly-in-2015-reversing-downward-trend/

11. http://www.pewresearch.org/fact-tank/2017/06/09/christians-faced-widespread-harassment-in-2015-but-mostly-in-christian-majority-countries/

12. *op. cit.,* p.3.

13. http://www.marrakeshdeclaration.org/

14. However, some Muslim thinkers totally reject this notion as an attack on God's sovereignty. Some contemporary scholars in Saudi Arabia and elsewhere see any attempts at constitutional or parliamentary government to be an act of apostasy. See the following chapter.

15. Grand Ayatollah al-Hakeem holds one of the highest offices in Shi'ite Islam.

16. https://en.wikipedia.org/wiki/Hikmeh_Center_for_Dialogue_and_Cooperation

17. http://csime.org

18. Erbil Declaration, ##1, 2, cf. https://www.prio.org/News/Item/?x=2074, http://csime.org/2016-events-updates/nggallery/thumbnails#1469590657227-9a0e3c75-4d71.

19. http://csime.org/blog/

VII

Jihad and Takfir in Contemporary Islam

During the second half of the 20th century and now in the 21st Islam has become an increasingly visible phenomenon and unfortunately, for the most part, not in a positive way. Several things have played a role in this development. Since the Six Day War in 1967, with Israel's occupation of the West Bank, the Israeli-Palestinian conflict, which is sometimes seen—with greater or lesser justification as a religious conflict between Jews and Muslims—has been a constant source of violence. There have been two *intifadas*, or Palestinian uprisings, several Israeli wars against Lebanon and Palestinian factions in Gaza, assassinations, collective punishments, etc. Sixty years after the occupation a solution seems as distant as ever. The conflict periodically bursts into violence and can recur at almost any time.

In 1979 Shah Reza Pahlavi was overthrown in a revolution whose guiding spirit was Ayatollah Ruhollah Khomeini. With more than a little brutality the Shah had tried to make Iran a modern state. The pushback came from the heretofore mostly quiet religious establishment. Ayatollah Khomeini developed the notion of the *vilayet-i faqih*, government by the (Islamic) scholar of jurisprudence. If the Shah was looking for a modern, Western-styled (though autocratic) state, Khomeini was looking for a state run totally according to the principles of Islamic law. With the establishment of the Islamic Republic of Iran in 1979, what is now called "political Islam" arrived on the world stage. While most Muslim countries see Islam as the basis of government and jurisprudence, most also employ Western legal systems in conjunction with Islamic law. Since the 1979 revolution, Iran claims its legal system to be based totally on Islamic jurisprudence, although Shi'ite jurisprudence differs in some aspects from Sunni jurisprudence. However, Iran not only claimed this for itself, it attempted to spread its understanding of Islam throughout the Muslim world. The fact that the Islamic Republic of Iran is Shi'ite practically guaranteed it little or no success in spreading its ideology in a Sunni world. Nevertheless, Iran became and remains a powerful force in the region and, indeed, the world.

For Americans the Immigration and Naturalization Act of 1965 (Hart-Celler Act)[1] reversed the increasingly restrictive immigration policies which the United States had enacted since the Chinese Exclusion Act of 1882.[2] These policies reached a peak with the Supreme Court case, United States vs. Bhagat Singh Thind, in which a naturalized citizen and veteran of World War I was stripped of his citizenship because his being from India disqualified him from the requirement of being "Caucasian."[3] Until the Hart-Celler Act of 1965 few immigrants from Asia entered the U.S. After 1965 large numbers of Asians arrived, many from Muslim countries like Pakistan. Although there had been Muslims in the U.S. for almost two centuries,[4] they constituted a small, almost invisible minority. After 1967 the visibility of Muslims in the U.S. changed greatly. The "Black Muslim"[5] movements arose in many African-American neighborhoods, often improving the lives of many living there. Immigration also brought large number of Muslims into many American cities. If in the 1950s Muslims were scarcely understood and more scarcely seen in the U.S., within 20 years there were very visible Muslim communities in parts of the U.S. In 2007 Keith Ellison of Minnesota was the first Muslim elected to Congress as a member of the House of Representatives.

Thus, there were two things happening. After the Iranian Revolution of 1979 and the emergence of what is sometimes called "political Islam," Islam became an important actor on the world stage. After the Immigration and Naturalization Act of 1965 Muslims grew more visible in the U.S. and began to participate in the overall society and body politic, including the legislative branch of the government. A similar but distinct phenomenon was occurring in different countries in Western Europe.

Although the U.S. had been involved in the Middle East for a good part of the 20th century, to a great extent because of its oil interests in Saudi Arabia and other countries in the region, U.S. involvement intensified in the second half of the century. The attack on the American Embassy in Teheran and the taking of diplomatic hostages by Iranian students of the group Muslim Student Followers of the Imam's (i.e. Khomeini) Line traumatized the U.S. For 444 days (November 4, 1979 through January 20, 1981) the public was faced almost nightly with images of blindfolded hostages and young crowds shouting, "Death to America." For some Americans it was their first and for many their dominant impression of Islam. The term "ayatollah," previously unknown in the U.S., became a household word and not a positive one.

Starting with Operation Desert Storm, or the First Gulf War,[6] U.S. military intervention in the region intensified. Attacks on U.S. installations in Beirut, Kenya and Yemen and ultimately the attack of September 11, 2001, caused some in the U.S. and other parts of the Western world to believe there was an assault on the West (and Western values and civilization) by "Islamic forces." The jihadi "freedom fighters" that the U.S. had supported against the Soviet invaders in Afghanistan morphed into various groups calling for terrorist attacks against their enemies, which now included the U.S.

The vacuums caused by the three wars in Iraq and the civil war in Syria, together with the general endemic instability of the region, provided a rich medium in which violent ideologies and terrorist groups could arise, metastasize and cause incredible havoc in the region and beyond. Al-Qaeda and its many local variations, ISIS and its other names; al-Shebab; Boku Haram; and numerous other groups became words known to almost all and groups feared and hated by almost all, too.

In what follows I avoid the term Islamic terrorism or extremism for several reasons. First, it is understandably a highly emotionally charged term, which is not helpful. It also does not get to the core of who these groups are, what they believe and why. Tragically, it also does not differentiate from the overwhelming majority of Muslims who suffer under them and reject all they stand for. Lastly, it generates two very unhelpful and misleading responses. The first response is that terrorism is the sum total of what Islam is about. This response is used to engender Islamophobia, bigotry against all Muslims and hatred. The counter response is that these movements have absolutely nothing to do with Islam; the perpetrators are "not Muslims." Each response is simply not true as it stands, and each response makes it more difficult to analyze these movements dispassionately and accurately, and ultimately to understand and eradicate them.

Overly simplistic approaches which consider these movements "just" political, or "just" religious certainly touch upon important elements but do not see the total picture. Ultimately, the groups are both political and religious. However, their ideological and symbolic world is Islamic. It must be absolutely clear that this is not meant to identify absolutely any of these groups with Islam. However, their ideo/theology, the language they use (or in all the following cases also *abuse*), their symbolic world and their attempts at warfare and governance, where appropriate, are drawn from Islamic sources. Each of the groups will draw on Islamic sources differently and to a lesser or greater extent. All, however, draw on them in one way or another.

Recognizing the—as we will see—often deep ideological roots of these movements, it should become clear that attempts to eradicate them militarily will never be successful. As ideo/theological movements they must be encountered also, indeed primarily, with arguments which are drawn from Islamic sources. While one can kill people with ideas, one cannot kill ideas. Ideas have a tendency to spring back up. Ideas are most effectively encountered by other, better, more convincing ideas.

Christians should at least be aware of similar phenomena in European history where centuries of anti-Semitism provided one of the conditions for enabling the rise of Nazi anti-Semitism. It is crucial to differentiate between direct causality and the creation of conditions for the possibility of something arising. In causality there is a direct relation of cause and effect. With conditions for the possibility the relationship is different. An attitude or a theology, for example, can provide conditions which make certain outcomes—intended or not—possible or even likely. The outcomes are neither inevitable nor directly created by the condition. However, the condition does make the outcome possible and stands in relation to the outcome. The outcome and the conditions for the possibility are clearly linked.

Drawing on ancient caricatures of Jews which had arisen--often in Christian preaching—the Nazis found ready-made stereotypes with which to dehumanize, demonize[7] and ultimately kill Jews. Perceptions of Jews as deicides (God killers), cursed, etc., all arose out of Christian theology, which became called a "theology of contempt." After the Holocaust the Catholic Church struggled with the anti-Semitism which had been a part of its theology for centuries. The decree *Nostra Ætate* (October 28, 1965) was the first fruit of the Catholic Church's long struggle with this history. Every pope since John XXIII (June 3, 1965) has worked to overcome the past and forge new relations—personal but most importantly also theological—between the Catholic Church and the Jews.[8] The work of the Jewish philosopher and theologian Jules Isaac and his meeting with Pope John XXIII played an important role in this development. The pope's encounters and relationships with Jews throughout his life gave him a deep and personal understanding of their plight.[9]

The journey has been long and painful. A study of documents issued by the Church since 1964 shows a clear growth in its understanding and appreciation of Judaism.[10] The journey is still not complete, but it has begun and, thank God, begun well, because of great spirits on both sides. Other Christian churches, the Lutherans, for example, have engaged in similar struggles. These struggles demonstrated how a religious group can grapple with an unfortunate past, see the theology of the past in a new and different context in order to overcome it and move to a better future. The history of Catholics with the Jews can also help Catholics be more understanding as Muslims deal with similar problems in the present. One of the great results of the interreligious movement is the increased possibility of learning from each other.

At the outset, I want to be clear about several things. First, ISIS and to a lesser extent other movements are politically motivated. One of the things which makes ISIS so effective and dangerous is that it has an infrastructure built out of the remains of the Ba'athist Party[11] which governed Iraq under Saddam Hussein. ISIS consists not only of religious fanatics but of highly educated military people, former government bureaucrats, computer scientists, etc. One need only look at ISIS's sophisticated use of multi-media communications to see that educated, highly trained people are involved. Much of ISIS's military strategy also shows that its commanders are not new to the field of military tactics and war.

After World War II the allies used "de-Nazification" to separate the bureaucracy of the Third Reich from Nazi ideology and to re-educate it to function in the new, democratic Federal Republic of Germany. Thus, a major part of the reason Germany was able to recover after World War II was the presence of a trained and educated infrastructure. The U.S. plan for the "de-Baathification" of Iraq took place under Paul Bremer, the head of the Coalition Provisional Authority in Iraq, and took a fatefully different approach. Two decisions were made to disband the Iraqi Army and to bar from government work the top four levels of the Ba'ath Party. One study[12] estimated that the "de-Baathification," ordered on May 16, 2003 "…eliminated the leadership and top technical capacity for universities, hospitals, transportation, electricity and communications." The total "amounted to between 85,000 to 100,000 people."[13] The disbanding of the Iraqi Army, ordered on May 23, 2003, had the effect of throwing "…hundreds of thousands out of work and immediately created a large pool of unemployed and armed men who felt humiliated…."

What made ISIS different from al-Qaeda and other similar groups was its ability to draw on a huge reserve of highly trained, alienated people to run its infrastructure. In a real sense, ISIS had an impressive political component of alienated Iraqi bureaucrats and military people. ISIS was clearly political in a way not seen in such groups previously. It was clearly not a group of wild-eyed fanatics striking out blindly in every direction. It was professional, tactical and political. But it was definitely not only political. Even when a religious movement is pathological, that does not mean it is not religious or even seriously religious. In refusing to see ISIS as either just religious or just political, we need to recognize it as both. It is as important to take the phenomenon as seriously religiously as it most definitely deserves to be taken politically.

In attempting to analyze and understand contemporary violent movements which trace their roots to Islam, I think it is important to analyze two concepts, *jihād* and *takfīr*. It is my belief that these are critical for understanding the Islamic theological and ideological underpinnings of the movements. This will serve to clarify the operative ideologies of these movements. It will also clarify that these ideologies are neither the only possible ones nor even the dominant ones in Islam as a world-wide religion.

The words *jihād* and *jihādī*, "one who practices *jihād*," are relatively familiar to non-Muslims in the West, although they may not be familiar in any depth. The Arabic root *j-h-d* carries the meaning of "to labor, struggle, endeavor, fight." It appears in phrases like "to do one's utmost" in Arabic. There has been a great deal written about *jihād* from the seventh century on. Muslims speak of the "greater" or spiritual *jihad* and "lesser" or physical *jihād*. According to a *hadith* or story about the Prophet Muhammad, which according to some scholars arose only in the 11th century, Muhammad returned to Medina after a battle and declared, "You have come from the Lesser Jihad to the Greater Jihad—the striving of a servant of God against his (own baser) desires." In contemporary discussions about *jihād* this is often brought up. Regardless of whether this tradition is strong or weak in Islam, *jihād* in the Qur'an and writings of early Muslim scholars almost exclusively has the meaning of armed conflict.

Since the Qur'an was revealed over a period of more than 20 years, and since the situation of the Prophet and Muslim community changed greatly over that time, the notion of *jihād* not surprisingly develops from the earlier parts of the Qur'an to the later.[14] In the earlier, Meccan period, the community was small, weak and persecuted. The message was primarily a call to submit to Allah, the one and only God. With the *Hijra*, or Emigration to Medina in 622, Muhammad went from being the head of a small, powerless and persecuted community to being the political and religious leader of Medina. The Encyclopedia of Islam[15] sees four different, chronological stages of *jihād* in the text of the Qur'an: "those which enjoin pardon for offenses and encourage the invitation to Islam by peaceful persuasion; those which enjoin fighting to ward off aggression; those which enjoin the initiative in the attack, provided it is not within the four sacred months; those which enjoin the initiative in the attack absolutely, in all times and in all places." Traditionally the common position was that the earlier texts were abrogated (*mansūḫ*) and the later, aggressive texts were obligatory. As the Encyclopedia of Islam notes, this is derived from the principle that Islam is a universal religion which is to embrace the world, if necessary, by force. Of course, in the actual working out of things, mitigating circumstances such as the toleration of the "People of the Book" and others led to a less than absolute application of the principle. Nevertheless, for many Muslim leaders and scholars, the aggressive understanding of *jihād*—at least theoretically—was the dominant one. Clearly, when one speaks of *jihādis* in the modern world, this would be their understanding of the relationship between the Muslim and non-Muslim worlds.[16]

Recently, however, one finds a development in the notion of the relationship of Muslim to non-Muslim countries among some Muslim scholars. In some cases the topic is clearly and expressly *jihād*, whereas in others the treatment is more generic, though no less important.

On October 13, 2007, 128 Muslim scholars published a letter entitled *A Common Word*. The title is a reference to the Qur'an 3:65. The letter was addressed to an impressive array of Christian leaders, from the pope to Eastern patriarchs, the Secretary of the World Council of Churches and many others. Perhaps even more impressive was the array of Muslims who signed the letter.

While Muslims often give the impression of being united, there are, in fact, many serious divisions among them. Major divisions such as Sunni and Shi'ite do not exhaust the entire reality. Sufis, Salafis, Zaydis, and many others often do not interact or even interact in hostile ways to each other. Nevertheless, the 128 signatories of *A Common Word* represented a more diverse group of Muslims than has probably ever been the case in the history of Islam.

The topic of the letter is a call for closer cooperation and understanding between Christians and Muslims. However, in the specific concept of *jihād* as a traditionally quasi-permanent state of war between Muslim and non-Muslim countries, *A Common Word* breaks new ground. The document's statement on war and peace between Christians and Muslims deserves to be cited in full.

> Finding common ground between Muslims and Christians is not simply a matter for polite ecumenical dialogue between selected religious leaders. Christianity and Islam are the largest and second largest religions in the world and in history. Christians and Muslims reportedly make up over a third and over a fifth of humanity respectively. Together they make up 55% of the world's population, making the relationship between these two religious communities the most important factor in contributing to meaningful peace around the world. If Muslims and Christians are not at peace, the world cannot be at peace. With the terrible weaponry of the modern world; with Muslims and Christians intertwined everywhere as never before, no side can unilaterally win a conflict between more than half of the world's inhabitants. Thus our common future is at stake. The very survival of the world itself is perhaps at stake.

Not content to merely underline the practical and the obvious, the authors of *A Common Word* recognize the existence of those in the communities who advocate violence and stress in the strongest terms the religious and moral importance of peace: "And to those who nevertheless relish conflict and destruction for their own sake or reckon ultimately they stand to gain through them, we say that ***our very eternal souls are all also at stake*** if we fail to sincerely make every effort to make peace and come together in harmony."

The importance of *A Common Word,* not only for Christian-Muslim relations but also for the "development of doctrine" of the concept of *jihād* in contemporary Islam, simply cannot be overestimated.

However, it is not merely the Muslim authors of *A Common Word* who have been grappling with the concept of *jihād* in the context of a globalized, interconnected planet. Less well known scholarly attempts are also being made to understand *jihād* in a new context. Because such studies are often not translated into English and employ categories unfamiliar to all but Islamic scholars and scholars of Islam, such studies rarely enjoy a wide readership. One such study is *The Islamic Law of War* by Ahmed Al-Dawoody (New York: Palgrave Macmillan, 2011). Al-Dawoody looks carefully at Islamic sources—scriptural, legal and historical—to come to a clear understanding of war in a context which is both Islamic and contemporary.[17]

While there are clear and hopeful signs that the notion of *jihād* in contemporary Islam is undergoing a renewal that in the long run can only benefit the security of the planet, it would be naïve to think that the work of these brave scholars has reached many who are referred to in *A Common Word* as those who "relish conflict and destruction for their own sake...." Violence in the Middle East, terrorism in Western Europe and elsewhere has not only not abated but seems to be increasing. In what follows we will look at part of the ideo/theology which inspires these people. We will investigate *takfīr* and its clearest manifestation in ISIS.

The word *takfīr* is derived from the Arabic root *k-f-r*, "to be an infidel, to not believe in God, to be ungrateful." As such it is related to the word *kāfir* (plural: *kāfirūn* or *kuffār*), "infidel, non-believer." The noun appears some 134 times in the Qur'an; the abstract noun *kufr* appears 37 times, and the verbal form appears 250 times. The words are often connected with *mušrik*, "polytheist," *širk*, "polytheism,"[18] and both groups are always condemned to hell fire in the afterlife. In this life they are called to convert to Islam and upon refusal are to be killed. The word *takfīr*, on the other hand, is a form of the verb which is used to express, among other things, declaration. Hence, *takfīr* is to declare someone a *kāfir*, an infidel, unbeliever or apostate. This is an extremely serious thing since, according to the law, the blood of infidels, unbeliever or apostate, is legal, i.e. they can be killed. The concept of *takfīr* in the sense of declaring another Muslim to be an infidel or apostate is very old and very controversial in Islam. The question of when a Muslim is no longer a Muslim and, therefore, worthy of death has been debated since the first generation of Islam. Clearly there are times when a Muslim leaves Islam and converts to another religion. Traditionally, such a person has been considered as having committed a capital crime and worthy of death.[19] Such cases are, however, clear. The problem arises when scholars ask if there are any other actions or intentions, internal or external, that render a Muslim an infidel. Historically, Muslim scholars have been extremely reticent about *takfīr* and, if they allow it at all, place many restrictions on such a declaration.

The question about what renders a Muslim *kāfir*, "infidel, apostate," goes back to almost the very beginning of Islam. The third caliph or leader of the Muslim community after the death of Muhammad was Uthman ibn Affan (ca. 577-June 17, 656). 'Umar ibn Khattab, the predecessor of Uthman, had been a severe and strict administrator of the affairs of the community, making sure that neither he nor his family profited from his being caliph. Uthman had been a wealthy businessman all his life and was a bit more relaxed in his administration. Even before becoming caliph, Uthman was known for favoring his family, the Umayyad Clan. It was not long before his nepotism caused resentment among Muslims in the outer regions of the growing Muslim Empire.

Resistance to Uthman was especially strong in Egypt and soon grew into open rebellion. The rebels approached 'Ali ibn Abi Mutallib, son-in-law of the prophet, offering him the caliphate upon the removal of Uthman. From the time of the Prophet's death in 632 there have been some Muslims who believed that 'Ali was the legal successor of Muhammad and not the three caliphs who had been chosen instead. 'Ali refused their offer and his sons, Hassan and Hussein, were among Uthman's body guards. After a short siege, the rebels broke into Caliph Uthman's house in Medina and killed him on June 17, 656. 'Ali was then elected the fourth caliph.

Almost immediately there was a serious division in the Muslim community. Some held that Uthman had been unjustly killed, that 'Ali supported the rebels and was, therefore, illegitimate as caliph. Others, however, held that Uthman had abused his power as caliph and was worthy of death. 'Ali did not help his side by refusing to condemn and punish those who had killed Uthman. Battles were to ensue and ultimately 'Ali would be assassinated (January 27, 661) by one of his disgruntled followers.

'Ali's followers included a group of people who rejected 'Ali's willingness to negotiate with his opponents. These followers, later known as the Kharijites (Arabic: "those who went out, left"), believed that the followers of Uthman were infidels and apostates and that negotiation with infidel/apostates was a sin against God. Until today, the expression Kharijite refers to a type of unbending, non-negotiable Islam, especially vis-à-vis other Muslims. It was ultimately a Kharijite who assassinated 'Ali.

Some Muslims living in the outer reaches of the empire were unfamiliar with the events at Medina. When pushed to decide whether Ali or Uthman were sinners and, therefore, infidels, they refused to do so. Insisting that judgment belongs to God, these Muslims held that judgment on Ali and Uthman had to be deferred (Arabic: *'rjā*) and so these were referred to as Murji'ites. The Murji'ites held that although Muslims could be sinners, they did not necessarily lose their status as believers but became misguided sinners whom God might punish or forgive.

Although this controversy was specific to the question of the legitimacy or illegitimacy of the caliphates of Uthman and 'Ali, the question of what, if anything, rendered a Muslim an infidel/apostate has been a recurring one in Muslim thought. Because there is a lively polemic in classical Islam against "Murji'ism," the Hanifiyah (one of the four Classical "Schools" of Jurisprudence in Islam) officially rejects it and denies that it is a description of its own position. However, since they tend to exclude external acts from faith, the Hanifiyah end up with a position very similar to that of the Murji'ites, without having the name.

In the late 13th and early 14th centuries Taqī al-Dīn ibn Taymiyya (1263-1328) was a prolific thinker and writer. Some see his thought—with differing degrees of justification—as leading to the contemporary *salafi-jihādi-takfīrī*[20] movement in Islam. In fact, ibn Taymiyya has had a profound impact on modern Sunni Islam and is considered by many to be the theologian upon whose work Wahhābism, the official form of Sunni Islam in Saudi Arabia, is based.

The context of ibn Taymiyya's thinking is based on the fact that after the Mongol invasions many of the Mongols converted to Islam but kept many non-Islamic, Mongol practices. Vastly oversimplified, the question was did/ could that render them infidel/apostates? Ibn Taymiyya sees Murji'ism—without necessarily using the name—to be the dominant position of the Sunni theology of his time. He argues that faith is indivisible and that external acts can render a Muslim an apostate without necessarily requiring the internal disposition of rejection or permission.[21]

The importance of ibn Taymiyya's thought is his attack on what he sees as the widespread Murji'ism in Sunni Islam, with its concurrent reticence towards *takfīr*. He puts great renewed stress on outward actions as an indication of whether one is a believer or an infidel worthy of death and eternal damnation. It must, however, be admitted that ibn Taymiyya was, for a variety of reasons, not nearly as extreme in the application of his theory as would be those who followed him.

The thinking of ibn Taymiyya remained a minority that attracted little official following in Sunni Islam until the advent of Wahhābism[22] in the 18th century. The movement, often described as "puritanical," is based on *tawhīd*, "the (radical) unity of God." It is now the only legal form of Islam in Saudi Arabia. Of the three aspects of this *tawhīd*,[23] it is the unity of lordship and the unity of divinity which are most pertinent here. The unity of lordship stresses the sovereignty of God over everything. The problem arises when almost any human political agency, such as constitutions and parliaments, is seen as challenging God's sovereignty. Such things are considered polytheism (*širk*, "association" of anything with God) and acts of apostasy.

The 20th century saw a further development of this thinking in the work of Sayyid Qutb (1906-1966). A pious Sunni Egyptian writer and educator, Qutb spent three years abroad, including two in the United States, from 1948-1951, where he earned a master's degree in education. Qutb was deeply shocked and disturbed by life in the U.S., which he found to be racist, sexually promiscuous and Zionist. This had the effect of deepening his commitment to Islam. Upon his return to Egypt, Qutb joined the Muslim Brotherhood and became its director of propaganda. His and the Brotherhood's relations with the Egyptian government deteriorated over time, and Qutb spent several years in jail. On August 29, 1966, he was executed by the Egyptian government and is considered a martyr by his followers.

Perhaps Qutb's greatest influence derives from two of his works, *Milestones* and *In the Shade of the Quran*. Deeply conservative and puritanical in nature, Qutb viewed the Muslim society of his day with an attitude that was, not surprisingly, almost as negative as his attitude towards Western society. Qutb was not trained in classical Islamic thought and showed a certain disdain for it. However, he took from it the concept of *jāhilīyya*, literally "foolishness" but also the traditional term for the period of time before the arrival of Muhammad and Islam in the Arabian Peninsula. For Qutb to accuse Muslim societies of *jāhilīyya* is tantamount to accusing them of being pagan and infidel, i.e. apostate. It is a type of global *takfīr* of entire Muslim societies. Qutb uses the term *ḥākimīyya*, "sovereignty," to make his point. In his work *In the Shade of the Quran,* Qutb states that Muslims have abandoned God by rejecting the legitimacy of God's sovereignty and claiming it for themselves, "whether this be claimed by individuals, legislative bodies or peoples."

Qutb bases his theory on an idiosyncratic reading of the Qur'an 5:44, "they who do not *yaḥkum* by what God has revealed, they are among the infidels (*kāfirūn*)" The key word here is *yaḥkum*, whose root *ḥ-k-m* can mean "to judge or to govern." Traditionally Muslims have read the verse, "those who do not judge according to what God has revealed...." Qutb translates it as "those who do not govern according to what God has revealed...." Thus, all Muslim societies striving for a constitutional, to say nothing of democratic, form of government, are infidel and apostate. This is *takfīr* on a scale never imagined in classical Islam or, perhaps, even by ibn Taymiyya.

There are several sayings in classical Islamic thought to the effect that "sixty years of tyranny are better than one day of *fitna*."[24] *Fitna* is rebellion, the total breakdown of ordered society, the rejection of God's plan for society. Muslim thinkers had always been aware that Muslim governments—including during the time of the caliphate—often did not live up to the standards of the Medina of the Prophet. However, the fear of *fitna* was so great that they could live with a corrupt Muslim government as the lesser of two evils. Qutb attempted—and in some places succeeded—in ending that tradition. *Takfīr* with Qutb became something it had rarely, if ever, been in classical Islam—a global judgment on Muslim societies.

Because Qutb was not trained in the traditional Islamic sciences and because he was often critical of those who were, his thought was generally not well received in Saudi Arabia. However, Safar ibn Abd al-Raḥmān al-Ḥawālī, a Saudi scholar who studied under Muhammad Qutb, Sayyid Qutb's brother, was able to connect Qutb's thought with traditional Muslim sources, making Qutb's ideas more acceptable to a much larger audience.

Daniel Lav[25] sees Ḥawālī's work as accomplishing several things: 1) Ḥawālī places ibn Taymiyya in the framework of Qutb's understanding of Islam in the world; 2) he extends ibn Taymiyya's critique of the opponents of his time to include those of later times and much contemporary Muslim scholarship as well; 3) he applies this to the *takfīr* of rulers; and 4) he accuses other scholars, even other *salafi*, of Murji'ism[26] with its implication of apostasy.

In a reference to *ḥākimīyya*, or God's sovereignty, Ḥawālī "considers any act of popular sovereignty—for example, parliaments—to be the replacement of the Shari'a with infidel law…even if these parliaments enact some laws that are identical to those of the Shari'a, because the validity of the law comes from the parliament and not from God's command." Nevertheless, Ḥawālī does not call for *takfīr* of other Muslim governments, perhaps because he has great respect for the Islamic tradition's reticence towards it, a reticence that Qutb seems not to have shared.

ISIS: The Practical Application of Jihad and Takfir

In what has preceded we have treated the categories of *jihād* and *takfīr* abstractly and academically. However, they are most definitely not merely abstract and academic. The Islamic State or ISIS is the product of the coming together of new understandings of *jihād* and *takfīr* in the 21st century. Certainly neither category is new. However, as I hope to have shown, in some quarters these categories are being reinterpreted in a new and very toxic way.

ISIS appeared up front and center on the world stage when on June 29, 2014, in the al-Nuri Mosque in Mosul a man introduced himself as Caliph Ibrahim, Commander of the Faithful. This man, otherwise known as al-Baghdadi, underwent a fascinating and calculated series of name changes. Born Ibrahim Awad al-Badri al-Samarrā'i, the name indicates he belonged to the Badri clan and was born in the city of Samarra on the Tigris roughly half way between Baghdad and Tikrit, the home of Saddam Hussein. A prisoner of the Americans, who did not think him important or dangerous enough to keep in captivity, al-Baghadi began to change his name to give himself an increasingly important Islamic "pedigree." He took on the name Abu Bakr, the first caliph and one of the "Rightly Guided" caliphs. To that he later added al-Hashimi and al-Qurashi. Hashimi and Qurashi refer to the clan and tribe respectively to which the Prophet Muhammad belonged.[27] It is highly unlikely that a Muslim would have such an ancestry and that it would appear only later in his life. It does seem, however, that al-Baghdadi was highly educated in Islamic jurisprudence, unlike most of the leaders in other groups like al-Qaeda.

ISIS conquered almost all of northeastern Syria and large parts of Iraq, including Mosul, Iraq's second largest city, within a matter of months. It then set up its capital in Raqqa, Syria. The spectacular military successes of ISIS shocked the world, and there was a tendency to believe that it had appeared out of nowhere. This is simply not the case. Rather, ISIS, or simply the Islamic State, as it called itself, had been evolving for several years before 2014.

Its origins are connected with Abu Musab al-Zarqawi, a notorious terrorist famous for bombings and for targeting civilians. Born in Zarqa in Jordan, al-Zarqawi seems to have been in constant trouble with the police as a young man. He spent some time as a *jihadi* in Afghanistan but ultimately ended up in Iraq where he formed the Organization for Tawhid[28] and Jihad. Al-Zarqawi brought his organization under the aegis of al-Qaeda, and for that reason it was sometimes referred to as al-Qaeda in Iraq (AQI). Al-Zarqawi's incredible brutality, his obsessive hatred of Shi'ites and his penchant for attacking civilians cost him whatever popular support he might have had. Ironically his brutality became a public relations problem for al-Qaeda, which considered him and his movement too violent! Al-Zarqawi was killed by an American bomb on June 7, 2006. He was succeeded by Abu Omar al-Baghdadi, and the Islamic State in Iraq (ISI) was formed.

With the death of al-Zarqawi, his movement suffered setbacks. In the central al-Anbar province of Iraq the Sunni leadership was chafing under the harsh puritanism of AQI and they began to rebel. A movement called "the Awakening" began in which the Sunni tribes rejected al-Zarqawi's movement. This also coincided with the American "surge," which brought some stability to the area. By 2006 the movement was in major decline. Beginning in 2007, however, some things started to change which would affect the future of al-Zarqawi's movement. The American surge of troops came to an end, and between 2007 and 2011 the number of American soldiers in Iraq was greatly reduced. At the same time the government of Nuri al-Maliki, the Iraqi Prime Minister, began to greatly favor Shi'ites over Sunnis. In another example of incredibly inept leadership, al-Maliki managed to alienate the Sunni part of Iraq. By 2009 AQI had reached a low point. On April 18, 2010, Abu Omar al-Baghdadi was killed and was replaced by Abu Bakr al-Baghdadi, who would later become the Caliph of ISIS.[29]

Several things worked in Abu Bakr's favor. Sunnis in Iraq were increasingly alienated from the government in Baghdad; a series of prison breaks in Iraq between 2012 and 2013 released a large number of people favorable towards revolt against al-Maliki, and the de-Baathification actions of Paul Bremer, the head of the Coalition Provisional Authority in Iraq in 2003, created a huge reserve of highly trained bureaucrats, strategists and military who were more than willing to offer their services to al-Baghdadi's organization. This is something which cannot be overlooked in understanding ISIS's spectacular successes, at least initially. It was composed not only of cadres of religious fanatics. It possessed also a highly educated and professional infrastructure. It was not long before al-Baghdadi started negotiations with other groups such as the Syrian *Jebhat al-Nusra* and tensions with al-Qaeda increased. In April 2013 AQI changed its name to the Islamic State in Iraq and Sham (ISIS), and on February 3, 2014 al-Qaeda repudiated the "new" organization.

ISIS is known not only for its spectacular military successes in Iraq and Syria but also, if not especially, for its incredible brutality[30] which it deliberately cultivated and promulgated through social media. Public beheadings on a massive scale, stonings, crucifixions, burnings, drownings and throwing people off tall buildings—all carefully "justified" by references to classical Islamic sources became the hallmark of ISIS.[31]

The impact of ISIS on Christians in Iraq and Syria has been devastating. After having conquered Mosul in June 2014, from August 1-15 ISIS extended its control to the north, south and east of the city. East of Mosul is the Plain of Nineveh, which has been home to thousands of Christians for over 1500 years. Christians of both Orthodox and Catholic Churches populated many of the towns on the plain. On the night of August 6 between 100,000 and 120,000 Christians had to flee, literally with only the clothes on their back. They escaped, many on foot, to the east to the safety of Irbil in the Kurdish part of Iraq. The soldiers of ISIS plundered what the refugees had left behind, desecrated the churches and cemeteries and often mined the houses with explosives and improvised explosive devices (IED). Those who were unable to flee were forced to convert, pay a tax which many could not afford or be killed. Others, like the Yazidis, fared even worse. Even with the 2016 defeat of ISIS in the Plain of Nineveh, it is still unknown if Christians will ever populate the Plain of Nineveh again to the extent they did in the past.

Since 2016 ISIS has been experiencing serious setbacks militarily. Mosul has been liberated, although at a terrible cost in both lives and property, and Raqqa in Syria is on the point of falling to Kurdish and other forces. There is talk about the defeat of ISIS, although at the same time so-called "sleeper cells" are creating havoc in places like Germany, France, Spain, the UK and elsewhere.

ISIS is the ideo/theological program of *jihād* and *takfīr* taken to its logical extreme. Unmoored from the restraints which Muslim scholars exercised over both for centuries, groups like ISIS can and do use the powerful symbolism of ancient Muslim categories to attract the young, idealistic and gullible and to reduce all dissent—especially but not exclusively in the Muslim world—to *kufr*, "infidelity, apostasy," and the whole world to the *dār al-ḥarb*, "the realm of war." The care with which movements such as ISIS take to set themselves up as ideal Muslims, perverse as it may be, has proven successful. As such, therefore, it should be clear that the military defeat of ISIS troops can never be equated with the defeat of ISIS and an ideo/theological movement. As such it presents perhaps the greatest challenge to Sunni Islam in centuries.

Lav concludes his study by stating that contemporary "jihadists…hold to a minoritarian interpretation of a minoritarian tradition…."[32] This is, I believe, extremely important in what it says and what it excludes. It affirms that the ideo/theology of much of the *jihādi/salafi/takfīri* movement(s) in contemporary Islam does, in fact, have deep roots in Islam. This is not a modern, rootless aberration of Islam. However, it also makes something else clear which is extremely important. Lav describes this movement(s) as a minority within a minority in Islam. The importance of this cannot be overstressed. On the one hand, by showing the clear Islamic roots of this phenomenon, it is clear that one ignores its religious basis at one's peril. If this problem is to be solved in the modern world, it is imperative that religious solutions play a major role. The religious component of the phenomenon explains its attractiveness to some people and also explains why it keeps returning after it is declared dead or defeated, especially by military means. However, it is equally important to see the phenomenon as a "minority within a minority" in Islam. Neither in the past nor in the present is this type of thinking typical of Islam. Those who see the phenomenon as the true face of the faith are simply ignoring or ignorant of the history of Islamic thought.

It is often noted that the vast majority of the victims of groups like ISIS and al-Qaeda are other Muslims. This is undoubtedly true. When one looks at the ruins of Aleppo, Raqqa, Mosul and other cities, the majority of these cities had Muslim majority populations. Christians and other minorities in the Middle East continue to suffer greatly. Because they are demographically much smaller and weaker, these communities often find themselves faced with an extinction that is not a threat to the Muslim population. Nevertheless, Muslim victims in the Middle East do not get the same media coverage in the West as do the religious minorities in the region. While regrettable, it is understandable. However, it also is a clear indication that, while this phenomenon is a world-wide problem, it is also profoundly a Muslim problem—a problem that deeply impacts and victimizes Muslims and a problem that requires a Muslim ideo/theological response.

In a world of increasing interreligious dialogue one may dare to hope that, without being self-righteous or paternalistic, religions can share experiences of overcoming their own internal problems and provide insights into how similar problems might be solved in other traditions.

STUDY QUESTIONS

1. What is *jihād* and what is *takfīr* in Islam?
2. What are some of the Islamic militant groups around the world?
3. Where are they to be found?
4. What are the differences, if any, among them?
5. What are some of the religious minorities present in the Middle East and how are they faring?
6. Al-Qaeda "disowned" ISIS. Why?
7. How do all religious people, including Muslims, suffer under ISIS and similar groups? What are the similarities and what are the differences?

SELECT BIBLIOGRAPHY

Daniel Lav, *Radical Islam and the Revival of Medieval Theology*. Cambridge: Cambridge University Press, 2012.

Majid Khadduri, *The Islamic Law of Nations: Shaybānī's Siyar*. Baltimore: Johns Hopkins Press, 1966.

Shaykh Muhammad al-Yaqoubi, *Refuting ISIS: A Rebuttal of its Religious and Ideological Foundations*. United States: Sacred Knowledge, 2015.

Khaled Abou El Fadl, *The Grand Theft: Wrestling Islam from the Extremists*. HarperCollins, 2005.

Rebellion and Violence in Islamic Law. Georgetown University Press, 2001.

"Conflict Resolution as a Normative Value in Islamic Law: Handling Disputes with Non-Muslims," *Faith-Based Diplomacy: Trumping Realpolitik* 178-209, edited by Douglas Johnston. Oxford: Oxford University Press, 2003.

"Between Functionalism and Morality: The Juristic Debates on the Conduct of War," *Islamic Ethics of Life: Abortion, War, and Euthanasia* 103-128, edited by Jonathan E. Brockopp. Columbia, SC: University of South Carolina Press, 2003.

NOTES

1. http://www.history.com/topics/us-immigration-since-1965

2. https://history.state.gov/milestones/1866-1898/chinese-immigration
   https://history.state.gov/milestones/1866-1898/chinese-immigration

3. https://supreme.justitia.com/cases/federal/us/261/204/case.html

4. New York City had a neighborhood called "Little Syria" in the second half of the 19th century. Cf. newyork-onmymind.com/little-syria-new-york-city.

5. Ultimately two movements. The first, the Ministry of Warith ud-Deen Mohammed, moved into mainstream Sunni Islam. The second, the Nation of Islam under the leadership of Louis Farrakhan, remains independent and differs from mainstream Islam in some ways. A search for "Islam and African Americans" provides a wealth of academic and sociological studies on this phenomenon.

6. There is some confusion in terminology here. People and the media in the Middle East speak of three "Gulf Wars:" 1) the Iran-Iraq War (September 22, 1980-August 1988); 2) the U.S. led war to drive out Saddam Hussein's troops from Kuwait, "Operation Desert Storm" (January 17, 1981 -February 28, 1981), often referred to in the West as the "First Gulf War;" 3) the U.S. invasion of Iraq on March 20, 2003 under George W. Bush. In the U.S., on the other hand, the media refer to the last two as the First and Second Gulf Wars respectively.

7. Cf. Jules Isaac, *The Teaching of Contempt: The Christian Roots of Anti-Semitism* (New York: Holt, Reinhart and Winston, Inc. 1964. Also, https://en.wikipedia.org/wiki/Jules_Isaac

8. Cf. the diary account of Jules Isaac of his meeting with Pope John XXIII, http://www.ccjr.us/dialogika-resources/documents-and-statements/jewish/1123-isaac1960 and, secondarily, https://jsawrite.com/2014/09/01/how-pope-john-xiii-and-jules-isaac-struck-a-blow-against-anti-semitism/comment-page-1/

9. The same can be said of Pope John Paul II, who in his youth in Poland had Jewish friends. Pope Francis had a close friend who was a rabbi in Buenos Aires, Argentina.

10. http://forward.com/culture/178873/the-evolution-of-the-relationship-between-catholic/

11. The Ba'ath ("resurrection, renaissance") Party was founded by Michel Aflaq (1910-1989), an Orthodox Christian from Syria. It was originally founded as a non-sectarian, secular party which would allow equality of citizenship for all. Although for several decades it was the governing party in Syria and Iraq, the two countries were often hostile to each other.

12. James P. Pfeiffner, "US Blunders in Iraq: De-Baathification and Disbanding the Army," *Intelligence and National Security,* Vol. 25, February 2010, 76-85.

13. *Op. cit.,* p. 79,

14. Like the books of the Prophets in the Hebrew Bible and the Letters of St. Paul in the New Testament, the chapters (*sura*) of the Qur'an are listed according to size, starting with the longest. Thus, the Letter of Paul to the Romans appears first in the New Testament, although it is much later than the letters to the Thessalonians, which are smaller and the Surah of the Cow, the second chapter of the Qur'an, with 287 verses is much later than the last chapter, Mankind, with seven verses.

15. *EI*, Vol. II, pp.538-540.

16. Traditionally one spoke of the *dār ul-islām,* "the House/Realm of Islam" and the *dār ul-ḥarb,* "the House/Realm of War," The former refers to those countries under the rule of Islam—understood in different ways—and those not, i.e. the non-Muslim world.

17. Khaled Abou El Fadl, professor of law at UCLA, received a JD from the University of Pennsylvania, a PhD in Islamic Law from Princeton University and studied jurisprudence for over 10 years in Egypt and Kuwait. He has written extensively on Islam in the modern world. Cf. *The Grand Theft: Wrestling Islam from the Extremists,* HarperCollins, 2005; *Rebellion and Violence in Islamic Law,* Georgetown University Press, 2001; "Conflict Resolution as a Normative Value in Islamic Law: Handling Disputes with Non-Muslims," *Faith-Based Diplomacy: Trumping Realpolitik* 178-209 (edited by Douglas Johnston, Oxford University Press, 2003); "Between Functionalism and Morality: The Juristic Debates on the Conduct of War," *Islamic Ethics of Life: Abortion, War, and Euthanasia* 103-128 (edited by Jonathan E. Brockopp, Columbia, SC: University of South Carolina Press, 2003).

18. The root š-r-k has the meaning "to associate." In this context it means the association of any person or thing with the Transcendent God, i.e. polytheism.

19. The basic human right of being able to follow one's conscience and leave or join a religion is today still hotly debated in Islam and in some Muslim countries is still a capital offense.

20. There is a great deal of confusion about these terms, especially in the media. Rarely, if ever, does one find all three together, with *salafi-jihādi* probably the most common usage with *takfīrī* appearing alone occasionally. They function primarily as synonyms for "terrorist" or "Islamic terrorist" with little, if any, differentiation.

21. The opinion of the Jahmite school of Sunni theology held that to be guilty of apostasy one had to openly reject the validity of a command

of God or to openly declare that something God had forbidden was permitted.

22. Wahhābism, named after its founder Muhammad ibn Abdul Wahhāb (1703-1791) is not the preferred name which the group gives itself. Its preferred self-nomenclature is *salafi* from the Arabic expression *al-salaf al-sāliḥ* "(the practices of) the worthy ancestors."

23. *tawḥīd al-rubūbīyya,* "unity of lordship, sovereignty;" *tawḥīd al-asmā,̛* "unity of names and attributes;" and *tawḥīd al-ilāhīyya,* "unity of divinity."

24. *Fitna* is civil war, discord, social chaos. *Cf.* also Qur'an 2:191 *"fitna* is worse than killing…"

25. Daniel Lav, *Radical Islam and the Revival of Medieval Theology* (Cambridge: Cambridge University Press, 2012).

26. Lav, *op. cit.,* p. 88.

27. The kings of Jordan belong to the Hashemite clan. Hence, the official name of the country is the Hashemite Kingdom of Jordan.

28. Tawhid, Arabic *tawḥīd,* is the proclamation and belief in the absolute unity and transcendence of God. This is the core belief of ISIS.

29. *Cf.* http://www.cnn.com/2014/08/08/world/isis-fast-facts/index.html; https://www.vox.com/2015/11/19/9760284/isis-history,

30. *Cf. Management of Savagery Cf.* https://counterjihadreport.com/the-management-of-savagery. It is a blood-chilling 260-page work that develops a highly sophisticated, if barbaric, as the title might indicate, program of ISIS's strategy on how to take over cities, from the initial infiltration to the final takeover, listing things such as how to break down the town's sense of security and to assassinate its leaders, first secretly and progressing to executing them publicly.

31. *Cf.* the careful legal reasoning ISIS used to justify burning to death the downed Jordanian pilot, a punishment universally condemned by Muslim scholars; *Cf.* http://16004-presscdn-0-50.pagely.netdna-cdn. com/wp-content/uploads/isis-doc-justify-torching-.jpg.

32. Lav, *op. cit.,* p. 203.

...and Muhammad Is His Prophet

For Christians, the Gospels provide the story of the life and teachings of Jesus. Every Christian knows the stories of the birth of Jesus, his miracles, the Sermon on the Mount, his passion, his death, and his resurrection even if only in the broadest detail. An understanding of Christianity would be impossible without an understanding of the life of Jesus. Muhammad holds a similar place in Islam. The reader here is introduced in broad outline to the life of Muhammad which is known to every Muslim. His life, struggles, and victories are presented. The life of Muhammad is very different from that of Jesus and the reader is given some insight into the difference. Although not revered as divine, Muhammad is deeply loved and revered by Muslims who try to pattern their lives on his.

- *Birth and early life of Muhammad*
- *The beginning of the revelation of the Qur'an*
- *Resistance to Muhammad's message in Mecca and persecution of Muslims*
- *The Hegira or Emigration to Medina*
- *Muhammad as religious, political, and military leader*
- *Victory of Islam in Arabia*
- *Death of Muhammad*

Chapter Timeline

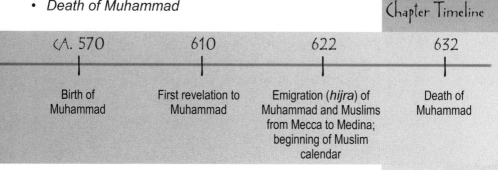

CA. 570	610	622	632
Birth of Muhammad	First revelation to Muhammad	Emigration (*hijra*) of Muhammad and Muslims from Mecca to Medina; beginning of Muslim calendar	Death of Muhammad

Source Material for a Biography of Muhammad

The life of Muhammad ibn Abdullah, the Prophet of Islam, is probably better known than that of Moses, Buddha, Jesus, or the founders of the other major traditions of the world. It would, however, be a mistake to think that the material which exists on the life of Muhammad is of the same character as that of a modern critical biography. There are several sources for information on the life of Muhammad and each of them brings with it certain difficulties. The first source is, of course, the Qur'an itself. However, much if not most of the material in the Qur'an relating to the life of Muhammad is oblique and often very difficult to understand. The Prophet, for example, receives a revelation concerning a problem facing the community or about a decision with which he is struggling. However, unless one is familiar ahead of time with the problem or the decision, the Qur'anic reference is not something which would attract the attention of the uninformed reader. Hence, there is a certain circularity about using the Qur'an to provide biographical material about the Prophet. Far more importantly, the Qur'an is not intended to be a biography of Muhammad nor is it intended to be a private revelation for Muhammad, a record of his problems and his decisions. It is intended to be a revelation for its hearers and ultimately for the entire world. Thus while the Qur'an does provide some useful information about the life of Muhammad, it is not a particularly rich or exhaustive source for biographical material.

A second source of information about Muhammad is the *hadith*. These are brief stories about what the Prophet said or did in a particular circumstance. Although Muslims and the Qur'an itself are quite clear that Muhammad is only a human being, he is, nonetheless, the Seal of the Prophets, that is, the last of God's prophets. Due to his special relationship with God, Muhammad led a life that is exemplary in the deepest sense of the word. Muslims try, therefore, to pattern their lives as closely as possible on the life of the prophet. The result is an attempt to present the life of the Prophet in great detail, a detail which modern people might find surprisingly earthy.[1] These *hadith* have been collected into encyclopedic volumes. Six collections of *hadith* came to be accepted by Sunni Muslims, with the collections of al-Bukhari and Muslim receiving special honor. A standard edition of al-Bukhari consists of nine volumes of several hundred pages each.[2] While the *hadith* present a tremendous amount of information on the life of Muhammad, they, too, do not intend to write a biography in the modern understanding. Although there was considerable effort in classical Muslim scholarship to insure their validity,[3] the purpose of the *hadith* is not so much to present a biography of Muhammad as it is to present an exemplar and a way of life to the Muslim believer.

A third source of information about the life of Muhammad is the *sirah*, or what has traditionally been understood as the accounts of the life of the Prophet of Islam. Two works stand out in particular, that of ibn Ishak and ibn Hisham, the latter depending on the former for many traditions. The *sirah* has several purposes including stories about the military exploits of the Prophet, stories about the Companions of Muhammad, commentaries on sections of the Qur'an, and even prophetic legend including stories of miracles. Early Muslim scholars were not unaware of the possibility of spurious or conflicting traditions. However, they did not always opt for one tradition over another if each had arguments in its favor. As a result it is not unheard of for two mutually exclusive stories about the life of the Prophet to exist side by side in a *sirah*, the author leaving it to the reader to decide which was the more valid.

As a result there are two very general attitudes towards biographical material on Muhammad. One attitude can be found, for example, in the monumental *Encyclopedia of Islam* (*EI*) in its article on Muhammad.[4] Recognizing a difference between the historical Muhammad and the Muhammad of Muslim faith, the *EI* sees little historical value in the stories about the early life of Muhammad, his trips to Syria, and a merchant and his encounter with Christian monks who recognized the prophethood of Muhammad. The *EI* holds that the traditions "are important historical sources for understanding early stages in Muslim perceptions of the Prophet...but they have little value as sources for the historical Muhammad...."[5]

A far more optimistic view of the *sirah* can be found in Karen Armstrong's biography of Muhammad.[6] Armstrong relies heavily on the work of A. Guillaume in *The Life of*

Muhammad.[7] Guillaume's work is extremely important. However, it must be kept in mind that there is no complete text of ibn Ishaq's work and Guillaume reconstructs his work on the basis of citations from ibn Hisham's work. This is entirely justifiable; however, it does add another layer which requires one to exercise caution about being uncritical about material found there. While Armstrong's work is very interesting and lively to read, and while it provides a good deal of useful information about the life of Muhammad, it probably does so with more certainty than the case warrants.

In what follows there is no attempt to write an exhaustive or historically critical biography of the Prophet of Islam and as a book for Catholic educators, neither would it be appropriate to write a type of inspirational biography about what the *EI* refers to as "the Muhammad of Muslim belief." In treating the early life of Muhammad it is inevitable that legendary material will be commingled with historical material. One can notice the same thing to a far greater extent in the "biographies" of other founders of the great religions of the world. It is to be hoped that the reader will get a fair and adequate understanding of the life of Muhammad, realizing all the time the difficulties which the sources provide. Thus, while the overall picture is and should be historically verifiable, individual details may be less so.

A Profile of the Life of Muhammad

It is not known exactly when Muhammad was born. Some traditions connect his birth with the "Year of the Elephant," which is the theme for Surah 105 of the Qur'an.[8] The Year of the Elephant refers to an unsuccessful attack on Mecca by Abraha, the Christian ruler of Yemen. According to the story, Abraha brought a war elephant against Mecca. However, the elephant knelt before the Ka'aba and refused to move. A miraculous flock of birds then dropped stones on the attacking forces, putting them to flight. Many scholars, however, would place the Yemeni attack on Mecca in or about 560 CE, making it too early for the birth of Muhammad. A generally accepted date for his birth is in or about the year 570.

Muhammad was the son of Abdullah ibn Abdi-l-Muttalib of the clan of Hashim and Amina bint Wahb. The clan of Hashim, whose name is found in the modern Hashimite Kingdom of

Jordan, was a clan of the larger Quraysh tribe. It seems to
have been one of the poorer of the Quraysh clans in Mecca
when Muhammad was born. Several months before the birth
of Muhammad, his father died on a trip to Syria. In pre-Islamic
Arabia, one's relationship to clan and tribe were especially
important. Lacking an overall form of government and penal
system, relations between Arabs were regulated by the tribe
and clan. One of the most important functions of the clan
was protection and vengeance. Violence was common in the
world into which Muhammad was born and homicide was a
constant threat. What kept the violence in check was the fact
that the members of a clan came under the protection of its
leader. If a member of one clan was killed by the member
of another, it was incumbent upon the clan of the deceased
to kill a member of equal status of the murderer's clan. To
be without protection was to be in a very dangerous and
precarious state. As an orphan and a widow, Muhammad
and his mother came under the protection of his grandfather
Abdu-l-Muttalib, who to all accounts was greatly fond of his
grandson.

According to the traditions Muhammad was given to a
Bedouin woman to be nursed. Although the clan of Hashim
was settled in the urban setting of Mecca, they were not
far from the traditions of the desert. It was believed—and
probably rightly—that life in the desert was purer and
healthier and that children nursed and reared in the desert
were stronger and healthier. Little or nothing is known of
the period Muhammad spent with the Bedouin, although
there are stories about how his foster family miraculously
prospered because of the presence of Muhammad. It is not
known how long Muhammad was supposed to have lived
among the Bedouin, but in any case his mother Amina died
when he was about six years old and he went to live with
his grandfather Abdu-l-Mutallib. Muhammad was to spend
only a brief time with his grandfather since about two years
later he died and Muhammad was once again bereft of his
home. It is not surprising that the Qur'an and Islamic law in
general devote a great deal of detailed attention to the state
of orphans. Care of the widow and the orphan is considered
an obligatory virtue, as it is in the Hebrew Bible, and the

oppression of the widow and the orphan is considered one of the greatest sins.

After the death of his grandfather, Muhammad was taken in by his uncle Abu Talib, leader of the Hashim clan. Abu Talib had four sons, one of whom, Ali ibn Abi Talib, was to be one of the earliest converts to Islam and to play a major role in the history of Islam. Despite stories about trips to Syria and encounters with Christian monks who publicly proclaimed his prophethood, little is known of the early years of Muhammad's life. Around the age of 25 Muhammad came into the employment of Khadija bint Khuwalid, a relatively wealthy merchant widow some years older than Muhammad. It seems that Muhammad was successful with Khadija's business and because of his honesty received the nickname Amin, "the honest, reliable one." Not long afterwards Khadija made an offer of marriage to Muhammad which he accepted. Khadijah and Muhammad had six children, two boys and four girls. The two sons, al Qasim and Abdullah, died as children.[9] The four daughters, Zaynab, Ruqayya, Umm Kulthum, and Fatima, each played a greater or lesser role in the history of Islam, with Fatima playing the greatest role of the four. In the polemics against Muhammad, his marriage to Khadija has often played a role. Although it is known that she was a widow and older than he, the fact that she bore him six children would indicate that she was not elderly. It is also clear that Muhammad was quite devoted to Khadija. Although polygamy was common in the Arab world and although Muhammad himself would later marry several wives, he never married another woman while Khadija was alive. Likewise there are stories about how some of his wives later became irritated and jealous of his constant praise of the deceased Khadija.

Religious Milieu in Mecca at the Time of Muhammad

There are some indications that at the time of Muhammad the religious situation in Mecca was in a state of flux. As merchants who traveled to Syria and Mesopotamia, Arabs were familiar with Christianity and Zoroastrianism, the religions of the superpowers of the day (viz., Byzantium and the Sassanid Empire respectively). Arabs were aware of the machinations of both superpowers in the lands surrounding the Hijaz. Both the Byzantines and the Persians had tried to exercise control over the southern, fertile part of the Arabian peninsula with varying success. Jews were also familiar to the Arabs and probably more so than Christians or Zoroastrians.[10] Although the exact history is not clear, there were Jewish tribes in Arabia at the time of Muhammad. What is not clear is whether they were Jewish tribes that migrated to Arabia after the final destruction of Israel by the Romans in the first half of the second century C.E. or whether they were Arabs who converted to Judaism. In any case, it seems that in some places, such as Yathrib, the later Medina, Jews formed a considerable and powerful part of the population.

Since pre-Islamic Arabia was not a literary culture that left behind documents, it is difficult to reconstruct what the religious situation was at that time. Muslims refer to the pre-Islamic period as the *Jahiliya*, meaning "state of ignorance." It is clear that the religious life of the Meccans and other Arabs in the peninsula revolved around the Ka'aba, a cubic structure in which a large stone, perhaps of meteoric origin, was embedded. Arabs would circumambulate (*tawaf*) or ritually walk around the Ka'aba seven times. Within the same sacred area[11] as the Ka'aba was the Well of Zamzam, which Arabs believe dated back to the time of Abraham and his son Ishmael. The entire shrine or "house" (*al-bayt*) was dedicated to the god Hubal, probably an astral deity, whose function it was to reveal the future through the throwing of sacred arrows. This practice is explicitly condemned in the Qur'an.

> "...And forbidden is also that you seek to divine with sacred arrows. This is a sin." (5:3)

> "Oh you who believe! Wine, gambling, idols and the sacred arrows are abominations, work of Satan." (5:90)

Hubal was by no means the only deity honored in the sacred precincts. Allah, the God of heaven and earth, was also revered there together with 360 other idols representing different deities. Among these were the "daughters of Allah," Al-Lat, Uzzah, and Manat, who were to become notorious because of the so-called Satanic verses.[12]

There was another religious group at the time that is much more difficult to define: the *hanifiya*. A *hanif* was technically a monotheist who was neither a Jew nor a Christian. Later in Medina as Muhammad become more familiar with the traditions of the Jews, he came to the conviction that since Abraham believed in one God but predated Jesus and Moses, he could not be considered a Christian or a Jew. Because Arabs considered themselves descended from Abraham through Ishmael, the faith of Abraham in one God was the original faith. Since Abraham and Ishmael had built the Ka'aba and opened the Well of Zamzam, the Ka'aba itself was originally monotheistic. To be sure, the *hanif* did not have a special revelation, as did the Jews in the Torah and the Christians in the Gospel, but served this one God in the way they knew best.

Muhammad seems to have been a *hanif* early in his life. Although he would regularly go and circumambulate the Ka'aba, he had nothing to do with the other divinities represented there. It also appears that he would spend nights in prayer and meditation outside the city in a cave, known as the cave of Hirah. At the time of Muhammad, the influences of Christianity and Judaism had been felt by some people who began to believe that the same God who sent prophets to the Jews and Christians would also send a prophet to the Quraysh. It is not clear how widespread this belief was, although it is clear that before his call Muhammad never considered himself to be that prophet. According to Islamic tradition, on the seventeenth night of Ramadan, Muhammad had the experience which changed his life and was to change the world. That night is called *laylatu l-qadr*, "the night of Power" and is remembered every year during Ramadan, the month of the Fast. According to the tradition, on that night Muhammad had an overwhelming experience of the Transcendent. In that experience he heard the command: 'iqra'! "Recite!" Not knowing how to respond and resisting the command Muhammad found himself being squeezed by a supernatural being until the words came out:

Recite in the name of your Lord who created
Created man from a clot of blood
Recite for your Lord is the most Generous
Who taught man by the pen
Taught man what he did not know. (96:1-5)
Although there are some who question the accuracy of

the tradition, most Muslims believe that 96:1-5 is the first revelation which Muhammad received and was the beginning of the Qur'an, "the Recital." Muhammad is said to have been terrorized by the experience and, thinking he was possessed,[13] climbed to the top of the mountain either to flee or to hurl himself from the summit. At-Tabari recounts that halfway up the mountain, Muhammad experienced a vision of a gigantic figure who filled his entire field of vision. Wherever Muhammad looked, the figure was there, striding the horizon. A voice informed Muhammad that it was Gabriel whom he was seeing and that he, Muhammad, was the apostle (*rusul*) of God.

The experience was profoundly unsettling for Muhammad and he returned to Khadija for help and support. Shaking and in terror, he clung to Khadija until the fear subsided. The tradition is unanimous that it was his wife's help that he sought and received. She assured him that he was not possessed by *jinn*. On the contrary, he had lived a God-fearing life of kindness to the poor, justice in business, and worship of the one God. Although the traditions are not unanimously[14] agreed as to the details of what happened next, they are all agreed that Khadija's cousin Waraqa ibn Nawfal, who is described as a *hanif* and sometimes as a Christian was involved. In any case, Waraqa informs Muhammad that he is a prophet within the great tradition of the prophets whom God had sent over the ages. What he had experienced was the same as what Moses had experienced.

It seems that after the first few revelations there was a break of several years. One of the earliest revelations—there are some who hold it to be the first—can be found in 74:1-7.

You who are wrapped in the mantle,
Arise and warn.
Glorify your Lord
Purify your heart
Avoid all uncleanliness
Do not give to get more
But for the sake of your Lord be patient!

These verses use a concept that is often found in the Qur'an, *viz.,* the concept of Muhammad as one who warns the people of the punishment of God.

Since it seems that Muhammad experienced opposition early on but not immediately, W. M. Watt in his biography of the Prophet[15] attempts to extract the earliest message and, hence, the earliest chapters. Relying on the work of earlier scholars, Watt sees five themes which characterized the earliest message: (1) God's goodness and power (80:17-22; 88:17-20, 25-31; 90:3-8); (2) Judgment on the Last Day (96:8; 84:1-12); (3) the proper response to God: thanks and adoration; (4) the proper behavior of the believer: generosity (51:17-19; 69: 33-35; 89:18-21; 92:5-11; 93:9-11), with special emphasis on generosity to the poor and the orphan; and (5) the call of the Prophet.[16] Whether Watt is correct in all the details is immaterial, since he is clearly correct in isolating the very earliest message of Islam.

Response to Muhammad's message was limited. The first person to accept the message was Khadija and she ranks as the first one to make submission (*islam*) to God and become, therefore, a *muslima*.[17] Watt notes that later generations of Muslims would declare their "pedigree" by stating that their ancestor had become a Muslim "while Muhammad was in the house of al-Arqam,"[18] the indication being that one's family had been Muslim since almost the very beginning. However, it is fairly certain that there was a period of two to three years between the time when Muhammad received the revelation and when he went to the house of al-Arqam. Very few could trace their spiritual lineage "before Muhammad was in the house of al-Arqam." Nonetheless, there were important conversions between that of Khadija and the more public preaching of Muhammad. There is some disagreement over who was the second convert to Islam, with some holding that it was Ali ibn Abi Talib and others that it was Zayd ibn Harithah, who had been a slave in the household of Muhammad and Khadija and then had been freed and treated as a son. Watt notes that at this time Ali would have been a boy of nine or ten while Zayd was in his mid-thirties. Another convert was Abu Bakr ibn Abi Kuhafa as-Siddiq. Abu Bakr was two or three years younger than Muhammad and was a merchant of modest means in Mecca. Abu Bakr was a close friend and confidant of Muhammad and remained so during his entire life. After the death of the Prophet, Abu

Bakr was chosen to be the first Caliph or successor. All in all, the traditions list about 50 people (Watt, 39 followers) who converted to the message of Muhammad before he began his public preaching at the house of al-Arqam.

Al-Arqam was a wealthy young man of the powerful Mahzum clan from whom one of Muhammad's bitterest opponents came, Abu Jahl.[19] In any case, after a period of about two years of silence the revelations began again and Surah 93, "The Morning" was revealed.

By the bright light of morning
And by the night which is still,
Your Lord has not forsaken you and does not hate you
The latter will be better for you than the former.
Soon your Lord will give you what pleases you.
Did he not find you an orphan and give you guidance?
He found you poor and enriched you.
Therefore, do not oppress the orphan
Or repulse the one who asks (for help, alms).
But proclaim the graciousness of your Lord!

It seems that it was originally Muhammad's attacks against the "daughters of Allah" that aroused the hostility of some of his hearers. The original proclamation that Allah was God was not entirely strange to the Meccans. What became clear to them gradually was strange indeed: Allah was the *only* God. The earliest proclamation did not seem to threaten the pilgrimages to the Ka'aba with the lucrative fairs which surrounded them. However, the attack on the three goddesses, al-Lat, Uzzah, and Manat, was a direct attack on their shrines which were in different towns outside of Mecca.

It seems to be the unanimous opinion that at the time of Muhammad, Mecca was in a period of moral decline. The old Bedouin virtues of loyalty to the clan were giving way to urban individualism and its accompanying greed. Again and again the Qur'an condemns greed and the artificial sense of self-sufficiency which comes with wealth. In the older tribal system generosity and care for the weaker members of the tribe were seen not only as virtues but as absolute requirements of what it meant to be a good person. It also seems that the clans of the Quraysh experienced quite different fortunes with some, like Mahzum, wealthy and powerful, and others such as Hashim in considerably more modest circumstances. Although it is an anachronistic observation, the poor were becoming poorer and the rich were becoming richer and increasingly arrogant.

It became clear that the message of Muhammad was a direct challenge to the situation that was developing in Mecca. In the Qur'an there is constant mention of the unbeliever. The word used is *kafir,* from the root *kfr*, which has the meaning of "denying God's goodness, being ungrateful." The message of the Qur'an stood in stark contrast to the growing sense of self-sufficiency in Mecca. Surah 80 is extremely interesting on this point. The opening verses criticize Muhammad for having been brusque with a blind beggar. By verse 17, the familiar theme of gratitude/ingratitude develops:

Destruction on the man! How ungrateful he is![20]
(24) Let man look at his food
How we pour down water in abundance.
We break up the earth properly
And produce grains in it
And Grapes and vegetables,
Olives and dates,
Lushly planted enclosed gardens
Fruits and herbs
Provision for you and your cattle.

All the wealth and the good things which the Meccans enjoyed was not the fruit of their own labors and wealth but a gift from God, to whom the proper response is gratitude.

With the refutation of the "daughters of Allah" and its implied attack on their shrines and the pilgrimages connected with them, the opposition towards Muhammad became stronger. By 615, the situation had deteriorated considerably. A delegation was sent to Abu Talib asking him to withdraw his protection from Muhammad. Without the protection of the clan, Muhammad's life would have been in terrible danger. With no one to exact the blood vengeance, anyone could have killed Muhammad with impunity and without fear of retaliation. Although Abu Talib was not a Muslim, his sense of pride and clan unity did not allow him to give in to the request of Muhammad's enemies and remove the clan's protection.

However, not all of the followers of Muhammad enjoyed

the protection of a relatively powerful clan. It was they who suffered the most. It is related that the second adult to become a Muslim after Abu Bakr was an African slave named Bilal ibn Rabah.[21] He was owned by Umayya ibn Khalaf who was an ardent opponent of Muhammad. It is said that he exposed Bilal to the scorching heat of the sun by tying him down and placing a large stone on his body. Abu Bakr, so moved by Bilal's suffering and refusal to recant, purchased him from Umayya and freed him. Known for his beautiful voice, Bilal was the first muezzin, the one who calls Muslims to prayer. He was also a constant companion of the Prophet. Bilal is one instance of the suffering which some of the early Muslims underwent at the hand of the Meccans who opposed Muhammad.

The Mahzum clan also exposed the Amman ibn Yasir to the heat of the Arabian sun together with his father and mother, who died refusing to renounce Islam. The traditions also recount how Abu Jahl treated those Meccans of different social status who became Muslims: "When he (Abu Jahl) heard that a man had become a Muslim, if he was a man of social importance and had relations to defend him, he reprimanded him and poured scorn on him, saying, 'You have forsaken the religion of your father who was better than you. We will declare you a blockhead and brand you as a fool, and destroy your reputation.' If he was a merchant he said, 'We will boycott your goods and reduce you to beggary.' If he were a person of no social importance, he beat him and incited the people against him."[22] Thus the situation for the followers of Muhammad became increasingly intolerable and dangerous. Were it not for the protection of Abu Talib, even Muhammad's life would have been in great danger.

Poetry was extremely important for Arabs. Poetry was not only a literary form in which beautiful sentiments were expressed with beautiful words; it was also a powerful and often brutal political weapon. It is difficult for the modern Westerner to understand the power of poetry at the time of Muhammad and the bitterness which he often felt towards poets. While Muhammad enjoyed the protection of Abu Talib against physical harm, he was often the topic of polemical poetry which accused him of being a fraud, an atheist, and one who had abandoned the faith of his ancestors. These poems would have had a profound effect on their listeners and on the Meccan's attitudes towards Muhammad. Although poetry was the only way his enemies could get at Muhammad, it was one which deeply hurt him. Surah 26 of the Qur'an is entitled "The Poets." At the end of the Surah we read:

(224) And the poets—
It is those who wander in error who follow them.
Don't you see them wandering in every wadi?
What they say is not what they do.
But those who believe, who act righteously in
    remembrance of God,
Defending themselves when wrongly attacked.
But the evildoers will know their future state.

The situation of the Muslim community reached such a state that in 616, some 83 Muslims left Mecca for Abyssinia to take refuge with the Christian Negus, or king of the Abyssinians. Muhammad's enemies tried to have these Muslims returned to Mecca. Nonetheless, the refugees received a cordial welcome from the Abyssinian Christians. According to the tradition, when the Muslims recited Surah Maryam (Surah 19) which deals with Mary, the mother of Jesus, and recited the verses treating the conception and birth of Jesus (19:16-34), the refugees so impressed the Negus that he offered them his protection. This occurred despite the fact that their enemies had informed him that the Muslims, though greatly revering Jesus and his mother Mary, rejected any claims to his divinity which Christians might make.

In the time after 616, the situation for Muhammad deteriorated significantly, despite the fact of the conversion of some powerful Meccans. One of the most powerful converts had also been one of Muhammad's most ardent opponents, Umar ibn al-Khattab, of whom it had been said, "This man... will not become a Muslim until al-Khattab's donkey does."[23] There are two accounts of Umar's conversion. Although they are very different in detail, they have one very important point in common. In the first account, Umar was on his way, sword in hand, to confront Muhammad. While on his way, he was asked why he didn't put his own house in order first, since his sister had become a Muslim, together with his brother-in-law and cousin. Upon returning home, Umar heard them reciting a section of the Qur'an. Knowing Umar's attitude towards Islam, the reciter ran and hid and Umar's sister hid the page of the Qur'an which was being recited. When questioned as to what was going on, they denied everything. In a rage, Umar attacked his brother-in-law. When his sister tried to defend the brother-in-law, Umar struck her, drawing blood. Upon seeing his sister's blood, Umar immediately cooled down and the people in the room admitted that they were indeed Muslims. Umar asked to see the sheet, the recitation of which he had just called nonsense, and was given it. Umar was so impressed by the "fine and noble speech" that he asked to be taken to Muhammad to become one of his followers.

In the second account, before his conversion Umar liked to get together with his friends to drink wine. One night when his drinking companions did not show up, Umar went to circumambulate the Ka'aba. Upon arriving there, Umar saw Muhammad praying. He was facing "Syria," since the first direction (*qibla*) of prayer for Muslims was Jerusalem, with the Ka'aba in front of him. Umar hid himself under the covering of the Ka'aba and positioned himself unbeknown to the Prophet right in front of him. Muhammad was reciting parts of the Qur'an. When Umar heard the words of the Qur'an, his "heart was softened and Islam entered into" him. He then followed Muhammad and declared his willingness to profess Islam and become a follower.[24]

Two things are important about these accounts. First, of course, is the conversion of the impulsive Umar. Second is the theme of the power of merely hearing the Qur'an. This is an important theme which appears several times in the tradition and which also provides an insight into the Muslim understanding of the Qur'an. Muslims have an understanding of the Qur'an which is significantly different from the understanding which most Christians would have of the Bible and is, in fact, much closer to what Catholics would understand to be true of the sacraments. The Qur'an is not merely a revelation of information, some type of anthology of religious assertions. The very words of the Qur'an have a type of *ex opere operato* power in and for themselves. One of the expressions we find is that upon hearing the Qur'an recited, Islam "entered into the heart" of someone who was not a believer but who becomes a believer through the hearing. The Qur'an does not call for a merely intellectual response, indeed it seems it does not even need a hearer to be predisposed towards it. The force of the words and the force of the message do not merely "change the mind" of the hearer but enter his or her heart, transforming the person. This attitude towards the innate power of the Qur'an can be found in Muslims today. The Qur'an is not merely a text to be studied, analyzed, and affirmed. It is primarily a Recital, an encounter which needs to be experienced. The Qur'an is not a text that is to be read silently. It is a Recital that must be proclaimed and in that Recital the Muslim encounters the Word of God.

With the conversion of Umar, the enemies of Muhammad realized that they had to intensify the pressure on him. The clans united to form a boycott against the clans of Hashem and al-Muttalib. It seems many of the Muslims moved into the same neighborhood in Mecca during the boycott, which lasted two years. Like most boycotts it was not total since many of the clans had relatives who were either Muslims or married to Muslims. Nonetheless, for the two years it lasted, the boycott caused considerable suffering for the community of Muslims.

The end of the boycott did not improve Muhammad's situation. In fact, in the year 619, that situation became considerably worse. His wife Khadija died. The loss for Muhammad must have been tremendous. During her lifetime he never took another wife and he often spoke of her and praised her long after her death. The tradition does not recount the death of Khadija in great detail. It merely states: "...with Khadija's death troubles followed fast on each other's heels, for she had been a faithful support to him in Islam and he used to tell her all his troubles." In the same year Abu Talib, Muhammad's protector, died. The tradition recounts some details about Abu Talib's death. As he was dying, members of the Quraysh tried to use him to get Muhammad to mitigate the claims of Islam to allow for the traditional gods.

The Muslim calendar begins with Muhammad's Hijra, or Emigration, from Mecca to Medina. The three Semitic religions, *viz.,* Judaism, Christianity, and Islam employ a lunar calendar. Since the lunar year (twelve months of twenty-nine and thirty days) is eleven to twelve days shorter than the solar year, there is the need for correction. Western Christians calculate the calendar with Easter being the first Sunday after the first full moon (lunar) of Spring (solar). Hence, Easter is on a different date each year and the number of weeks in "Ordinary time" differ from year to year. Jews correct the calendar by adding an intercalculary month when such is necessary. Islam, however, does not correct the lunar calendar over against the sun. As a result, Ramadan, the month of fasting, moves "backwards" by about eleven days each year. More challenging is the fact that it is very difficult to correlate any given Muslim year (presented as A.H. [*Anno hegirae*]) with the Gregorian calendar which is universally used. Since the Islamic year is shorter than the Gregorian year, one cannot simply add 622 to the Islamic year. Hodgson provides a formula to convert the Islamic year to the Gregorian: $G=H-H/33+622$ (Hodgson, 20-22). Since it is highly unlikely that most (any?) readers will employ this short-hand formula, it is merely important for the reader to know: (1) the Islamic year is shorter than the year as we normally understand it; (2) dates in Islamic calendar calculations are difficult to translate into the Gregorian calendar.

This Muhammad was not prepared to do. It is interesting to note that Abu Talib does not die a Muslim. As he was dying, Abu Talib told Muhammad that he didn't want people to think that he had become a Muslim out of fear of death and that if he were to recite the Muslim creed it would merely be to please Muhammad. Abu Talib was moving his lips shortly before his death and Abbas told Muhammad that he had "spoken the word." Muhammad's response was "I did not hear it."[25] With the death of Abu Talib Muhammad's position became perilous in the extreme. Not only was his protector gone, the new head of the clan was his avowed enemy, Abu Lahb. Although Abu Lahb respected his role as protector even *vis-à-vis* Muhammad, it was a situation which could not last. In a calculated attempt to alienate Muhammad from Abu Lahb totally, Abu Jahl asked the prophet if Abdu-l-Muttalib was in hell. Abdu-l-Muttalib was the grandfather who had taken

Muhammad in as a child when his mother died; he was also the father of Abu Lahb. When Muhammad answered in the affirmative, the break was made. It was not enough that he repudiated the gods of his grandfather. Now he declared his grandfather (and Abu Lahb's father) to be in hell. It is hard to imagine the consternation which that would have caused. Abu Jahl had achieved his goal.

During the pilgrimage of the year 620, Muhammad had a fateful encounter with six of the pilgrims from Yathrib, a town about 120 miles northeast of Mecca. Yathrib was basically an oasis that had grown into an agricultural community. In addition to pagan Arabs, there were three major Jewish tribes living there: the Banu Nadir, the Banu Qurayzah and the Banu Qaynuqa. There were also two important pagan tribes: the Aws and the Khasraj. Life in Yathrib was far from peaceful and there was constant strife between the tribes. It seems part of the strife was sectarian. The Jewish tribes derided the pagan tribes because they did not have a prophet who could have brought them the revelation of God. When the pilgrims from Yathrib met Muhammad and heard his message, they became Muslims and saw in Muhammad the opportunity to bring harmony to Yathrib. They told Muhammad they would return to Yathrib telling the inhabitants of what they had experienced and the possibilities which Muhammad might offer as a neutral mediator between the feuding parties. They promised to return the next year to report on the response of the people of Yathrib. The six converts returned the following year bringing seven others with them. They made an agreement to accept Islam and obey Muhammad. In the meanwhile, Muhammad sent an emissary, Musab ibn Umayr, to Yathrib to teach the people the Qur'an. Musab was successful in his mission and many of the people of Yathrib became Muslims. After his encounter with the pilgrims from Yathrib, Muhammad added practices such as fasting on what would have been the tenth day of the Jewish month of Tishri. In addition, the *qibla*, or direction of prayer, had been towards Jerusalem. Since this did not compromise the austere monotheism of Islam, there was no reason not to add something which would make the new faith more acceptable to the Jews of Yathrib. At this time, Yathrib began being

known as the "city of the Prophet," madinatu-n-nabi or, in its
short form, Medina.

The following year, 622, a large contingent of pilgrims
came from Medina to Mecca. During this pilgrimage the
Pledge of War was sworn. The leaders of Yathrib swore: "We
pledge ourselves in war to complete obedience to the apostle
(Muhammad) in weal and woe, in ease and hardship and
evil circumstances; that we would not wrong anyone; that we
would speak the truth at all times; and that in God's service
we would fear the censure of none."[26] The Pledge of War was
connected with the revelation which Muhammad had received
concerning war. Until this point the Muslims had not engaged
in hostilities with their enemies even though they had been
harshly treated and some had been killed. The revelation is to
be found in Sura 22:39-40.

To those against whom war is made
permission is granted to fight, because they have been
    wronged.
Indeed God is powerful to help them.
Those who have been expelled from their homes
in defense of what is right, (expelled for no reason other
    than that)
they say "Our God is Allah"...

With the permission to fight their enemies and with the
agreement of the people of Medina,[27] the Hijra had begun.
In July and August of 622, about seventy Muslims with their
families left Mecca and headed for Medina. Although it
does not seem that Muhammad's enemies were particularly
alarmed by their exit, they nonetheless, tried to travel without
drawing a great deal of attention to themselves. Muhammad,
Abu Bakr, and Ali remained behind. The enemies of
Muhammad did not remain indifferent long. Several of them
realized that Muhammad could become a powerful adversary
if he were allowed to leave the city. At a secret council,
several of the younger members of the clans were chosen to
kill Muhammad. If all the young men were to kill Muhammad,
no one tribe would be liable to blood vengeance, since all
the tribes would have taken part in it. The conspirators then
went to carry out the assassination. According to the tradition,
the angel Gabriel alerted Muhammad to the danger and he

was able to escape with Abu Bakr. Ali remained behind to put things in order. The conspirators did not attack because they heard women's voices in the house where Muhammad was supposed to be and it was dishonorable to kill a man in the presence of the female members of his family. In addition, Ali was sleeping wrapped in Muhammad's cloak, giving the conspirators the impression that Muhammad was still there. It was only the next day when they saw Ali leave the house that they realized that Muhammad had escaped unharmed. A reward of one hundred camels was offered by the Quraysh to anyone who could capture Muhammad and bring him back.

The move from Mecca to Medina was a turning point for Muhammad and Islam. This is recognized in the Qur'an where the heading of a Chapter tells whether the Sura was revealed in Mecca or Medina and there are some differences between the two, as we shall see. Sura 2, the longest Sura in the Qur'an was revealed a few months after Muhammad arrived in Medina. When he arrived in Medina, Muhammad gave his camel free rein and said he would live wherever the camel stopped. As the arbitrator of a sometimes bitterly divided community at Medina he wanted to show no partiality. In Medina, Muhammad was no longer the despised leader of a small group of Muslims in a sea of enemies. He was at first the religious leader of the community and was well on his way to becoming the political leader of Medina.

Although Muhammad had expected and hoped for a friendly reception for his message by the Jews, this was not to take place. The Jews saw the differences between the Qur'an and the Hebrew Scriptures. Stories about biblical events and figures in the Qur'an were considerably different from those of the Bible. Nor did the Jews feel the need for another prophet, much less an Arab prophet. At this point in history it would have been considered very strange for any Jew to proclaim himself a prophet. The polemic against Jews which we find in the Qur'an is an indication of how disappointed Muhammad was in this rejection by the people he thought would support him. In this period we notice an increased emphasis on Abraham, who was neither Christian nor Jew. One of the more dramatic signs of the break was the change of the *qibla*, or direction of prayer, from Jerusalem to the Ka'aba which took place in January 624 about fifteen months after Muhammad's arrival in Medina. The relationship between Muhammad and the Jewish tribes of Medina would deteriorate as time went on.

Muhammad as Military Leader

Perhaps one of the most difficult things for Christians to understand about Muhammad is his leadership of military campaigns. Accustomed to the stories about Jesus, Christians find it incongruous for a religious leader to fight battles. This overlooks the fact that Christian leaders over the centuries have often engaged in warfare. The Crusades were religious wars and Pope Julius II often led his troops against rebellious parts of the Papal States, to cite merely two instances. In the Pentateuch, Moses leads the Israelites in many battles against their enemies. The great Hindu sacred book, *The Mahabharata*, deals with a war between two rival families. History shows that religious leaders often engaged in military endeavors and Muhammad is no exception. In this he is closer to the figure of Moses than that of Jesus.

The accounts of Muhammad's military successes over his Meccan enemies are very important for Muslims. The victories of the Prophet are signs that God is with him. They are analogous to what are referred to as the "mighty acts of God" in the Christian and Jewish traditions. While it is not necessary for Christians to know all the details of Muhammad's military exploits, it is crucial that they be able to integrate them into the Muslims' overall understanding of Muhammad and of Muslim foundational history.

Once in Medina, Muhammad was able to embark on a more aggressive program against his Meccan enemies. It was not unusual in Arabia for tribes to engage in raids on each other. In 623, Muhammad sent out a party to raid the caravans of the Meccans. Although the raids were not very successful, it became clear to the Meccans that Muhammad was quickly becoming a force to be reckoned with. In March of 624, Muhammad led a large force to intercept the caravans of Abu Sufyan, one of his Meccan opponents. Abu Sufyan was an experienced trader and when Muhammad and his forces reached the Well of Badr he took a different route and sent on to Mecca for help. The other raids the Muslims had made against caravans were relatively minor. Abu Sufyan's caravan was one of the largest and when the Meccans heard of the temerity of the Muslims, they were incensed. About a thousand leading Meccans marched out to the aid of Abu Sufyan. Both sides met at the Well of Badr. It appears that neither side was overly anxious to start a battle. The Battle of Badr began in the traditional way with a single combat in which three Muslims were pitted against three of the Quraysh. When all three of the Quraysh were killed, the general battle began. Although the Meccans outnumbered the Muslims, the discipline and order of the Muslim forces made them superior to the free-wheeling tactics of the Quraysh. By noon, the Quraysh had broken ranks and fled, leaving Abu Jahl, one of Muhammad's longest standing opponents, dead on the field. The Muslims had gone from being a despised and persecuted minority in Mecca to overcoming a Meccan force in the field. However, the Qur'an warned the jubilant community: "It was not you who killed them; it was God. When you threw the dust it was not your act but God's. In order that He might bestow a grace upon the believers from Himself. For God is the one who is all-hearing and all-seeing" (8:17). Like the Israelites' victory over the forces of Pharaoh, the Muslims saw in the victory of the Battle of Badr a sign of God's favor, a sign that God was intervening in history on their behalf. The small community that met at the house of al-Arqam was now becoming the *umma*, the Community of the Faithful, which was built on faith and transcended the traditional bonds of family, clan, and tribe.

After the Battle of Badr, Muhammad went out of his way to treat the prisoners of war humanely. Prisoners were either to be held for ransom or released (47:4). If the prisoner's family did not have the means to ransom him, he was to be allowed to work to earn the money to ransom himself. It was clear that Muhammad was not out to destroy the Meccans but to convert them.

The victory which Muhammad achieved at Badr was not universally greeted with acclaim in Medina. Ibn Ubbay, backed by the Jewish tribes of Medina, had lost prestige with the arrival of the Prophet and was not happy to see that Muhammad was now gaining in stature among the people of

Medina. One of the poets of the Banu Nadir went to Mecca and started to compose verses hostile to Muhammad and to encourage the Quraysh to avenge the 50 men they had lost at Badr. Abu Sufyan, whose caravans the Muslims had attacked, and who had assumed a role as leader of the opponents of Muhammad in Mecca, had a meeting with the Banu Nadir at the outskirts of Medina. After the meeting, the Meccans destroyed some fields and palm trees and killed two Muslims. Muhammad pursued the raiders but without success. He was later informed that the smallest of the Jewish tribes, the Banu Qaynuqa, was extremely hostile to the Muslims and their cause. After a brawl at the market place, Muhammad was called in to exercise his role as arbitrator. The Banu Qaynuqa refused to acknowledge him and barricaded themselves, expecting help from Ibn Ubayy. When this help was not forthcoming they were forced to surrender unconditionally after a two-week siege. The tribe knew that the traditions of warfare permitted the victor to massacre them. However, Muhammad spared them on the condition that they leave Medina immediately. Expulsions of tribes from a town or oasis was not unheard of in the time of Muhammad, and the Banu Qaynuqa left Medina and emigrated to live with another Jewish clan along the Syrian border. This was the first instance of serious conflict between the Jewish and Muslim communities in Medina which resulted in the expulsion of Jews.

When the poet of the Banu Nadir returned to Medina and once again began composing hostile poetry again the Prophet, Muhammad had him assassinated. When the Banu Nadir saw the expulsion of the Banu Qaynuqa and the execution of their inflammatory poet, they approached Muhammad to complain. He offered them a special treaty in addition to the one which he had with all the people of Medina. They accepted this and Muhammad's position was secured for at least a little while.

In the Spring of 625, the Meccans prepared another attack against the community in Medina. A large force appeared outside the city on March 21, camped on the plain by Mount Uhud. With a force of about one thousand men, the Muslims went out the next day to meet a force that was more than three times their size. Ibn Ubbay went out with the forces of Medina and then deserted with 300 of his followers. The Jewish tribes refused to take part in the battle because it was the Sabbath. The battle was engaged and the Muslims broke ranks. Muhammad was knocked unconscious in the melee and the rumor spread that he had been killed. Once the Quraysh heard that Muhammad had been killed, they stopped pursuing the Muslims who were then able to make a successful retreat. The victory was not a great one for the Quraysh and when Abu Sufyan heard that Muhammad had not been killed, he offered a challenge to meet the Muslims the following year at Badr, the scene of the Muslims' previous victory.

Sixty-five Muslims had been killed in the Battle of Uhud and their spirits sank. The feelings of optimism and of God's favor that they experienced at Badr were replaced with a sense of despair and abandonment. At this point the third Sura was revealed to Muhammad. The defeat at Uhud had not been an act of God. The reason for the defeat was the Muslims themselves with their lack of discipline and inner quarrels. The defeat at Uhud also made it clear to Muhammad that not everyone in Medina could be trusted. The Qur'an begins to speak of the *munafiqun* or "hypocrites," who secretly or not so secretly rejoiced at Muhammad's defeat.

Some time after the defeat in Uhud, Muhammad was engaged in a council with members of the Banu Nadir. He was informed in a revelation that members of the tribe were planning to kill him, probably in revenge for his execution of the tribe's poet earlier. According to the tradition, the Banu Nadir planned to drop a large rock on the Prophet to kill him. Muhammad gathered a force and marched against them. They had broken both treaties which they had made with Muhammad and the time of reckoning was at hand. The Banu Nadir took refuge in their fortress, as had the Banu Qaynuqa earlier. Muhammad ordered the palm trees be cut down and burnt which was a sign of all-out war. When help from Ibn Ubbay once again failed to materialize, the Banu Nadir sued for peace, asking only that their lives be spared. Muhammad agreed to spare their lives on condition that they leave Medina immediately, taking with them only that which they could carry on their camels.[28] The expulsion of the Banu Nadir is recalled in Sura 59:2: "It is He (God) who drove out the Unbelievers from among the People of the Book from their homes." And in verse 3, "And had it not been that God had decreed banishment for them, he surely would have punished them in this world. And in the Hereafter they shall certainly have the punishment of the Fire. (4) That is because they resisted God and His Messenger. If any one resists God, God is severe in punishing."

The last major battle that Muhammad fought against the Meccans was the so-called Battle of the Trench. In March of 627, the Meccans gathered their forces and began to march on Medina. Muhammad had notice of the attack and there was time to prepare the defenses of Medina. In order to defend the one weak northern side of the city, a large trench was dug, hence, the Battle of the Trench. Once again the Quraysh outnumbered the Muslims by more than three to one. However, the cavalry upon which the Meccans were heavily relying were of little or no use because of the trench which they could not get over. When the Meccans realized that force would not accomplish their goals, they resorted to treachery. They attempted to get the last Jewish tribe left in Medina, the Banu Qurayza, to allow their forces into the southern part of the city. The Banu Nadir, who had been banished previously, aligned themselves with the Meccans and had sent troops to support them. Although the Banu Qurayza were initially hesitant, recalling what had befallen the other Jewish tribes of Medina, they gave in when faced with the large Meccan force. The treachery of the Banu Qurayza was reported to Muhammad and it seems that they actually did make an attack against one of the Muslim positions where the women and children were kept. Muhammad tried to use diplomacy to secure his flanks by neutralizing the Banu Qurayza. For the most part, his efforts were arrogantly rejected. As the siege went on, both sides became exhausted and the Banu Qurayza were beginning to distrust their Meccan co-conspirators.

It must be remembered that neither the Meccans nor the Muslims had anything near to a standing army which could maintain a siege. For the most part they were merchants. Attacks and raids were possible for their forces but long, drawn-out sieges were not. It seems that the weather changed for the worse and the Meccans simply lost heart and went home. The Muslims were saved; the trench had accomplished its task. However, Muhammad was now faced with the problem of the treachery of the Banu Qurayza, a treachery which could have resulted in the destruction of the Muslim community. The Banu Qurayza took refuge in their fortress and held out for 25 days. When it became clear that the situation was hopeless, they sued for peace, offering to leave the area as had the other two Jewish tribes. Muhammad refused and demanded unconditional surrender. Muhammad suggested that the fate of the Banu Qurayza be decided by one of the Muslim allies from Medina. The Jews agreed and Sa'd ibn Muadh, who had been wounded in the battle, was appointed. He was brought to Muhammad and all swore to abide by his decision. His judgment was that all the males of the Banu Qurayza should be killed and the women and children sold into slavery. The sentence was carried out the next day.[29]

For the contemporary person in the west, the story of the Banu Qurayza is very unsettling. It is often said that it is unthinkable that Jesus would have taken part in such a massacre and that is true. However, there were different mores prevalent in Arabia at that time. Even in the Hebrew Scriptures there are accounts of entire cities being put under the ban (*herem*) according to which every living thing was destroyed. Christians too have engaged in massacres. The stories of the Crusaders' sack of Jerusalem, the murder of the Rhineland Jews by Crusaders, and the massacre of the Albigensian heretics are examples enough to show that no religion is innocent of often terrible violence. This does not excuse the violence but hopefully puts it into a context which makes an unjustified sense of superiority more difficult.[30]

In the year following the Battle of the Trench, Muhammad worked to strengthen his position by forming alliances with tribes in the area and by continuing to raid the caravans from Mecca. It is clear that Muhammad had no intention of destroying the Quraysh and defeating them in the military sense. He did engage in campaigns against some of the tribes which had been allied with the Quraysh, but the overall plan seems to have been to strengthen the position of the Muslims and weaken the position of the Meccans.

In pre-Islamic times as well as in Islam, there are two types of pilgrimage that can be made to the Ka'aba. The first is the Great Pilgrimage, the *hajj*. The *hajj* is one of the Pillars of Islam[31] incumbent upon all Muslims who are able to perform it. In addition to the *hajj*, there was and still is the Lesser Pilgrimage, the *'umrah*, that a person makes out of devotion. On March 16, 628, Muhammad, having been instructed to do so in a dream, set out for Mecca to perform the Lesser Pilgrimage. According to the tradition, he took 70 sacrificial camels with him and some 700 men. He was careful to dress in the garb of a pilgrim to signify that he was really making a pilgrimage and had no intention of attacking Mecca. Needless to say, the Quraysh were not happy with Muhammad approaching Mecca even with only 700 men, and they went out to meet him. Abu Bakr, however, helped the Muslims take an alternate, though more difficult, route until they arrived at a place near al-Hudaybiya from which there was easy access to Mecca. When Muhammad reached the Pass of al-Murar, the tradition recounts that his camel knelt and refused to go further. The Prophet took it as a sign from God and stated "the One who restrained the elephant from Mecca is keeping it (*i.e.*, the camel) back." At this point Muhammad realized that God did not want him to make the pilgrimage that year. The Meccans sent a man, a polytheist Bedouin known for his piety, to speak with Muhammad. Upon seeing the sacrificial camels decorated for sacrifice, he was convinced of Muhammad's sincerity and returned to Mecca with the opinion that Muhammad's intentions were sincere. The Meccans were not happy with the report and took to insulting the man, who threatened to pull out of his tribe's alliance with the Meccans until they apologized. The Meccans sent a second envoy to Muhammad and the situation became very tense. The envoy was struck by one of the Muslims for touching Muhammad's beard in an act of familiarity. At the end, the envoy was

From War to Truce with Mecca

impressed by the Muslims' intense loyalty and devotion to
Muhammad, indicating they were willing to fight for him to
the death. Muhammad then sent an envoy of his own to the
Meccans. They killed his camel and would have killed him
had not the followers of the pious polytheist come to his aid.
Muhammad then sent Uthman to negotiate with the Quraysh.
Uthman informed them that Muhammad really had come to
perform the pilgrimage and should be allowed to do it. The
Meccans refused but told Uthman that they would allow him
to circumambulate the Ka'aba. When he refused to do it
before Muhammad, the Meccans took him hostage and the
story went out that he had been killed.

Muhammad had the Muslims who were with him swear
a special oath of loyalty to him, the Pledge of ar-Ridwan, or
Good Pleasure. While it may have been that the Muslims
believed they were taking the pledge to proclaim their loyalty
in the battle to come, that was not to be the case. In fact, the
Muslims' loyalty to Muhammad was to be tested in a way
they never expected. After the pledge, the news arrived in
the camp that Uthman had not been killed.

Shortly after the Pledge, Muhammad saw one of the
Quraysh approaching the camp. He knew that the Meccans
were now willing to negotiate. What follows is perhaps the
best example of Muhammad's extraordinary skills. While
uncompromising in his faith, he was prepared to compromise
on many non-essentials, even if that compromise might
cause him problems. An agreement was made with the
Meccans, known as the Treaty of Hudaybiya. According to
the treaty, there would be a ten-year cessation of hostilities
between the Meccans and the Muslims. Muhammad would
not make the pilgrimage that year, thus allowing the Meccans
to save face. The following year, however, the Meccans
would abandon the city for three days to allow the Muslims to
make the rites of pilgrimage. The fact that Muhammad was
really serious about making the pilgrimage must have deeply
impressed on the Meccans that he was not out to destroy all
of the ancient traditions. While Islam would have nothing to
do with other gods, the pilgrimage and the circumambulation
of the Ka'aba were not in danger. It was also agreed that any
member of the Quraysh who became a Muslim and went to

Medina would be returned to Mecca, although Muslims who recanted would not be returned to Medina.

As the treaty was being formulated, Ali was writing it. Muhammad began dictating by saying, "In the name of God, the Most Merciful, the Most Gracious."[32] Suhayl, the Meccan negotiator, objected to this and demanded that it begin solely "In your name, O God." Muhammad agreed. When Muhammad continued to dictate: "This is the agreement which Muhammad, the Apostle of God, has made...," Suhayl again objected saying, "If I had witnessed that you were the Apostle of God, I never would have fought against you." Again Muhammad complied. At the conclusion of the treaty a refugee to the Muslims was returned to the Quraysh much against his will.

The Treaty of Hudaybiya was a tremendous disappointment to the followers of Muhammad. They had expected to make the pilgrimage and were not able to that year. Some of them certainly must have expected to attack the Meccans and instead a treaty was made with them. The treaty did not seem favorable at all to the Muslims. The ten-year non-aggression pact effectively prevented the Muslims from raiding Meccan caravans, one of their main sources of income. The provision of the return of refugees was one-sided in favor of the Meccans and even in the writing of the treaty Muhammad had been humiliated. Nonetheless, at the end of the negotiations, Muhammad sacrificed the animals and shaved his head as a sign that he had completed the rites of the pilgrimage. Some of his followers shaved their heads, others merely cut their hair, a sign that all was not well. In fact, Hudaybiya was the closest that Muhammad ever came to experiencing mutiny among his followers. It was simply impossible for them to see or understand how wisely and cleverly the Prophet had acted in this matter. On the way back to Medina, Surah 48 was revealed which begins "Truly we have given you an obvious victory. So that God may forgive you your past faults, fulfill his favor in you and guide you on the Straight Path" (48:1-2).[33]

In March of 629, Muhammad made the lesser pilgrimage to Mecca without event. Because of the piety which he showed, many Meccans were favorably impressed and some leaders made submission to Islam. Khalid ibn u-lWalid, later to be one of Islam's most famous generals and strategists, became a Muslim at this time. Muhammad was also able to secure a reconciliation with his uncle Abbas, who had formerly been one of his major opponents. It was clear that Meccan opposition to the Prophet was beginning to wane.

The Treaty of Hudaybiya began to unravel about November 629. The details are complicated and intimately connected with the customs of the time. A tribe which had allied itself with Muhammad killed a man of another tribe who had written hostile poetry against Muhammad. The assassinated man's tribe was an ally of the Meccans. Some of the Meccans gave arms to the offended tribe which then attacked and exacted vengeance on members of the tribe allied with Muhammad. The ten-year non-aggression pact had technically now been violated. When Muhammad learned of the situation, the Meccans knew they were in a difficult position especially since they had armed the enemies of Muhammad's allies. Abu Sufyan was sent to Medina to negotiate with the Prophet, who was in a much more powerful position than were the Meccans. Although there are several differing accounts about what went on between Muhammad and Abu Sufyan, there is good reason to believe that Abu Sufyan was a practical man and realized that the situation was hopeless. Abu Sufyan, however, was not totally without resources. His daughter Umm Habiba was one of Muhammad's wives. It is possible that he came to some sort of an agreement with Muhammad because later at the siege of Mecca he worked to have the city surrender without fighting.

In January of 630, the Muslims marched on Mecca. The resistance which a few of the Meccans offered was minimal and Muhammad entered the city in triumph. He pitched his tent near the Ka'aba and rested. After resting he rode his camel seven times around the Ka'aba proclaiming *Allahu akbar*, "God is the greatest!" According to the traditions, Muhammad then destroyed the 360 idols which surrounded the Ka'aba. One of the traditions recounts that there were also pictures, two of which were of Jesus and Mary. The tradition states: "The apostle ordered that the pictures be erased except those of Jesus and Mary."[34] A general amnesty was declared and with the exception of a few people the population of Mecca was spared. Muhammad spent two weeks in Mecca. Parties were sent out to destroy the shrines of two of the "daughters of God in towns surrounding Mecca." Except for installing Islam as the religion of Mecca and removing all signs of polytheism, Muhammad did little to change things. This strengthened his position with families and clans who feared losing all in a Muslim takeover. In fact, they lost little if anything.

Upon hearing of the fall of Mecca to Muhammad, enemies of the Meccans, the Hawazin, gathered to attack what they thought was a weakened city. Muhammad, now the leader of Mecca, responded. The two forces met in the Battle of Hunayn on January 31, 630. The two forces were the largest yet gathered. One tradition holds that Muhammad had two thousand troops to encounter the enemy's 20,000. Although it seemed to go badly for the Muslims at first, the steadfastness of Muhammad and the strategy of the recently converted Khalid ibnu-l-Walid won the day. The opponents surrendered and ultimately accepted Islam. Muhammad had shown himself not only capable of capturing Mecca but also capable of defending it.

In March 632, Muhammad decided to perform the *hajj* to Mecca. This was the first time the pilgrimage would be performed by believers in the one and only God. Islam changed the rites of the *hajj* very little, although the deepest meaning of it had been radically changed and made monotheistic. After the *hajj*, Muhammad preached what later became known as the Farewell Sermon. When he returned to Medina, he began experiencing headaches, which became worse until one day he collapsed in the cabin of one of his wives. He signaled that he wished to be with Aisha, his favorite wife, and was taken to her quarters. On Monday, June 8, 632, it seemed that Muhammad had suddenly recovered from his illness. Although Abu Bakr had been ordered by Muhammad to lead the prayers, Muhammad now appeared in the mosque. Afterwards he returned to Aisha's quarters and once again rested his head on her lap. In that position he quietly died. The loud lamenting of Aisha alerted the people to the unthinkable—the Messenger of God was gone. There was tremendous grief and confusion. It was then that Abu Bakr declared, "if anyone worships Muhammad, Muhammad is dead. If anyone worships God, God is alive, immortal." He then recited Sura 3:144, "Muhammad is not more than a Messenger. There have been many messengers before him that passed away...."

STUDY QUESTIONS

1. How do the figures of Jesus and Muhammad function within the Christian and Muslim communities respectively? How are they similar and how are they different?
2. How is the information we have about Jesus in the Gospels and about Muhammad in the Sirah and the traditions different? How does this affect how the two communities look at each other, at Jesus, and at Muhammad?
3. What relationship might Muhammad have to the prophets of the Hebrew Scriptures, for example Moses, that we do not find in Jesus?

SELECT BIBLIOGRAPHY

Armstrong, Karen. *Muhammad: A Biography of the Prophet.* San Francisco: Harper, 1993.

Guillaume, Alfred. *The Life of Muhammad: A Translation of Ibn Ishaq's Sirat Rasul Allah.* London: Oxford University Press, 1955.

Schimmel, Annemarie. *And Muhammad Is His Messenger: The Veneration of the Prophet in Islamic Piety.* Chapel Hill, NC: University of North Carolina Press, 1985.

NOTES

1. A similar attention to detail can be found in the Talmud which has a prayer and blessing for the most intimate of occasions and bodily functions in an attempt to sanctify the entirety of human existence.
2. *Sahih al-Bukhari*, Muhammad Muhsin Khan, ed., (New Delhi: Kitab Bhavan, 1984).
3. The word *sahih* in Khan's work above means "healthy, strong, certain, admissible," *i.e. hadiths* with the best verifiable chain of transmission as opposed to *da'if*, "weak or unreliable."
4. *The Encyclopedia of Islam, New Edition*, Vol. VII, C. E. Bosworth, et alii, (Leiden: Brill, 1993), 360-387.
5. *EI*, Vol. VII, 362.

6. Karen Armstrong, *Muhammad: A Biography of the Prophet* (San Francisco: Harper, 1993).

7. Alfred Guillaume, *The Life of Muhammad: A Translation of Ibn Ishaq's Sirat Rasul Allah* (London: Oxford University Press, 1955). Armstrong has 102 footnotes referring to citations, *etc.,* from Guillaume's work.

8. The Qur'an is divided into 114 chapters which are called Surah and each Surah is divided into *ayah* (plural: *ayat*) or verses.

9. After the birth of al Qasim, Muhammad would have been known as Abu l-Qasim Muhammad ibn Abdullah.

10. Zoroastrianism was the official religion of the Sassanid (Persian) Empire. Zoroastrians exist today mostly in India, though there are small Zoroastrian communities in Europe and North America.

11. A *haram* is a sacred area. The *haramaynu,* or "Two Sacred Places," refers to the Mosques in Mecca and Medina. The "Noble *haram,*" or *al-haram ash-sharif* is the Temple Mount in Jerusalem where Al-Aqsa Mosque and the Dome of the Rock are found.

12. These three goddesses were seemingly popular in the Hijaz. The Meccans were willing to accept the concept of Allah as God, since it was a term already familiar to them. However, they saw no reason to reject the "daughters of Allah." According to the Qur'anic commentator at-Tabari, Surah 53 was revealed to Muhammad with the verse "Have you seen/considered al-Lat, and Uzza and Manat, the third, the other one" (53:19-20). At-Tabari states that at this point Satan had Muhammad include this line which would seemingly endorse a role for the goddesses: "they are the exalted cranes whose intercession is allowed." (Hence, the expression the "Satanic verse.") Cf. Armstrong, 113-114. Regardless as to the truth of at-Tabari's story, the goddesses are clearly not allowed in 53:23, "they are only names which you and your ancestors have named for which Allah has handed down no authority..."

13. Arabs at the time of Muhammad believed in the *jinn*. They are minor spirits and in the pre-Islamic times were seen as the forces that inspired the ecstatics and poets, not unlike the *daimonia* of the ancient Greeks. When one was possessed by the *jinn*, one became *majnun*, which is today the Arabic word for "mad, crazy." We recall here that in the Middle Ages, epilepsy was considered a "divine" disease.

14. *Cf.* Chapter 2, note 2.

15. W. Montgomery Watt, *Muhammad, Prophet and Statesman*, (London: Oxford University Press, 1961).

16. Watt, 23-33.

17. Feminine form of *muslim*, "one who submits (to God)."

18. Watt, 56.

19. This was not his actual name. His real name was Abu-l-Hakam. Abu Jahl means "the father of ignorance." Sometimes the Meccan opponents of Muhammad were given polemical names. One sees this also in the case of Abu Lahb, "the father of (hell) fire" whose real name was Abdu-l-Uzza. *Cf.* Surah 111.

20. Some translations have "what made him reject God?" However, given what follows, it seems that *kfr* here should retain its sense of ingratitude.

21. *Cf. EI*, Vol. I, 1215; Guillaume, 143-144.

22. Guillaume, 145.

23. *Ibid.,* 156.

24. *Ibid.,* 158.

25. *Ibid.,* 192.

26. *Ibid.,* 208.

27. Traditionally the people of Medina who supported the prophets are referred to as the *ansar* or "the Helpers." The earliest Muslims are called *sahaba*, "the Companions." The *muhajirun* are those who made the *hijra* or "emigration" from Mecca to Medina.

28. Guillaume, 437-438.

29. Guillaume, 461-466; Watt, 171-175; Armstrong, 204-209.

30. In a post-Holocaust and post-Nazi world it is important to stress that what happened to the three Jewish tribes of Medina was not the beginning of a program of anti-Judaism. As members of the People of the Book, Jews together with Christians enjoyed a protected status in Muslim society and were permitted to practice their religion, albeit under restrictions which were sometimes more and sometimes less stringent. It was the Muslims of the Ottoman Empire who welcomed the Jews who had been expelled from Spain in 1492. While the history of Jewish-Muslim relations in Medina during the time of Muhammad was not only not happy but also tragic, it is simply unjustified to draw parallels between it and the history of the Jews in Nazi Germany.

31. For the Pillars of Islam, see the chapter on "Islam As a Religious System."

32. Called the *bismilla*, literally "in the name of God..." the phrase is used by pious Muslims at the beginning of any important act, lecture, treaty, *etc.*

33. For the events of Hudaybiyah, *cf.* Guillaume, 499-507; Watt, 182-188; and Armstrong, 214-224.

34. Guillaume, 552.

IX

Islam as a Religious System

In this chapter the reader is given a view into Islam as Muslims believe, practice, and live it. Those values and practices which provide identity, spiritual strength, and the way to God for Muslims are described.

- *The Qur'an, God's Word revealed to Muhammad: eternal, perfect, and the rule of life for Muslims*
- *Pillars of Islam: Creed, Prayer, Almsgiving, Fasting, and Pilgrimage*
- *The Tradition: Sunna and Hadith*
- *The Four "Schools" of Sunni Islam · Sunni and Shi'ite Islam*

I n treating the topic of Islam as a religious system we are attempting to look at Islam fairly and objectively as a coherent system of beliefs, values, and practices. Of course, there is a certain distancing which takes place when treating any religion as a "system." Religions are systems but they are also far more than systems. They are spiritualities, ways of life, ways of finding meaning in life, of achieving holiness, and of encountering the Transcendent. For 14 centuries Islam has spiritually nourished hundreds of millions of people. It has produced saints, mystics, artists, and some of the most beautiful products of the human spirit. As such Islam can never be—and should never be—"reduced" to a mere system. That is not what we are attempting to do. What we are attempting to do is provide the reader with an accurate portrayal of Islam "from the outside." To understand Islam or any religion "from the inside," one must know believers.

An introduction to any religion written by someone who does not belong to that religion runs the risk of looking at the phenomenon from the outside. That is not to say that a non-believer cannot have a grasp of a religion, its history, and its values. Indeed it is possible for a scholar to know more about a religion that is not her or his own than someone who practices that religion. Nonetheless, that scholar will never have the same "feel" for the religion that the believer has. The scholar will never have been touched at his or her deepest core by the call of that religion. Religion can be an object of study but it is far more than that to its adherents. One can learn a great deal about what adherents of a particular religion believe and do from reading about that religion. In order to learn about how that religion penetrates and transforms the lives of its believers, one has to get to know those believers and acquire a deep appreciation and understanding of the religion. Regardless of what one holds about the origins of a particular religion, a religion is **something that people believe in and live out in actions**.

Beliefs and Practices of Islam

It must be remembered, however, that Islam extends across a huge spectrum of cultures, geographies, and languages. It is likewise a religion that is over 1400 years old. While every believer in a religion likes to think that nothing in the religion changes and perhaps the essentials do not change, as living realities, religions do change considerably in many ways. What follows may be compared to a black and white snapshot of a long, rich, colorful, dramatic film. It may portray the reality—and hopefully it will—but it lacks the color, the texture, the depth, the movement, and the dynamism of the original.

Points of apparent connection between this or that belief or practice in Roman Catholicism are often helpful in initiating dialogue, but they can be seductive and misleading. So, *caveat lector!* "Let the reader beware!" When too much stress is placed on what Catholics and Muslims have in common, there is the temptation to begin to look upon the Muslim as "just like me." To some extent that is true. Falling for such a temptation, however, fails to take into account what I call the irreducible particularity of the religion of the Other. Islam is Islam. It is not an exotic form of Christianity. John of Damascus was simply mistaken in thinking that Islam was a Christian heresy. There is at the core of Islam that which makes it Islam and not any other religion, that which it does not share with any other religion. One must grasp this irreducible particularity of Islam to understand it properly.

The Qur'an

The Qur'an is at the very center of Islam. An Islam without the Qur'an is simply unthinkable. Jews, Christians, and Muslims speak of the "word of God." For Muslims, the Qur'an is the word of God *par excellence*. Catholics and many other Christians believe that the Bible was revealed by God using human language and human writers. Those writers lost none of their individuality in writing the books of the Bible. For Muslims, the Qur'an is the word of God in a far more concrete sense. It is literally the word that God spoke to the Prophet Muhammad. Early on in Islam, the angel Gibra'il, Gabriel, became the one who dictated the revelations to Muhammad. Islamic tradition has held that Muhammad was illiterate. While he was the conduit of the Qur'an, he did not write it; indeed, as illiterate, he could not have written it. Therefore, Muslims will never say: "Muhammad says in the Qur'an." Muhammad was the *rasul*, the messenger, who delivered the message. He did not compose it. Muslims often speak of the "miracle of the Qur'an." Unlike the founders of other religions, Muhammad is generally not presented as having performed miracles. When this was brought up to question the validity of his prophethood, it was the miracle of the Qur'an which was used to show Muhammad's position. Several times in the Qur'an, those who oppose or doubt the veracity of Muhammad are challenged to produce a Surah[1] that would be similar to those of the Qur'an (2:23; 10:37-38; 11:13; 52:33-34).

"This Qur'an is not such
As can be produced
By anyone other than God.
On the contrary it is
A Confirmation of
That which went before it,
And a fuller explanation
of the Book—in which there is no doubt

From the Lord of the Worlds" (10:37).

The Qur'an functions very differently from the Bible. As the literal word of God, the sounds of the Qur'an are important for Muslims. Almost 85% of Muslims are not speakers of Arabic. Nonetheless, because it is the word of God, the Qur'an can never be translated. Any translation is an "interpretation" and of necessity of lesser value than the Arabic. During prayers, the Qur'an is recited in Arabic regardless of the language of the worshiper. The recitation of the Qur'an has a power of its own. Complicated rules regulate *tajwid,* the ritual recitation of the Qur'an. Merely hearing the sound of the Qur'an beautifully recited is a deep and powerfully religious experience for a Muslim, whether or not he or she can actually understand the text that is being recited. The words of the Qur'an themselves have power. Like the Bible the Qur'an has content. It has statements, regulations, criticisms, laws, and so forth. However, it is far more than a book with a content. The Qur'an has a certain *ex opere operato*[2] quality to it. It has a power above and beyond its content and assertions.

The Qur'an is written in what is called *saj'u* or rhymed prose. Thus Surah 1 has seven verses of different lengths (verse 2 has two words while verse 6 has eight) all of which end in the sound "-im" or "-in." This imposes a certain restraint on the language and makes the Qur'an very elliptical. That is to say, the language is often "telescoped" and a lot must be assumed before one understands the text. A certain tension exists in the Qur'an between the meaning of words and the sounds of them, both being important in a way foreign to the Christian understanding of the Bible.

The Qur'an is roughly the size of the New Testament. It contains 114 Sura or chapters and each chapter contains *ayat* or verses. The Suras of the Qur'an are arranged roughly according to size. Thus the second Sura, *The Cow,* is the longest, although it was not revealed until Muhammad had already moved to Medina, while the closing Suras of the Qur'an tend to be the earliest and from the Meccan period[3] The Qur'an was revealed in pieces. When Muhammad received a revelation, he recited it to his followers who then memorized it. Even today it is considered a virtue—and a necessity for a scholar—to memorize the Qur'an in its entirety. The smaller Surahs were often revealed as whole.

However, the longer ones were often put together after several revelations had been given. The most traditional copies of the Qur'an take account of this.

Muslims tend to resist describing other Muslims as "fundamentalists" because they assert that every Muslim is a fundamentalist since every Muslim believes that the Qur'an is the literal and hence infallible word of God. Having said that, however, it would be a mistake to think that Muslims do not have a critical approach to the Qur'an. They do. It is, however, different from what is often called the critical method in biblical scholarship. A very traditional edition of the Qur'an will provide the reader with a great deal of information and aides for understanding. For example, in a traditional Arabic-only edition of the Qur'an from Cairo, the heading of Surah 29, "The Spider," reads: "Surah The Spider, Meccan except for verses 1 to the end of verse 11 which are Medinan; it (the Surah) has 69 verses and was revealed after Surah 'The Romans' (Surah 30)." Traditional texts of the Qur'an are very careful to situate each Surah within a historical context. In order for the reader to properly understand the chapter, he or she must understand the chapter's history. Awareness of the impact of historical context on interpretation is not usually a hallmark of what is commonly understood as fundamentalism. In addition, the copy has footnotes explaining spellings in the text that diverge from the common spelling of Arabic words.

The whole text of the Qur'an is often centered on the page and then surrounded by one of the traditional commentaries (*tafsir*), such as al-Tabari. Muslims have never held that the Qur'an is easy to understand. Although one frequently finds in the Qur'an that the message is "plain," Muslims very early on developed an elaborate and detailed method for interpreting and understanding the Qur'an which includes grammar, lexicography, and what were called the *asbabu-l-tanzil*, "the occasions of the revelation," the setting in which the particular revelation was given to the Prophet and not unlike the *Sitz im Leben*, "the setting in life" of biblical scholarship.

One of the most interesting techniques for interpreting the Qur'an is *naskh* or abrogation, replacement. It is also a phenomenon that has played a considerable role in pre-modern Christian polemics against Islam. Surah 4:82

indicates that there is no discrepancy in the Qur'an; a divine book cannot be self-contradictory. Faced with that conviction, Muslim scholars had a problem in that several verses of the Qur'an were in fact not compatible with each other. The Qur'an seemed to be contradicting itself. Working on the chronology of the Surahs in which the contradictory verses were found, the later verse was declared to be *nasikh*, "abrogating," and the earlier verse *mansukh*, "abrogated." According to Qur'anic scholars, a classical example of abrogation can be found in 8:65-66. In verse 65, God says that 20 patient Muslims can overcome 200 adversaries and 100 will vanquish 1,000. In verse 66, it is 100 who will vanquish 200 and 1,000 will conquer 2,000—considerably better odds than in the previous verse. Likewise it is held that 4:10-11, which gives detailed instructions as to how the inheritance is to be apportioned, abrogates 2:180, which regulates inheritance in a very general way.

The notion of abrogation is not without some impact on Christian-Muslim relations. The Qur'an shows differing attitudes towards Christians. In 5:82 we read, "...And those nearest among them in love to the Believers you will find among those who say 'We are Christians,' because among these are men dedicated to learning and men who have renounced the world. They are not arrogant."[4] Yet some 30 verses earlier we read "Oh you who believe! Do not take the Jews and the Christians as your friends and protectors. They are not friends and protectors. They are only friends and protectors to each other. Any of you who turns to them for friendship is one of them. God does not guide an unjust people" (5:51). Likewise in 9:29 Muslims are commanded to fight against the People of the Book until they pay the tax with willing submission and feel themselves subdued. The Qur'an states that there is to be "no compulsion in religion" (2:256); it advises "let him who will, believe, and let him who will, reject," (18:29); it recognizes plurality of faith as God's work "...if God so willed it, He could have made you a single people...the goal of you all is to know God. It is He who will show you the truth of the matters in which you dispute" (5:48). Muslims are advised: "Do not dispute with the People of the Book except in the best way" (29:46).

Contemporary Muslims, therefore, might find themselves in a quandary as to the proper way to interact with Christians (and Jews). While the vast majority of Muslims have no problem with friendly interaction with Christians and are committed to interreligious dialogue, there are those who are opposed to friendly relations with Christians and who see all positive mention of Christians in the Qur'an to be *mansukh*, that is, abrogated by other later hostile verses.

Each of the Surahs of the Qur'an has a name. There are animal names like "The Cow," "The Spider," and "The Ants." There are Surahs bearing the names of people in the Bible: "Jonah," "Joseph," "Abraham," and "Mary." Some of the Surahs get their names from the opening line. This is frequently the case with the earlier Surahs from Mecca. In any case, the name of a Surah does not necessarily guarantee that the Surah deals with the topic of the title. To be sure, the Surahs named after biblical characters do deal with that particular character, but there is usually a great deal of additional material that may or may not have to do with the title character.

Stories in the Qur'an which refer back to biblical characters or events are often very different from the "same" story in the Bible. This was one of the points of early disagreement between Muhammad and the Jews. It can also be a point of contention between Christians and Muslims. In addition to those sections of the Qur'an which deny the divinity and sonship of Jesus,[5] there is also the claim that he was not crucified. "They say in boast, 'We killed Christ Jesus, the son of Mary, the Messenger of God,' but they did not kill him. Only a likeness of what was shown to them...for certainly they did not kill him" (4:157). Needless to say, this poses considerable problems for Christians for whom the crucifixion is not only a matter of faith but also a verifiable historical event. For Muslims, the Qur'an is the word of God. If anything contradicts the Qur'an, in this case the Crucifixion of Jesus, the Qur'an as the word of God must take precedence.

The division of Surahs between Meccan and Medinan which we find in the Qur'an itself is reflected more or less in the Surahs themselves. The earlier Surahs tend to be shorter. The language is vibrant, highly descriptive, and elliptic. It is not unusual for an early Surah to have less than ten verses, as opposed to the 286 verses of Surah 2. Thus the last five Surahs of the Qur'an have three, five, four, four, and five verses each. One of the earliest descriptions of Muhammad is "the Warner." The earlier Surahs reflect this, for with vivid, often apocalyptic, language the Qur'an calls the hearer to submit to God, to recognize God's goodness, to recognize that God is one, and it warns against miserliness, unbelief, and an exaggerated sense of self-sufficiency.

> *Say! He is God*
> *The One*
> *God, the Eternal, the Sublime*[6]
> *He does not beget*
> *Nor is he begotten*
> *And there is none*
> *Like Him (112:1-4)*

The later Surahs that were revealed in Medina are different and reflect the different situation of the Prophet and the community. They are not only considerably longer; they also often deal with very practical topics such as laws of inheritance, division of plunder, and marriage. Muhammad had become the leader of a community, which had very specific needs, and presented different challenges to the Prophet than it did when it was a small, persecuted minority in Mecca.

If comparisons must be made, it might be said that the Qur'an does not function in Islam like the New Testament functions in Christianity. The Qur'an for Muslims functions much more like the figure of Christ functions for Christians. For Christians, Christ is the perfect revelation of God, living and present in the community of believers. Christ is "God among us," leading the Church, mediating God to humans as one who is both divine and human. Christ is the primary reference for Christians. So, too, with Muslims and the Qur'an. Regarding the actual, physical text of the Qur'an, it would function similarly to the Eucharistic elements in Roman Catholic theology. The text of the Qur'an is not merely a book any more than the Eucharistic bread is just merely bread for Roman Catholics.[7]

The Pillars of Islam

The five pillars of Islam are those practices that are considered essential for every Muslim. They are (1) *Shehada* or Creed, (2) *salat* or Prayer, (3) *zakat* or Almsgiving, (4) *sawm* the Fast of Ramadan, and (5) *hajj* or Pilgrimage.

THE SHEHADA OR CREED

The first Pillar of Islam is the *shehada* or Creed. The root *šhd* in Arabic means "to give witness."[8] It consists of the solemn profession: "There is no god but Allah and Muhammad is the Messenger (*rusul*) of God." Said in the presence of adult witness, the profession of the *shehada* is what makes one a Muslim. There are no ceremonies involved. It is the act of profession and submission to God itself that makes one a Muslim.

The first part of the *shehada* is connected to what is called the *tawhid*, the profession and belief that God is radically one. There is no other god but God and God is utterly unique, single, and transcendent. For Muslims the mortal sin is *shirk*, which means "association." To associate anything with God is polytheism and is radically opposed by Islam. Muslims have always rejected the divinity and divine Sonship of Jesus precisely because it seems to posit a partnership in God. If Christians generally have a difficult time understanding the Trinity and a much more difficult time explaining it to non-Christians, Muslims generally understand the Trinity to be three gods. Surah 5:73 declares "They are disbelievers[9] who say: 'God is one of three;' for there is no god except One God. If they desist not from the word a grievous punishment will befall the disbelievers among them." For the most part, this determines the attitude which most Muslims would have towards the Christian belief in the Trinity. Therefore, it is probably better not to initiate a dialogue on the Trinity at an early stage of dialogue.

The second part of the *shehada* proclaims that Muhammad is the messenger of God. Again and again in the

Qur'an and in the traditions it is stressed that Muhammad is human and only human. Thus, Muslims strongly disapprove of any portrayal of the Prophet in painting or sculpture. Calling a Muslim a "Muhammadan" is offensive. Muslims object to this and will be quick to point out that what makes them Muslim is their submission to God and not to Muhammad. Christians worship Christ and we are called Christians. Muslims do not worship Muhammad and do not want to be called Muhammadans.

Having said that, however, it is important to stress that Muslims have a tremendous devotion to the person of the Prophet. He is still the perfect model for what the human life should be and the safest way to discern God's will. The words, deeds, practices, likes, and dislikes of the Prophet have been gathered to provide a *sunna*, a path by which the Muslim can walk in righteousness, pleasing God. After pronouncing the name of the Prophet, the pious Muslim will always add "peace be upon him." Pious texts will follow the name of Muhammad with a cartouche-like device which reads "God bless him and grant him salvation" in Arabic. Conversely, insulting Muhammad is considered a grave sin, punishable by death in many countries even today. While most Muslims living in a Western, pluralistic culture do not expect non-Muslims to totally share their reverence for Muhammad, they do expect that in dialogue and conversations reference to him be respectful.

SALAT OR PRAYER

The second Pillar of Islam is *salat* or Prayer. This is not prayer in general but the obligatory prayer, which is said five times a day by every healthy adult Muslim. According to Muslim tradition Muhammad had a mystical experience in 620 in which he miraculously traveled to Jerusalem and from there to God's throne in heaven. According to the tradition, as he ascended the different levels, he met Jesus and the different prophets of the Hebrew Bible. On reaching God's throne he was told that Muslims were to perform the prayers 50 times a day. On his way down from the throne he encountered Moses who told him that 50 was too burdensome and that he should return to ask God for a lower number. This he did several times until the number was reduced to five. Moses thought that the number was still too high, but Muhammad was embarrassed to go back to God again and so the number was fixed at five.[10] The prayers are said at dawn (*fajr*), noon (*zuhr*), afternoon (*'asr*), sunset (*maghrib*) and night (*'isha*). The time of prayer is announced (*adhan*) by a muezzin (*mu_adhdhin*) who calls to prayer, proclaims *allahu akbar*, "God is Greater (than everything)" and the *shehada.* Slight variations occur during the day. For example, the call to prayer at dawn has the phrase, "prayer is better than sleep."

Before the beginning of the prayer, the believer is to purify him or herself by washing feet, hands, forearms, face, and head. The intention (*niyah*) is very important. Muslim scholars hold that the believer must make a conscious decision that he or she is praying to fulfill the obligation of the *salat*. Lack of intention or an improper intention can invalidate the prayer. Some jurists say that the performance of the obligatory prayer begins with *takbir*, the proclamation *allahu akbar*, and ends with *taslim*, the *assalam 'aleikum*, "peace be upon you" that each believer says to the person on either side of him or her at the end of the prayers. The obligatory prayer consists of recitations from the Qur'an, some out loud and others in a whisper, bows, and prostrations. The opening Surah of the Qur'an, the *Fatiha*, is recited. Each prayer remains constant and does not change from day to day except for the noon prayer on Friday, which is accompanied by a sermon.

Muslim communal worship takes place in a mosque or *masjid*, literally "the place where one prostrates," although Muslims can and do perform the prayer anywhere.[11] An imam, literally "the one up front," leads communal prayer. An imam needs no special education; he merely needs to know how to lead the prayer so that the faithful can follow his actions in a dignified and orderly fashion. In some Muslim countries there are preaching and non-preaching imams. The preaching imam is ideally educated and often licensed by the state to preach. The non-preaching imam simply leads the prayers. In the United States, one notices a definite trend towards more educated imams. Muslims will often stress that Islam has no hierarchy or clergy. To some extent—at least for

Sunni Islam—that is true. If by clergy one means mediators or dispensers of sacraments, Islam clearly does not have a clergy. If one understands clergy as an educated and, to some extent, separate class within a religion, Islam seems to be developing such a clergy in North America, regardless of how they might name the development.

In addition to the obligatory prayers, Muslims also have a rich tradition of other personal prayers and devotions, which have developed over the centuries. One of the more common ones is the recitation of the Ninety-nine Beautiful Names of God. Often performed with a type of a rosary, this recital recalls ninety-nine names and characteristics of God. Very much like the rosary or Jesus prayer in the Christian tradition, it is a type of meditation technique that helps the believer center her or himself in God.

ZAKAT OR ALMSGIVING

The third Pillar of Islam is *zakat* or Almsgiving. All Muslims are required to give a certain percentage of their holdings to the poor. The four different schools of jurisprudence that will be mentioned below have different ways of calculating what percentage of goods must be donated, but each Muslim is required to perform the *zakat*. Traditionally the *zakat* is given at the time of the Feast of 'Eid al-Fitr or the Breaking of the Fast of Ramadan.

SAWM OR THE FAST OF RAMADAN

The fourth Pillar of Islam is the fast. This is not any fast, but specifically the solemn fast of the holy month of Ramadan. The fast prohibits taking anything into the body. Eating, drinking, smoking, and sexual activity are forbidden during the month of Ramadan from sunrise until sunset.[12] At the setting of the sun, the fast is broken (*iftar*) and normal activity may resume until sunrise. The Muslim attitude towards the fast is quite different from the Christian attitude, which is penitential. For Muslims, Ramadan and its fast are a time of self-discipline, focusing, and re-dedication. Pious Muslims try to recite the entire Qur'an during the month of Ramadan and to visit the mosque more frequently. The fast of Ramadan is a strengthening of one's dedication to God and one's submission (*islam*), if you will. Ramadan is not a solemn period in the sense that Lent is. In fact, it is a joyous time for most Muslims. Finally, the celebration of the Feast of the Breaking of the Fast, 'Eid al-Fitr,[13] is one of the happiest holidays of the year for Muslims. In many countries, houses are decorated with lights, there is feasting, and families visit each other and exchange gifts.

There are two major holidays in Islam: 'Eid al-Fitr and 'Eid ul Adha. 'Eid al-Fitr is the Feast of the Breaking of the Fast of Ramadan. 'Eid ul Adha is the Feast of Sacrifice. It takes place at the end of the Hajj and commemorates the sacrifice that Abraham made instead of his son.[14] 'Eid ul Adha is theologically the greater of the two feasts and is sometimes referred to as "The Greater or Bigger Feast." However, it is 'Eid al-Fitr which seems to have captured the emotions of most Muslims in terms of celebrations. One finds a similar phenomenon in Christianity with Christmas and Easter. Easter is by far the more important feast theologically, but it is Christmas that has captured the emotions of most Christians.

HAJJ OR PILGRIMAGE TO MECCA

The fifth Pillar of Islam is the *hajj* or Pilgrimage. Every able-bodied Muslim is required to make the *hajj* to Mecca and perform the rites of the Pilgrimage once in his or her lifetime. However, it is a reasonable obligation; it obliges only the Muslim who can physically make the pilgrimage without causing undo damage to health, family, or person. Until very recently, the performance of the *hajj* was extremely arduous, especially when the month for it (*dhu-l-hajj*) fell in the summer time. Even today it is a fairly strenuous undertaking and people die during the Pilgrimage every year. The ill, weak, elderly, poor, those in debt, or those with pressing family obligations are not required to make the Pilgrimage. At the close of the *hajj* pilgrims perform (or have performed) the ritual sacrifice mentioned above. A Muslim who has made the Pilgrimage then has the right to the title al-Hajji or al-Hajjiya (feminine).

Tradition: The Sunna and Hadith

In addition to, but not equal with, the Qur'an, Muslims have a source of tradition called the *sunna*. Originally, the word *sunna* in Arabic referred to the path that animals regularly took to waterholes and oases. In its specialized meaning, it refers to the huge collection of material that has to do with the life, sayings, and opinions of the prophets. The *sunna* is a collection of *hadith* or stories about the Prophet.[15] Since for Muslims Muhammad is the perfect model for a life lived in conformity with the will of God, the imitation of Muhammad is the surest way a Muslim can also live such a life. The collection of the stories about the Prophet has produced a tremendous literature. One of the so-called "canonical" collections of *hadith* is that of Bukhari and consists of nine volumes. Each of the *hadith* is preceded by a list of the people through whom the tradition has been transmitted. "The chain of transmitters," or the *isnad*, became an important area of study for Muslim scholars of later centuries in order to determine the authenticity of the *hadith*. There are different levels of authenticity which a particular *hadith* may enjoy, with *sahih*, "healthy, reliable," being the highest and *da'if*, "weak, unreliable," being the lowest acceptable level.

The Qur'an and the *Sunna* provided the sources from which Muslim jurists began to develop a theory and practice of law, the *shari'ah*. The purpose of the *shari'ah* was to order society according to the will of God; in other words, to achieve the perfect society. Needless to say, this was a monumental effort and the differences in understanding the Qur'an and the *Sunna* provided much opportunity for disagreement among scholars. The *shari'ah* took several centuries to develop and is not a codified law in any sense of the word. Precedent, analogy, and agreement play a role in the development of the practice of jurisprudence in Islam. In the western press one often reads that this or that political movement wants to install the *shari'ah* as the law of the land in a particular country. One gets the impression that the *shari'ah* is a concrete code of law like the Code of Theodosian or the Napoleonic Code. One gets the impression sometimes that some of the Muslims advocating the *shari'ah* have the same mistaken opinion. The *shari'ah* is more a hermeneutic than anything else. It is a specific way of interpreting the Qur'an, the *Sunna*, and other legal precedents and applying them to a given situation. To be sure, the Qur'an is quite clear in some legal areas such as adoption and inheritance. In the vast majority of instances, however, no such clarity is to be found in the Qur'an or the *Sunna* and the Muslim jurist must use the best interpretive skills he has at his disposal.

The Four Schools of Sunni Islam

Four schools of interpretation arose around four different scholars. Each of the four schools is called a *madhhab*, or "(chosen) way." The followers of Abu Hanifah formed the Hanifi School whose adherents were originally mainly in Iraq. The followers of Malik ibn Anas formed the Maliki School, prominent in the Hijaz. Al-Shafi'l founded another school, the Shafi'l, which was popular in Egypt, and lastly Ahmad ibn Hanbal formed the Hanbali School.[16] These four schools of jurisprudence are to be found among Sunni Muslims and not among Shi'ites.

The four different schools do not differ radically, although there are some significant differences in details. Although each school was prevalent in a particular area, every Muslim was free to choose a particular school. However, one was not permitted to choose from several different schools at the same time. Once one, for example, had opted to follow the Shafi'l School, one could not use a Maliki reasoning because it was more favorable. In point of fact, most Sunni Muslims chose to be either Hanafi or Shafi'l.

Groupings in Islam

I have chosen to use the neutral word "grouping" to describe the following phenomenon. Often one reads of "sects" within Islam. While there are certainly small sects within Islam, the word "sect" is inappropriate in discussing Sunni and Shi'ite Islam. In addition to having the connotation of illegitimacy, sect also has the connotation of marginal and even ephemeral, neither of which is applicable here.

The *ahlu-l-sunna* or People of the *Sunna*, the Sunnis, comprise the majority of Muslims throughout the world with 80-85% of Muslims. As their name implies, they follow the *Sunna* and have accepted the Caliphate of the Ummayads and later the Abbassids and Ottomans. For demographic and other reasons, Sunni Muslims are the Muslims one encounters most frequently in the Catholic-Muslim Dialogue.

The *shi'at 'ali* or the Shi'ites, the Party or Faction of Ali, forms a large minority in Islam. Historically, the Shi'ites held that the Caliphate should remain within the family of the Prophet. They accept the first four "Rightly Guided Caliphs," the fourth of whom was Ali, the cousin and son-in-law of Muhammad. After the death of Ali, hostilities began between his followers and the followers of Muawiyah who had been chosen to succeed Ali. The hostilities culminated in the year 680 with the slaughter of Hussein, Ali's son and the grandson of the Prophet, at Karbala in modern day Iraq. For several centuries after the death of Hussein, a member of the family of the Prophet, an imam,[17] was found to lead the Shi'ite community. A considerable mystical theology developed around the person of the imam. As the direct descendant of the Prophet, he enjoyed many of the characteristics, which Sunni Muslims would ascribe only to the Prophet. The Imam infallibly guided the community and assured it of its faithfulness.

The two largest groups of Shi'ites are the "Seveners" and the "Twelvers." These names arise from the number of imams they accept. The Seveners, better known as the Ismaili, hold that Ismail ibn Ja'far, the son of the sixth imam appointed his son as imam. Ismail died before his father, so before 765, and his father appointed Musa al-Kazim as his successor, whom most Shi'ites accepted. The Ismaili exist today largely in India and Pakistan, although they are also to be found in the United States. They are probably best known as followers of the Agha Khan.

The eleventh imam, Hasan al-Askari (846-873/4), was a virtual prisoner of the Abbassids and was imam for only six years. Upon his death there was considerable confusion as to whether he even had a son. The Twelvers hold that Muhammad al-Mahdi (the Guided One) al-Muntazzar (the Awaited One) went into occultation[18] and will return at the end of time. In the meantime, the Shi'ites are without a visible imam. Twelver Shi'ism is the state religion of Iran and the religion of most Shi'ites in the Middle East. Until recently in the Middle East they were an ignored and often persecuted minority. Saddam Hussein massacred tens of thousands of Iraqi Shi'ites during his time as dictator in Iraq.

In all the basic tenets of belief the Shi'ites are identical to the Sunni Muslims. Their belief in the Qur'an and the observance of the Five Pillars of Islam is indistinguishable from that of the Sunnis. However, there are considerable differences between the two groups. For one thing, the Shi'ites over the centuries have developed an extremely sophisticated mystical theology and philosophy. Karbala in Iraq and Qum in Iran are famous centers of learning to which students flock to prepare to become leaders in the community. While not hierarchical in the same sense as Roman Catholics, Orthodox, and Anglicans, the Shi'ites do recognize levels of religious authority within the community which are not found in Sunni Islam. The highest level is that of the Ayatollah, a title that means "Sign of God." Although most Americans spoke of "the" Ayatollah Khomeini during the Iranian Revolution as if he were the only Ayatollah, that was not the case at all. Khomeini was one of several Ayatollahs in Iran and Iraq and was not ever the senior or the most important one, who held the title of *marja'u-l-taqlid*, or "reference of emulation." A second level of leadership is the Hujjatu-l-Islam, or "Proof of Islam." More numerous than Ayatollahs, the Hujjatu-l-Islam is a man who has undergone at least eight years of rigorous training in one of the great Shi'ite centers of learning, where he studied the Qur'an, exegesis, Islamic law, history, philosophy, and hermeneutics.

Because of the martyrdom of Hussein the son of Ali and the grandson of the Prophet and because of their own history, Shi'ites have developed a theology of suffering which is not to be found among the Sunnis. Likewise, they have a rich mystical tradition that manifests itself, for example, in some Persian poetry, which is among the most beautiful poetry in the literature of the world.

Although Shi'ite Muslims live in the United States, for the most part they have not taken extensive part in the Catholic-Muslim dialogue. There are a number of reasons for this with demography, Shi'ite reticence, and Sunni prejudice both play a greater or lesser role. On the international level there have been extensive contacts between the Vatican, the Pontifical Council for Interreligious Dialogue, and the Islamic Republic of Iran. Dialogues are taking place and there are exchanges of professors between Catholic and Iranian theological faculties. Mohammed Khattami, the President of Iran, a Hujjatu-l-Islam and the son of Ayatollah Khattami, was present at the funeral of Pope John Paul II in an extraordinary manifestation of how far relations have come between Shi'ites and the Roman Catholic Church.

Two other groupings in Islam need to be mentioned at least briefly, viz., Sufis and Wahhabis. Sufi is the generic term for a movement in both Sunni and Shi'ite Islam. A mystical movement in which personal experience and even absorption into the Divine is important, Sufism took and continues to take the form of different orders (Arabic *tariqah;* plural *turuq*, "a way, method") that use different disciplines to attain their goal. Sufism has often pushed the boundaries of orthodoxy in Islam and Sufis have been executed for apostasy because of their theology. Perhaps the most famous Sufi martyr is al-Hallaj who was executed in 922 and whose life was researched and published by Louis Massignon.[19] There are many Sufi groups to be found in the United States, although it is sometimes not clear if it is a genuine Sufism or a group of non-Muslims who are using Sufi spiritual disciplines. Nonetheless, Sufis are often held suspect by Sunni organizations. Beginning in the late nineteenth century, Islamic reformers tended to look upon Sufi practices as backwards, superstitious, and the reason why Islam had not prospered in the modern era. This attitude is intensified in Wahhabism,[20] the official form of Islam found in Saudi Arabia. It is not always clear if Wahhabism even considers Sufism as a part of Islam. The exuberance of Sufism and its openness towards other forms of mysticism, which often brings the accusation of syncretism,[21] is in sharp contrast with the stern austerity of Wahhabism. As a result Sufis or Muslims who admit to following a Sufi order are rare in the Catholic-Muslim Dialogue. Nonetheless, there are several prominent Muslims—both male and female—in the US who are publicly following a Sufi order or tariqah.

STUDY QUESTIONS

1. How does the history of the text of the Qur'an make it different from that of the New Testament?
2. How does the Qur'an function in the life of the believing Muslim?
3. Are there any similarities between prayer and fasting in Islam and Christianity? What are the differences?

4. How do Christians and Muslims look upon the authority of their respective scriptures?

5. How might Judaism, Christianity, and Islam remain faithful to their tradition and still show the commonalities that we all have as monotheists?

6. How might a Christian in dialogue with a Muslim respond to a statement in the Qur'an which he believes to be incorrect, for example, that Jesus was not crucified?

7. In what ways do I stereotype Muslims, which get in the way of seeing them, as I would want them to see me? How do they impede my capacity to love my neighbor as myself?

SELECT BIBLIOGRAPHY

Cragg, Kenneth. *Muhammad and the Christian*. London: Darton, Longman and Todd, 1984.

Esposito, John. *Islam the Straight Path*. New York: Oxford University Press, 1988.

Gätje, Helmut. *The Qur'an and Its Exegesis*. Oxford: One World Press, 1996.

Momen, Moojan. *An Introduction to Shi'I Islam: The History and Doctrines of Twelver Shi'ism*. Oxford: George Ronald, 1985.

Speight, Marston. *God is One*. New York: Friendship Press, 2002.

NOTES

1. The Qur'an is divided into 114 Surahs (Arabic *surah;* plural *surat)*, or chapters. Each chapter is divided into Ayat (Arabic *'ayah*; plural *'ayat*, literally, "signs") or verses.

2. In Roman Catholic sacramental theology, the expression *ex opere operato*, literally, "from the work already done," expresses the belief that a sacrament properly performed conveys God's grace independently of the faith or moral state of the celebrant and recipient. For the recipient there is only the condition that he or she not place an obstacle (*obex*) against the sacrament's administration. Thus the sacrament's efficacy depends on God's faithfulness and not human worthiness. Cf. Council of Trent (1545-1563), Session 7, Canon VIII.

3. A similar phenomenon can be seen in the Bible. The books of the prophets are also collected roughly according to size with no attention being given to chronology. Thus Isaiah is the first of the prophetic books whereas the Book of Micah appears in ninth place. Isaiah of Jerusalem and Micah of Moresheth were contemporaries. However, the Book of Isaiah is lengthy and the Book of Micah is relatively short and hence later in the collection.
The same phenomenon occurs with the letters of Paul. The first letter of Paul to be found in the New Testament is the Letter to the Romans and the last letter is the Second Letter to the Thessalonians. Romans is one of Paul's later letters, whereas First Thessalonians is his first. However, the Letter to the Romans is larger than the Letters to the Thessalonians and hence appears before them.

4.   Cf. also 2:62; 61:14. However, 57:27 is critical of monasticism.

5.   There is even disagreement on the name of Jesus, although this rarely surfaces. In the Qur'an Jesus is 'isa, which etymologically is connected to the biblical character Esau. Although Arabic Christians use allah as the word for the God they worship, they refer to Jesus as yasu' in Arabic translations of the New Testament.

6.   The word here is not clear and there are many different translations.

7.   To understand the impact that the 2005 (incorrect) reports on the desecration of the Qur'an (Guantanamo Bay) had on Muslims, one needs only to think how a similar desecration of the Eucharist would affect Roman Catholics.

8.   It functions similarly to the Greek word martyr in Christianity. A martyr and a shahid are both witnesses and people who give up their lives for their faith.

9.   The word used for "disbelieve" is kfr which is quite strong.

10.   Cf. Armstrong, 138-142.

11.   It is not at all uncommon and can be inspiring to see truck drivers pulled over on the side of the road in Muslim countries performing the prayers alongside their trucks.

12.   Since Muslims are to be found increasingly in northern latitudes and since the Muslim month "moves backwards" through the solar year, the fast can be difficult for Muslims in summer time in the north where the sun rises very early and sets very late. The prohibition of drinking even water makes such a long time very arduous.

13.   It is significant to note that the U.S. Post Office for the past several years has been issuing a stamp for the celebration of 'Eid al-Fitr.

14.   This is an example where a biblical story in Islam differs from the one found in the Hebrew Bible. In the Hebrew Bible God commands Abraham to sacrifice his son Isaac. In the Muslim tradition it is Ishmael, the ancestor of the Arabs, who was ordered to be sacrificed.

15.   There are two types of hadith. By far the more common is the "prophetic hadith" in which there are words from Muhammad. The second is the hadith qudsi which contains words of God that are not to be found in the Qur'an. One thinks of Acts 20:35 in which Paul speaks of "the words of the Lord Jesus who said, 'It is better to give than to receive.'" This saying of Jesus is found nowhere in the four Gospels.

16.   Cf. Hodgson, The Venture of Islam, Vol. I, p. 335.

17.   The same word, imam, can have very different meanings among Sunni and Shi'ite Muslims. For both it can mean the man who "stands in front" and leads the prayers. For Shi'ites, however, it can also mean the descendant of the Prophet, chosen by God and born to lead the community infallibly.

18.   Occultation is the term to describe the "absence" of the imam. He is not considered dead but merely absent and invisible.

19.   Louis Massignon, The Passion of al-Hallaj, (Princeton: Princeton University Press, 1982).

20.   Wahhabism is a reform movement begun by Muhammad ibn Abdu-l-Wahhab (1703-1791). Wahhabis vehemently oppose anything, which might appear to be polytheistic. As a result they oppose any veneration of Muslim saints and especially their tombs. Any innovation which cannot be based on the Qur'an, the Sunna, or the Companions of the Prophet is considered heresy. Wahhabism became the form of Islam practiced by al-Sa'ud and later became the dominant form of Islam after World War I, when the descendants of Sa'ud took over the Arabian peninsula, which then became Saudi Arabia.

21.   Syncretism is the often-uncritical taking over of religious practices from one religion to another.

Epilogue

Any attempt to teach or learn about another religious tradition is a daunting task. It involves dealing with a history, a culture or cultures, beliefs, practices, and most of all assumptions. Initially, the most difficult part of teaching and learning about another religion is the assumptions that we bring to our study. Immersed as we are in our own culture and religion, it is easy to take them as "normal" in two senses of the word: normal in the sense that anything different is outlandish and weird; normal in the sense that they are the norm against which everything else is judged.

The American culture is rich, diverse, and seductive. For many Americans, even Roman Catholics, it is difficult to imagine a different culture, much less to appreciate it. As a culture, we Americans live very much in the present. History is "boring." The expression "that is so *yesterday*!" is a good gauge of our attitude towards that past. Yesterday is "ancient history." Whether that is good or bad is not the topic of this book. What is bad, however, is to simply assume that every culture and religion has the same attitude towards the past. For many cultures and religions and certainly for Islam, the past is vivid, alive, and determinative of the present. Ignorance of Islam's past, especially its foundational past, the life and times of Muhammad, is ignorance of Islam.

Although there is a great deal of information or data to be learned, a religion is far more than just data. Learning about the life of Muhammad and the Pillars of Islam is important. However, that is merely the beginning. The really difficult part is to learn how the information about Islam that we teach or learn as Christians lives deeply in the spirit of the believing Muslim. It is important that we be familiar with the life of Muhammad. The stories of the Prophet are as familiar to Muslims as the stories about the birth of Jesus are to Christians. Not to know the story of the birth of Jesus is not to appreciate an important part of Christians' spiritual life. Not to know the life of the Prophet is to miss a large part of the spiritual life of Muslims. It is not that Jesus and Muhammad function in exactly the same way in their respective communities. Muslims do not believe that Muhammad is divine. Muslims do not believe in Muhammad like Christians believe in Jesus. Nonetheless, the love that Muslims hold for their Prophet is tender, deep, and intense. Not to know the life of the Prophet is not to know a great deal about Muslims.

Beliefs and practices are an important part of any religion. It would, for example, be difficult to understand Roman Catholicism without having an understanding of the sacramental system. Having an academic understanding of the sacraments, however, does not provide insight as to how the sacraments form the lives of believing Catholics. There is a huge difference between reading a book on the sacraments and observing Catholics as they celebrate the sacraments. Knowledge about the Pillars of Islam is essential for any understanding of the religion. While an accurate understanding of the Pillars is crucial, it does not go below the surface of the phenomenon. An understanding of the Pillars of Islam (much like an understanding of Roman Catholic sacraments) tells us *what* the believer does. Such an understanding is of itself not able to tell us *why* Muslims believe what they believe or *how* it affects and transforms their lives.

Any book on a religious tradition is merely an introduction, regardless how erudite and lengthy it might be. It is an introduction because in a real sense religions live not in systems but in the lives of believing people. Objective information is indispensable both for teacher and student. The more one knows about Islam, the better one can understand it. Yet that information is an introduction. It is the indispensable introduction to getting to know the Islam that is believed and lived by Muslims. True understanding and appreciation of Islam comes when good information is complemented by the experience of living Muslims whose lives are transformed, given meaning, and ultimately made holy by their faith.

This book, written by a non-Muslim who is a Roman Catholic, is an attempt to give Roman Catholics, especially Catholic educators, as accurate a picture as possible of Islam *as Muslims understand it*. If a Muslim can recognize his or her faith in this book, it has been a success. If Roman Catholics can come to at least an initial understanding and appreciation of Islam, and from that feel comfortable enough to engage believing Muslims as neighbors, dialogue partners, and friends, it has been a great success.

REV. ELIAS D. MALLON, PH.D.

Elias D. Mallon, Ph.D., a native of New York City, was educated at Catholic University in Washington, DC, and Eberhard-Karls Univeristät in Tübingen, Germany. Dr. Mallon holds graduate degrees in Old Testament studies and a doctorate in Near Eastern Languages. He has taught at American University in Washington, DC, and the University of Washington in Seattle. He was also on the faculty at the Ecumenical Institute of the World Council of Churches in Switzerland.

Dr. Mallon has been involved in Interreligious Dialogue since 1985. An ordained member of the Society of the Atonement, he was Director of the Graymoor Ecumenical & Interreligious Institute and has been involved with the Christian-Muslim Dialogue in the Archdiocese of New York, the Secretariat for Ecumenical and Interreligious Affairs of the NCCB and the World and National Council of Churches.

Dr. Mallon has published several articles on the Christian-Muslim Dialogue and Interreligious Dialogue and is the author of *Neighbors: Muslims in North America.* He spoke on Islam at the NCEA Conference in Atlantic City in 2002, in Boston in 2004 and in Philadelphia in 2005.

At present Dr. Mallon is the External Affairs Officer of Catholic Near East Welfare Association (CNEWA), an agency of the Holy See founded in 1929 to accompany the Catholic Eastern Churches, providing support to their pastoral and humanitarian initiatives throughout the Middle East, Northeast Africa, India and Eastern Europe.